Business and the
Middle East

Pergamon Titles of Related Interest

Looney ECONOMIC ORIGINS OF THE IRANIAN REVOLUTION
Mossaver-Rahmani ENERGY POLICY IN IRAN: DOMESTIC
  CHOICES AND INTERNATIONAL IMPLICATIONS
Mroz BEYOND SECURITY: PRIVATE PERCEPTIONS AMONG
  ARABS AND ISRAELIS
Thorelli/Becker INTERNATIONAL MARKETING STRATEGY

Related Journals*

ECONOMIC BULLETIN FOR EUROPE
INTERNATIONAL JOURNAL OF INTERCULTURAL RELATIONS
OPEC REVIEW
SOCIO-ECONOMIC PLANNING SCIENCES
WORLD DEVELOPMENT

*Free specimen copies available upon request.

PERGAMON POLICY STUDIES ON BUSINESS AND ECONOMICS

Business and the Middle East:
Threats and Prospects

Edited by
Robert A. Kilmarx
Yonah Alexander

Pergamon Press
NEW YORK • OXFORD • TORONTO • SYDNEY • PARIS • FRANKFURT

Pergamon Press Offices:

U.S.A.	Pergamon Press Inc., Maxwell House, Fairview Park, Elmsford, New York 10523, U.S.A.
U.K.	Pergamon Press Ltd., Headington Hill Hall, Oxford OX3 0BW, England
CANADA	Pergamon Press Canada Ltd., Suite 104, 150 Consumers Road, Willowdale, Ontario M2J 1P9, Canada
AUSTRALIA	Pergamon Press (Aust.) Pty. Ltd., P.O. Box 544, Potts Point, NSW 2011, Australia
FRANCE	Pergamon Press SARL, 24 rue des Ecoles, 75240 Paris, Cedex 05, France
FEDERAL REPUBLIC OF GERMANY	Pergamon Press GmbH, Hammerweg 6 6242 Kronberg/Taunus, Federal Republic of Germany

330.956
B96

Library of Congress Cataloging in Publication Data
Main entry under title:

Business and the Middle East

    (Pergamon policy studies on business and economics)
    Bibliography: p.
    Includes index.
    1. Near East--Economic conditions--Addresses, essays, lectures. 2. Near East--Social conditions --Addresses, essays, lectures. 3. Near East-- Politics and government--Addresses, essays, lectures. I. Kilmarx, Robert A. II. Alexander, Yonah, 1931-   . III. Series.
HC415.15.B87   1982   330.956'04   81-13845
ISBN 0-08-025992-8   AACR2

90168

Printed in the United States of America

Contents

v

CHAPTER

Foreword

"Risk analysis" has at last made it into the lexicon of international business and banking as a needed requirement for the 20th century. This is encouraging news for those who have been working to persuade increasing numbers of international enterprise leadership that near-term decisions more and more must be based on longer term assessments of related geopolitical trends. Except for a few companies with long overseas experience, such as in oil or mining, most managements until recently have generally discounted this kind of linkage as more esoteric than practical for day-to-day operations.

The British withdrawal east of Suez in the early 1970s is a case in point. When these plans were first announced in the mid-1960s, little notice was taken by the U.S. business community - save for some of the major oils - as to what the likely consequences would be. This is understandable, because in those days, particularly, decolonization and self-determination were still the unfettered goals of enlightened internationalism. The mood of the times left little room for "what if" contingency planning as a serious element in policy thinking, both private and public alike.

Here and there, though, a few Middle East experts and geostrategists began thinking the unthinkables. Foremost among them was a team put together at Georgetown University's Center for Strategic and International Studies. By 1969 it had reached a basic conclusion. Unless a Western strategy were developed and implemented to fill the power vacuum caused by British withdrawal, the "lid" would come off. Centuries-old ethnic and religious rivalries would explode to engulf the region in new crises well beyond the already prolonged and tragic Arab-Israeli dispute.

At that time, efforts were made to convince both U.S. and British policymakers to develop a "strategy of replacement" sufficiently far enough in advance of the withdrawal so as to help contain the regional dislocations that were sure to come once these outside influences were removed. Similar attempts were made to involve the business and financial communities in advocating such a strategy. The hope was that a consensus for action could be built between the public and private sectors, so that vital economic and security interests of the United States and the West might be protected. But the preoccupations were many and perceptions of the consequences limited. (For example, I was part of a U.S. group which addressed this issue to certain members of the British Government in 1969 who received our assessments with courteous but noncommittal interest.)

Thus, no truly structured and coherent strategy ever emerged, except for the Shah of Iran's largely unilateral effort. For the most part, the fundamental destabilizing elements predicted in these early risk analyses have since come to pass.

One could argue endlessly over whether or not a comprehensive "strategy of replacement" would have made much of a difference in the scheme of things. The point is, however, that such predictions were made which proved reasonably accurate -- accurate enough at least to establish that risk analysis when properly defined and realistically structured is a legitimate tool in the art of forecasting. But like any tool, its degree of effectiveness cannot be known until it is tested and used constructively.

In any case, the 1973 oil embargo did occur. The Shah did fall. And the dislocations set in motion by just those two events alone are well charted on the account books of a host of multinational businesses and banks.

One result has been that in the intervening years, risk analysis has come into its own as a generally accepted practice by international enterprise. This is not so much because of the persuasiveness of its advocates but to a significant degree because of grim lessons learned through hindsight about Middle Eastern vagaries.

However it has won acceptance, risk analysis is only as useful as its core function is understood and applied. Quite simply, that function is to know where to look when one is attempting to isolate and assess the seeds of impending crisis.

In the case of the disintegration of Iran, for example, much of the American conventional wisdom was ever so busy looking at conditions in Iran through American eyes; thereby, basing its assumptions on American values; which ultimately led to American miscalculations as to the outcome, when the props were finally knocked from under the Shah. Things might have gone better for us had more Americans been steeped in enough knowledge, wisdom and humility to have been able to look at their own United States through two-thousand-year-old Persian eyes.

Because, leaving aside the seething Iranian rivalries (always a constant negative in the risk equation), it was essentially U.S. naivety about Persian folkways and mores that affected U.S. policy changes in the manner in which they occurred. That, of course, was to alter rather precipitously a 25-year-old policy in which unwavering support of the Shah had been its centerpiece (thereby muting the risk offset factor in the equation). Thus, the persuasive argument: The trigger mechanism for the disintegration as it occurred was quite possibly as much in the United States as Iran.

The U.S. defeat in Vietnam occurred not in that country but in Washington, where the two landmark decisions were made -- involvement and withdrawal. And if one is looking for clues as to how stable Central America is likely to be over the next decade, one had best be watching Soviet behavior, in addition to the political and cultural crosscurrents of, say, El Salvador.

Knowing where to look, then, can make the difference in assessing risk and the chances for economic survival in a traumatized world. The prerequisites for this are a combination of both insight and foresight. These human judgment factors can only come from personal in-depth knowledge about a targeted subject; knowledge based on reality, not subjective assumptions.

That is why this book is important. In this case, of course, the particular target is the Middle East. Those whose task it is to continue to make high-stake judgments about this still critically important region will find the chapters that follow truly valuable tools.

R. Daniel McMichael

---

*Mr. McMichael is Administrative Agent of the Scaife Family Charitable Trusts. He also is a director of the Center for Information Policy Research, Inc., Harvard University; a member of the National Security Advisory Board, Fletcher School of Law and Diplomacy, Tufts University; and member of the Advisory Board, Center for Strategic and International Studies, Georgetown University (1978-82).

Acknowledgments

The editors wish to thank the authors for their valuable contributions and Daphne Alexander, Stephanie Clipper, Robin Ehrlich, Tim Schey, JoAnn Vislocky and Nina Ostrovitz for their assistance in preparation of this volume. Special acknowledgement should be given to the Center for Strategic and International Studies (Georgetown University) and the Institute for Studies in International Terrorism (State University of New York) for their continued encouragement and support. These institutions, however, bear no responsibility for the views expressed by the authors and editors.

Introduction

Yonah Alexander
Robert A. Kilmarx

On October 6, 1981, in one of the most dramatic incidents in the history of contemporary ideological and political violence, Anwar el-Sadat, president of Egypt, was assassinated by member of Takfir Waihigra ("repentence and atonement"), a fundamentalist Islamic group which had planned to liquidate Egypt's political and military leadership with "sacred terror."

This sad event underscores most tragically the perpetual instability of the Middle East. Clearly, many factors contribute to this situation. Included in these are the crisis of legitimacy of various Arab and non-Arab regimes, the question of political participation and representation, the conflict between traditionalism and modernity, the idea of pan-Arabism, Islamic fundamentalist revival, the growing gap between the sparsely populated wealthy countries and densely populated poor countries, the escalating arms race, and numerous ideological and political disputes within the region.

Moreover, against the background of restless ethnic-religious-ideological minorities, boundary disputes, and other sources of tension in the region, the record indicates that there are hardly two countries without conflicts that have erupted or are about to explode. The list of inter-Arab confrontations is indeed long. It is sufficient to mention the current civil war in Lebanon. In addition to these inter-Arab and intra-Arab upheavals, crises, and hostilities, coupled with the current situation in Iran, the other lingering threat to Middle Eastern stability is the Palestinian question, which involves the Arab nations, the superpowers, and other interested states.

It is because of these indigenous and external pressures that violence - ranging from terrorism, to civil war, to open hostilities - has become a permanent feature in the struggle for power in Middle Eastern politics. That is, both established regimes and opposition groups, functioning under varying degrees of stress, have intentionally utilized instruments of psychological and physical force - intimidation coercion, repression, and, ultimately, destruction of lives and property - for the purpose of attaining real or imaginary ideological and political goals.

The purpose of this book is to examine the political security situation in this Middle East and its significance for business in the 1980s. The outlook for business in the region, while rich in opportunities, is more clouded in the 1980s than in earlier periods. The outlook is darkened by varying degrees of internal instability, deeply rooted rivalries and conflicts between states, profound religious and historical cleavages, and destabilizing forces of modernization, political terrorism, and uncertainty concerning the outlook for political evolution or revolutionary change. Increased big-power rivalry in the area feeds on these conditions. The rivalry stems mainly from Soviet penetration and subversion in its struggle for influence and its opportunistic exploitation of internal weaknesses that are exacerbated by internal and regional conflicts and tensions.

The persistent Arab-Israeli conflict, the civil strife in Lebanon, tension between South and North Yemen, the threat to Saudi Arabia posed by South Yemen, the Iran-Iraq war, Iran's threat to export its fundamentalist revolution, tensions between Syria and Iraq, and Libyan efforts to radicalize and destabilize the area all have the potential to trigger confrontation between superpowers. Dependence of the Western democracies and Japan on the oil resources of the area polarizes and magnifies the importance of local events in the diplomacy of affected developed states.

The response of U.S. foreign policy has not been equal to the challenge, in spite of the early success of the Camp David process. The Reagan administration faces many difficult choices as it seeks to increase its influence and security relationships with moderate Arab states hostile to Israel, as a response to Soviet threats, and at the same time maintain its special, historical commitment to Israel and to even strengthen it with new defense ties. Washington thus continues to walk on a policy tightrope. Miscalculation, misadventure, internal political weakness in Washington, or policy disarray could turn friends or potential allies into neutrals, at best, or increase the fragility of the leadership of traditional conservative regimes.

Multinational corporations and other commercial interests are at the center of the conflicting forces that will shape the area's orientation and political destiny in the 1980s and beyond. With the weakening effectiveness of traditional instruments of American foreign policy, U.S. business interests become more important factors in influencing the overall environment. As stated by Harold H. Saunders in his fine report for American Enterprise Institute entitled "The Middle East Problem in the 1980s" (released in December 1981): "American technology and managerial skill are having a greater effect in transforming societies and economics than could either diplomacy or military force."

Multinational corporate activities can both contribute to instabilities, because of its accelerated and pervasive impact on traditional cultures, and at the same time, create beneficial ties, common values, and interests that can bridge otherwise intractable rivalries. Business can be a positive force with favorable political influence. In some cases, business can become a partner of governments in addressing deep-seated problems or can work in harmony with the objectives of governments under economic conditions dominated by market forces. Business, however, also can be a destabilizing target for opposing groups of fundamentalists and radicals, and thus indirectly contribute to internal political upheavals.

The Middle East has become increasingly important to U.S. commercial interest, our balance of payments, and our economy. In 1980, U.S. exports to the Middle East totaled $9.8 billion, while U.S. imports totaled $15.5 billion. Exports to the Middle East significantly reduce the burden of oil dependence and the international financial problems associated with accumulated Arab dollar surpluses from oil sales.

The United States presently has a market share of sales to the Middle East of about 15 percent, about twice that of Japan. The market share of other major reporters is: over 17 percent for the Federal Republic of Germany; 12 percent for the United Kingdom; over 20 percent for France; and 11 percent for Italy. The share of other countries combined is about 15 percent.

Each contributor to this volume deals with a particular aspect of the problem. The book begins with an analysis of the sociological environment. Roger Savory provides an historical look at the Islamic religion which, he claims, has "assumed a new significance in the light of the continuing convulsions in Iran, the sectarian strife in Syria, Iraq, Lebanon, Turkey, and other parts of the Middle East, and the growing strength of Muslim fundamentalism in Egypt, Libya, Pakistan, and elsewhere." The author traces the expansion of European Christendom's oldest rival across Asia, North Africa, and into Europe by A.D. 711. The Christian counterattack that followed led to centuries of hostile contention with armies as disciplined as the Ottoman Turks before finally giving way to the Age of Exploration.

"As the West lost its fear of the Ottoman empire, it also lost its respect for Muslims, for Islam, and for Islamic civilization," he asserts. Suddenly neglected, many parts of the Muslim world reacted by cultivating nationalist movements which ultimately brought about the end of colonial rule and gave rise to independent Muslim states throughout the Middle East.

Dr. Savory makes the point that the current revival of Islam should be viewed as merely another "cyclical fluctuation" in the interacting evolution of these ancient religious rivals. Indeed, this revival has been developing since the start of the nineteenth century, but has only been cast to the forefront by the area's sudden accession of economic power from 1973 onward, made possible by the West's dependence on Middle East Oil.

Many of the current problems facing the Middle East derive from the conflict between classical Islamic tradition and the attempts by Muslim leaders to effect policies of local modernization and social reform. Without a fundamental knowledge of the Islamic view of the world, the author maintains, it is not possible to understand the torment facing the Middle East today. Islam, it is said, can be examined as a composite of three principal concepts, each of which has a substantial bearing on the Middle East's current state of affairs.

First, Islam as a religion and a faith primarily concerns the search for knowledge of God through His prophet Muhammad. With strict emphasis on ritual, the Islamic faith is rooted deeply in the day-to-day affairs of its followers, both as individuals and en masse.

Second, Islam is important in terms of law and tradition as well. The prophet Muhammad was not only the messenger of God, but the leader and first lawgiver of the initial Muslim community. Long ago the ancient Arab notion of normative custom was incorporated into the doctrine to supplement the movement's religious and moral elements. At least since the beginning of the tenth century, the followers of Muhammad have agreed that "at the very root of the Muslim conception of law lies the idea that law is inherently and essentially religious."

Third, Islam maintains a rudimentary posture in terms of state and nation. In Islamic tradition there is no separation between religion and politics. To preserve the religious aspects, to unify the faithful, and to codify divergent interpretations of Islamic jurisprudence, the movement developed into its own political structure.

Since Islam is no more a monolithic system than is Christianity, the author provides a brief reference to those components which he feels have had the most instrumental effect upon Islamic tradition in general. Significant are the Sunni-Shi i schism following the death of Muhammad in A.D. 632 (the effects of which are still visible in factional hostilities today), and the mystical aspect of Islam known as Sufism. Sufism embodies the symbolic and esoteric elements of the Muslim faith, and has found expression in the rich literature of Arab, Persian, Turkish, and Urdu theologians.

Following an updated historical perspective of the Islamic movement, during which Western ideas and colonialism dominated the concerns of those in the Middle East, the author addresses the Muslim response to the overwhelming tide of imperialism. Politically, responsibility for advancement was accepted by various nationalist movements. On the religious plane, however, the Muslim response was more complex.

After a period of submissive content, many thinkers of the Middle East began to identify a "process of social and cultural disintegration" with the import of Western institutions and standards. The fundamentalist Muslims espoused anti-Turkish as well as anti-Western sentiment, attempting to revive traditional Islam by "purifying" it from within. Resisting European domination by returning to religious fundamentals proved to be the motivating force behind the Muslim activism becoming commonplace during the nineteenth century.

Islamic "modernists," on the other hand, felt that some degree of modification was necessary if the faith was going to adapt itself to the modern world. Normative tradition, it was believed, had stagnated the Islamic movement. Furthermore, religion and law were essentially different, modernists claimed, and therefore had to be separated.

Dr. Savory points out that the modernized codes existing under Riza Shah in Iran were quickly reverted to their traditional format once the Islamic Republic of Iran was established in 1979. It is clear that the evolutionary cycle of religion in the Middle East continues to progress. All laws and regulations, in Tehran at least, have been refounded on ancient Islamic principles.

In confronting the state of religion, particularly Islam, in the Middle East today, the author challenges the opinion of those who claim the West is superior economically, militarily, and spiritually. For the Muslim world, political independence "inevitably encouraged a revival of religious fervor," due to the essential blending of politics and religion in Islam. To illustrate the different ways in which Muslims have responded to the opportunity of shaping their own destiny, Dr. Savory presents four specific examples.

Pakistani Muslims have, above all else, sought to create a concise Islamic state. At the opposite extreme, Muslims in Turkey have deliberately turned their backs on their Islamic heritage in order to establish a secular state. Egypt is mentioned as a state adopting a "gradual" response to Western influence, and Iran stands out as the only Islamic country in which Ithna Ashari Shiism is the official religious sect of the state.

Several important points are clarified in Dr. Savory's conclusion. First, Islam - the most popular religion in the Middle East - is not a succinctly defined and readily predictable force under any given set of circumstances. The dilemma

of how best to adapt to the technological age must be faced
by all religions, and the Muslims have yet to realize that they
need not abandon their religious faith in order to improve
their material standards. Also, one must accept the fact that
certain Muslim attitudes are unchanging. Despite the preachings of Islamic modernists, "the authority of the past" still
dominates the thinking of Muslims; their ultimate allegiance is
to God, not to a nation-state - as is common in the West. The
question of how or whether the fundamental principles of Islam
may be reformulated without destroying its essential elements,
unfortunately, remains unanswered.

The second chapter, by Waldo H. Dubberstein, is devoted
to several aspects of the complex Middle East security crisis.
A short historical background sets the stage for an examination of the following issues: the Arab-Israeli conflict; the
Egyptian-Israeli peace effort; the Palestinian question; the
ongoing tragedy in Lebanon; the Iran-Iraq war; and finally,
what the author refers to as "the overhanging Soviet threat"
in the Middle East.

The basis for deep-seated Arab-Israeli conflict was established in the 1940s after Britain had overzealously promised a
homeland to both the Arab congregation and the displaced
Jews. Arab-Israeli battles have occurred ever since Israel
achieved statehood in 1948. Israeli sovereignty was thereupon
perceived by the USSR as justification for Soviet intervention
in the region. While Palestinian refugees kept the tension
high between periods of large-scale fighting, Israel retaliated
as it saw fit, and violence escalated.

In August 1955 Egyptian President Nasser agreed to accept Soviet arms through Czechoslovakia. Britain and France
responded by teaming up militarily with Israel in October of
1956 in an attempt to reconquer the Suez Canal. The next
major fighting took place in mid-1967 after Egypt, Jordan, and
Syria joined to harass Isareli shipping operations. Israel
attacked the three Arab states, along with Iraq, and quickly
annihilated its enemies; no peace settlement resulted. The
Yom Kippur War of 1973 evidenced yet another stage in full
scale warfare, this episode having no clear victor. Also at
about this time, Yasir Arafat's Palestinian Liberation Organization began to achieve recognition as the sole representative
of the Palestinian people.

A formal Egypt-Israel peace treaty was finally signed in
March 1979 under the prodding of President Carter. Under
the agreement, all of Sinai was to be returned to Egypt within
three years. The pact seemed ill-fated, however, when
Jerusalem continued to permit new Israeli settlements to form
on the West Bank, and terrorist operations increased.

As the situation stands, Israel remains militarily the most
powerful of Middle Eastern nations. Yet it is hated and feared
by its neighbors, all of whom seem totally committed to the

destruction of the Israeli state. The situation is further complicated by the ambiguous status of the Palestinian population. Since 1964 this relatively small group of Arabs - some four to five million scattered across Lebanon, Syria, Jordan, Kuwait, and Saudi Arabia - has been officially represented by the Palestinian Liberation Organization (PLO). The PLO is composed of a number of active branches, and receives an exorbitant amount of funding from the wealthy oil-producing states and through a mandatory tax imposed on all Palestinians, regardless of where they live. There is also speculation as to what is called the "Moscow connection" with the PLO, but details have been kept discreet.

Since its creation, the PLO has waged its regional war on Israel through the practice of terrorism. Palestinian guerrillas operate sophisticated terrorist training camps throughout Libya, Algeria, Iraq, Jordan, Lebanon, and South Yemen, and often operate in collaboration with radical organizations based in other areas of the world. In addition to strikes against Zionism, it should be noted, intra-Arab terrorism has been a regular activity among a number of Arab entities.

Another factor of major importance to Middle East stability is the increasing state of Arab disunity. Since the time of Muhammad, Islamic unity has been a prominent theme throughout the Arab world; but, exacerbated by the creation of a formal Jewish state, the Arab dream has never come to be. Despite geographical similarities, pronounced cultural, regional, and religious differences exist between various segments of the Arab community. Tension over the past thirty years has escalated, evidenced in part at least by reports that former Egyptian President Nasser and Libya's Colonel Qadhafi had each taken direct measures to assassinate fellow Arab leaders. Political preferences among today's rulers have further stimulated increased hostilities among Arab nations.

Circumstances in Lebanon also have a significant effect on the overall Middle East situation today. The country's long and complex history has fostered an extremely diverse population mixture. Nonetheless, a stable and contented environment endured until masses of Palestinian refugees migrated to Lebanon following the creation of Israel in 1948. By 1970 this integrated country had become an operational base for Palestinian terror strikes against Israel. The conflict intensified in 1975 when the Arab League and outside states began to take active interest in the course of events. The United Nations Interim Force in Lebanon (UNIFIL) helped to tone down the violence, restricting large-scale border raids between the Palestinian factions and the Israeli military. Still, the fighting persists. Although Israeli troops pulled out in 1978, chances for a lasting peace seem less likely than ever. With the abundance of Syrian troops, Palestinian militants, Lebanese Christians, UNIFIL forces, and the official Lebanese government military, chaos and bloodshed are destined to continue.

Dr. Dubberstein concludes his report with an overview of current developments in the Middle East. The status of Iran is stressed because of the power turnover to Ayatollah Khomeini and the persisting Iran-Iraq military clash. To a limited extent, sides have been chosen among neighboring states, but many, especially the Gulf states, are anxiously trying to remain uninvolved in the contention between Iran and its neighbors. Finally, Dr. Dubberstein comments on the Soviet role in the Middle East, taking particular note of Moscow's long-standing interest in Iran. Soviet arms have begun to flow into the Middle East, and bilateral pacts appear to tie the Russian bear in the course of policymaking. It is apparent that the USSR is "determined to expand its influence" in the Middle East and is willing to undertake a variety of means and tactics to achieve its goals. The Middle East remains in a perilous condition and "if past patterns prevail, the present situations will be somewhat resolved . . . but there will be no definitive solutions."

Ibrahim M. Oweiss, in the third chapter (written before the assassination of President Sadat), asserts that understanding the strategic, economic, and political dimensions of Egypt is fundamental to comprehending the current domestic and international trends pertaining to this controversial state. Strategically, Egypt's importance is obvious. A geographical crossroads between Africa and Asia, the country is the most populous of Middle Eastern states, and in spite of its desert environment, Egypt enjoys an abundance of fertile valleys and navigable waterways.

Egypt has also become a prominent figure in the enduring Arab-Israeli conflict. Its leadership role, however, has cast Cairo out of favor with her Arab neighbors. Still, the lack of local retaliation suggests that Egypt has managed to maintain a position of respect in the region.

Egypt's strategic status is apparent also in its attraction to the superpowers. America views the nation as crucial to securing Washington's main Mideast objectives: resolution of the Arab-Israeli conflict, containment of Soviet influence in the area, and continued access to Middle East oil. U.S. concern for regional stability had prompted increases in military and economic assistance to President Sadat, especially after the loss of Iran as a strategic American friend. Furthermore, Soviet intervention in Afghanistan and Ethiopia, and deep-seated influences in South Yemen and Libya, make a staunch, pro-Western ally in Egypt, one of vital concern to policymakers in Washington.

Dr. Oweiss devotes a good deal of text to his economic analysis because "it is the success of domestic economic efforts which will determine the future of Egypt." All in all, consid-

erable progress was being made under the Sadat regime, and
this is most currently reflected in an economic growth rate of
8 to 9 percent since 1975. The author attributes such positive
gains primarily to the performance of the industrial and petroleum sectors, which in turn depend to a large degree upon the
increasing flow of foreign capital within the Egyptian economic
system. Advances in transportation and communications, and
increasing interest in tourism and banking have likewise stimulated economic growth in Egypt. Investment spending is up,
due to commercial tax exemptions, the removal of export license requirements, the establishment of free zones, and other
foreign trade incentives applied by the government.

Countering the economic progress and the increasing rate
of employment are a number of "monumental problems" which
the administration in Cairo must still overcome. The country's
actual rate of inflation has been estimated to be as high as 23
percent per annum, a result of the rapid increase in money
supply. Egypt continues to suffer a large balance-of-payments
deficit, and has been witnessing a devastating national population increase. Census bureaus report an additional one million
persons every ten months, and the pace is quickening despite
the migration of Egyptian workers to Saudi Arabia, Kuwait,
and Libya. What is worse, the tendency is for the most
highly educated and trained to leave the Egyptian labor pool,
resulting in something of a "brain-drain" malady.

External assistance has helped alleviate the strains imposed upon the Egyptian economy. Financial aid from the Gulf
Organization for the Development of Egypt (GODE), various
channels of support from the American government, and food
resources from the European community have notably contributed to the Egyptian cause at home. Assorted other aid programs have similarly proved beneficial.

The political stability of Egypt is described as being
"remarkably high." Since Anwar Sadat succeeded President
Nasser in 1970, domestic policies have been modified in the
direction of greater freedom. The country's 1971 constitution
describes it as a democratic socialist state, and its government
system is characterized by an elected president, an extensive
cabinet, a unicameral elected legislature, and an independent
secular judiciary.

Until 1976, Egypt maintained a single-party system.
Since that time, various groups espousing alternative postures
have represented different segments of the population. A few
of these have voiced considerable discontent concerning the
regime in power. Economic dissatisfaction, based upon sky-
rocketing population increases and runaway inflation, presents
the primary concern for unrest in Egypt.

Increasingly hostile Islamic sentiment was also an issue of
great concern to the Sadat administration. The area's traditional sensitivity to religion fomented a secular body opposing

the existence of Israel and led to a reemerging of the severe
polarization between Moslems and Christian Copts (the largest
minority in Egypt).

In an attempt to limit reactionary behavior and to ensure
long-term internal stability in Egypt, the existing government
has made several adjustments in the nation's sociopolitical
structure. To limit the activities of theological groups to
religious matters, the president has made it illegal for such
organizations to establish political associations. Constitutional
changes include the widely supported 1979 referendum allowing
Mr. Sadat to remain in office for life, the cancellation of mar-
tial law, and the official establishment of a multiparty political
system in the state of Egypt.

Cairo's domestic political stability, of course, was also
contingent upon the effectiveness of President Sadat's foreign
policy decisions. Egypt's position of relative isolation from her
Arab neighbors could possibly lead to the expulsion of Egyptian migrant workers from the Arab oil-producing countries.
An influx of dissatisfied laborers returning home may well
become a major source of domestic instability. Close alignment
with the United States may also represent a potential area of
political vulnerability for the present regime.

In conclusion, Dr. Oweiss reminds the reader that
Egypt's overall economic situation since 1975 has been "rather
impressive." Substantial assistance through the U.S. AID
program is expected to compensate for the downward trend in
agricultural productivity and the burden imposed by the lag-
ging public sector, a result of Nasser's nationalization of large
industries in 1961.

President Sadat's political future was assessed by Dr.
Oweiss as "relatively secure" in spite of its controversial political status in the international picture. However, "an optimistic view of Egypt's future will only be possible when her
deep-rooted historical and cultural relations with the Arab
countries are once again normalized and as she gradually resumes her position of leadership in the Arab world."

The chapter by Malcolm Peck examines the political and
security concerns of the seven Arab states of the Gulf region
(including Oman) in the wake of three highly charged events:
the Camp David talks and subsequent Egyptian-Israeli peace
treaty; the Iranian revolution; and the Soviet invasion of
Afghanistan. Dr. Peck also challenges American policy in this
part of the Middle East.

The invasion of Afghanistan has revived old fears of
Soviet expansionism to gain access to the Gulf. Although the
Soviets are seen as an ever-present threat, the Arab states
see no immediate danger from that quarter; what they fear
more are subversive movements supported by external interests. For this reason, the Iranian revolution and Khomeini's
efforts to spread the revolution have aroused feelings of dis-

quiet among the Gulf states. However, small Shia and Iranian communities, along with the development of modern political structures in some states and various other factors, have all helped them to control or impede any unrest.

For security reasons, a policy of accommodation with neighbors has been pursued by the smaller Gulf states, except for Oman. Saudi Arabia is especially sought out for support, be it financial or political. This type of policy means, though, that these Gulf states retain small armed forces. Kuwait and the United Arab Emirates (UAE) have embarked, however, on a military expansion program to maintain internal security and, in the case of the UAE, to symbolize unity.

The smaller Gulf states also seek to have good relations with the rest of the world. Kuwait has tried to strike a balance between the Americans and the Soviets; Bahrain maintains a U.S. naval command, MIDEASTFOR - both an embarrassment during strained U.S.-Arab relations and a powerful psychological security factor, and Oman enjoys a good rapport with the West, especially with Great Britain and the United States. Qatar prefers to pursue a low-profile external policy.

Iraq and Saudi Arabia are the two largest and most powerful states in the Gulf area. Iraq has molded a new role for itself, replacing Iran as the main security organizer for that region. The Iraqi government is now willing to work with a variety of Arab regimes, not just the radical ones, to attain common Arab goals. For the Iraqis, the Iranian revolution is feared because of its ability to destabilize the region, thus producing cause for a superpower intervention. This would frustrate Iraqi plans of regional domination. Dr. Peck sees the role of Iraq expanding and increasing in importance; it is an influential state to be paid particular attention to in the future.

Saudi Arabia, as a major military and economic power in the Gulf, plays a commanding role in regional politics. Major threats to Saudi security involve internal unrest spurred on by external forces - a threat shared by most of the smaller Arab states. Iraq is seen as an instigator of this type of unrest. The Saudis deal with external threats by a variety of means. Diplomatic accommodation as well as military and economic power to help to support favorable relations with most nations; a close relationship with the United States also serves as a deterrent. The principal threat to stability in Saudi Arabia and states throughout the Gulf region is their major dependence on expatriate skills; unrest among those who are denied citizenship is always a present danger.

Saudi Arabia enjoys a close military, political, and economic relationship with the United States dating back to World War II. Recently, however, serious economic problems between the two have developed, affecting political relations. Military relations have also become strained, with the countries espous-

ing different priorities. The author points out that the main
political strain on U.S.-Saudi relations is the Arab-Israeli
conflict. Any U.S. move in this affair colors relations with
the rest of the Arab world.

United States interest in the Gulf area has gained in
importance in recent years. Failure to actively counter threats
to American interests as well as those to American allies, however, has raised doubts of U.S. credibility. Also, the danger
of Soviet influence infiltrating this area cannot be ruled out.
A Soviet oil shortage may prompt a commercial venture, as
opposed to a military venture, into the Gulf States. Careful
scrutiny must be made of any relationship in the Middle East,
especially when considering ties between the Arab-Israeli conflict and the political and security concerns in the Gulf. This
linkage was underlined by the Arab response to the Egyptian-
Israeli peace treaty. Necessary and appropriate actions must
be taken only after all possibilities have been explored.

Chapter five, by Charles G. MacDonald, deals with the
Islamic Republic of Iran. Today, it is characterized by a
dynamic state of chaos thoroughly undermining any foundation
of social, political, or military stability that once existed in the
land. Factors such as rampant foreign intervention, internal
contention among political, ethnic, and religious forces, and a
distraught and fragmented populace have contributed to the
rapid weakening of Iran's defenses, in both a political and a
military perspective. As the Soviet Union's presence looms on
the northern horizon and Iraq eyes Iran's western provinces,
Dr. MacDonald addresses the country's political context and
security situation with particular reference to current developments, factors, and forces determining Iran's future.

In the past three years, Iran has been transformed from
what former President Carter once described as "an island of
stability in one of the most troubled areas of the world," to an
Islamic republic enduring a state of continuing revolutionary
upheaval. Since 1979 the country has experienced a series of
short-term governments. Prime Minister Azhari resigned on the
first day of that year, and his military government was replaced by the civilian regime of Shapur Bakhtiar three days
later. To the cheers of millions, Ayatollah Khomeini arrived in
Iran on the first of February, following a period of prolonged
self-exile in Paris. As head of the Islamic Revolutionary
Council, Khomeini immediately demanded Bakhtiar's resignation
and selected Mehdi Bazargan to head the country's "provisional" government. On the verge of civil war and without
military support, Prime Minister Bakhtiar consented, resigning
on February 11. Within the next month, Khomeini alternated
between supporting and criticizing the Bazargan government.
The Islamic Republic was officially established during late
March, bringing an end to Iran's 2,500-year-old monarchy.

Even at this time, internal dissension was becoming apparent. Summary courts and executions kept the domestic threat under control for Khomeini, but at the same time exposed his Revolutionary Council to scattered charges of despotism. Political polarization increased as the provisional government and the Revolutionay Council continued to act separately. Fearful of further internal competition, the Ayatollah published a new constitution in mid-June. To no one's surprise, the revised draft strengthened the power of the clerics at the expense of the president and the Majlis.

While the constitution was still under consideration, a group of militants calling themselves the "students who follow the line of Imam" seized the American embassy in Tehran and took hostages on November 4, 1979. This ended the reign of Bazargan's provisional government and resulted in Khomeini's order for the Revolutionary Council to assume governmental responsibility.

On November 15 the council announced a new government that included Abolhassan Bani-Sadr as minister of finance and economic affairs. Two months later, Bani-Sadr won the presidential election with an overwhleming 75.7 percent of the vote. His power was quickly compromised, however, as the Islamic Republican Party easily defeated Bani-Sadr's supporters in the Majlis (National Consultative Assembly) elections held during April and May. (Since that time, of course, the Shah has died, the American hostages have been returned, and the Ayatollah has managed to maintain his position of leadership with a forceful hand.) Usurped of power, ex-President Bani-Sadr was forced to flee his country under threat of execution, and this turnabout has led to an uncontrolled state of low-level domestic violence, including a surge of political assassination.

Iran's revolution has seen a number of disparate groups vying for power, most of which defy simple categorization because of crosscutting loyalties. According to Dr. MacDonald, it was the Shah's departure that brought the differences within the opposition to the fore. Among the politically active religious bodies are the Mujahhidin-i Khalq, "Iran's largest lefist group," and the clandestine Furgan-admitted assassins of a number of revolutionary figures. Holding a more central line are two nationalist organizations: The National Front of Karim Sanjabi, and the Freedom Front of Mehdi Bazargan.

Lesser political opposition is projected from the National Democratic Front, the Tudeh Party, and the Fedayin Khalq. Domestic chaos, however, is not all politically founded. Various ethnic minorities, led by the Kurds and the Azerbaijanis, have militarily sought autonomy from the central government. Numerous other ethnic groups have added to the country's growing disunity, but severe crisis has been delayed, it appears, by the national fear of Soviet invasion.

As time goes on, the number and makeup of Iran's pro-
tagonist groups continue to change and the list of casualties
continues to grow. As Ayatollah Khomeini has periodically
shifted his posture to maintain a delicate internal balance, he
has also attempted to "purify" all aspects of Iranian life with
the Islamic creed. This, the author feels, will lead to "the
gradual solidification of power by the hard-line clerics, the
vanguard of Iran's Islamic revolution."

The concept of legitimacy in revolutionary Iran is a fundamental aspect of Dr. MacDonald's assessment. The roots of
legitimacy are found in the revolution's two driving forces,
Islam and nationalism. In addition, opposition to the Shah had
initially served as a unifying factor among the people and the
evolving leaders in Iran. "By the fall of 1979 a new cohesive
factor was needed as the revolution seemed to be losing its
momentum and disintegrating." This came in the form of Khomeini's comprehensive anti-American campaign, and was dramatically highlighted by the militants' seizure of the American
embassy in Tehran.

MacDonald contends that legitimacy in Iran is currently
going through a transitional phase. The hostage incident has
contributed to serious disruption internally, as have the political executions and the widespread unrest among Iran's populace. A further revised constitution, placing "absolute power
in the hands of the 'Great Ayatollah Khomeini,' the faqih," is
establishing itself as the most recent symbol of legitimacy.
Under the new format, the faqih is constitutionally permitted
to exercise total authority if he so decides. The Council of
Guardians and 270-member Majlis provide for minimal checks
and balances, and the president serves primarily as an administrator.

With Iran's oppressed history of foreign influence and
domination, the nation has come to place great emphasis on
protecting its sovereignty and territorial integrity. Since the
revolution, however, security goals have become obscured,
with revolutionary objectives seemingly contradicting Iran's
traditional defensive concerns.

During the 1970s, Iran's military capacity mushroomed.
Yet, despite the presence of a highly sophisticated arsenal,
the military nearly disintegrated upon the Shah's departure.
Many ranking officers either fled, were assassinated, or were
purged, and regular rumors of coup plotting kept any plans
for military reconstruction in their most primitive stages.
Following the sixth actual coup attempt in four months, the
Revolutionary Guards took the initiative to maintain internal
security. After the guards opened fire on a Mujahidin rally in
June 1980, injuring 300, questions surfaced as to whose security interests were indeed being served.

There exist both external and internal threats to the
security interests of the Islamic Republic. Externally, the So-

viet Union and the United States are simultaneously perceived
as realistic threats and potential saviors. And of course,
neighboring Iraq presents the most immediate military threat to
Iran. Internally, any of numerous political, religious, and
ethnic minorities may further upset the already questionable
state of stability within Iran.

Revolutionary Iran has denounced its predecessors' regional security concerns. Instead, it appears to adopt a
destabilizing role by attempting to broaden and export its
revolution. Among its weapons are an Islamic attack on Zionism, deep anti-Western sentiment, and anti-imperialist outcries.
Whether or not the directing body can survive long enough to
carry out the movement's long-range aspirations remains to be
seen.

Beginning with a look at the basic economic setting of the
Middle East, Hossein Askari, in the sixth chapter, stresses the
"unusual dispersion of characteristics in physical size, population, GDP, GDP per capita, basic economic structure, and the
like" among the countries in this region. In order to most
effectively analyze the area's economic conditions, he divides
the component states into "oil-exporters" and "non-oil-exporters," with the former encompassing the OPEC nations as
well as the states of Oman and Bahrain.

Admitting that such categorization restricts one's evalu-
ative precision, Dr. Askari proposes several general conclusions in line with this compromise. First, the oil exporters of
the area show a significantly greater variance in all mea-
surable economic determinants. Second, "the major difference
between the oil exporters and the non-oil-exporters is a
tremendous gap in economic prosperity." Exceptions exist; but
for the sake of simplicity, these assumptions are practicable.

The author's main point is that oil-exporting countries in
the Middle East must maintain an acccumulation of productive
wealth or foreign assets to support their petroleum enterprises, in order to secure future economic stability. Among the
alternatives mentioned for transforming oil wealth into stable
productive assets are agricultural promotion (severely limited
by terrain and climate in most Middle East countries) and
industrial expansion (restricted by technological and educational capabilities in many areas). Solutions will not be simple
or obvious, but a sustainable productive bias is critical.

The unique characteristics of the oil industry are worthy
of mention. In the first place, the oil sector is not integrated
into the rest of the economy through backward and forward
linkages. Second, employment opportunities are limited to a
narrow range of skills which may not match overall national
aspirations. Third, since it is the government that receives
the oil-export revenues, income is not rationally distributed,
and this can ultimately lead to popular discontent.

Related problems arise because the government must select branches of economic diversification without the benefits of
receiving indications through the market mechanisms, as a
more broadly based and gradual process of private sector
industrialization would offer. Similarly, the "quantum increase
in income occurring over a short period of time has resulted in
a massive surge in imports and consequently an unbounded
rate of inflation." Dr. Askari contends "The oil exporting
countries find themselves in a vicious circle which . . . is not
caused by too little current revenues, but by too much current revenues from a nonsustainable source coupled with unattractive investment." International cooperation is suggested as
a necessary precondition to a feasible long range remedy.

In terms of existing economic structure, several contrasts
are made between the oil-exporting and the non-oil-exporting
groups. Due to rising oil revenue and general neglect, the
agricultual sector has deteriorated sharply for oil exporters
throughout the past decade or so.   And except for Algeria,
Iran, and Iraq, the level of manufacturing has also been significantly lower among the oil exporters. Related to this factor,
the export structure for non-oil exporters is considerably more
diversified than for the other group.

Expanding oil revenues have markedly affected the makeup of the labor force in a number of oil-exporting countries.
Expatriate labor accounted for nearly three-quarters of Kuwait's working force in 1971, and more than 80 percent of that
of Qatar (no current figures given). Apparently, the ratios
have been increasing ever since, and while there are certain
benefits to labor exchange, the costs of so massive an effort
have ranged from economic and commercial setbacks to widespread social disruption. Labor shortages have evolved where
surpluses once existed, and a high percentage of migrating
skilled labor never returns to the country that provided the
original training.

The most important fundamental distinction between the
countries of the Middle East is the existence and nonexistence
of oil.   Whereas oil has dramatically affected the economic
development of those countries possessing significant amounts,
the resource is nonetheless finite in quality and must therefore
be converted into productive non-oil domestic assets and attractive foreign interests in order to maintain successful
long-term national economies.

Enlarged petroleum revenues in the oil-exporting countries, then, have resulted in increased population growth
(largely from labor inflow), higher GDP, spurred inflation,
and increased national savings and investment rates – all to
varying degrees, depending on the particular country. The
question becomes one of time: How long will the oil phenomenon
endure? With proper economic and development guidance –
avoiding large-scale military expenditures and other prestige

projects and instead focusing upon agriculture, education, health, and other social services as well as stabilizing industrial ventures - future prospects appear favorable. Callous economic planning can only lead to unjust income distribution, popular frustration, and eventual political and social disruptions as seen in 1978-1979 Iran. The economic stability of the Middle East, though promising, remains uncertain.

The seventh chapter, by Peter Hale and Cherie A. Loustaunan, reviews the history of trade relations between the United States and the Middle East. The eighteenth century marked the beginning of these relations when the eastern United States was a British colony. Although the British Acts of Trade prohibited the colonists from trading directly with North Africa and the Levant, American products were shipped on British vessels or on American ships under British protection. American exports at this time included wheat, flour, and cloth; wine, salt, and Moroccan leather were imported.

The Declaration of Independence in 1776 cut the Americans off from British trading privileges and protection. Prohibited from dealing with any part of the British Empire, the Americans turned to the East. This became a costly endeavor due to the Barbary pirates. By 1800, one-fifth of America's revenues were paid to the North African states to ensure safe passage of American ships in the Mediterranean, and for payment of ransoms. This exorbitant amount forced the United States government to seek out a cheaper negotiation.

In 1787, a treaty of peace and friendship was signed by the Sultan of Morocco. This was the United States' first treaty with a non-European power (also, the longest unbroken treaty in U.S. history). Treaties with the other North African states did not come about so quickly; it was not until 1816 that a treaty was negotiated with Algeria. These treaties, however, did little to encourage trade between the United States and North Africa. Rather, they helped promote trade with countries of the eastern Mediterranean, since American vessels were no longer threatened in those waters. Yet despite easy passage, trade was slow to grow. It was not until after World War I that trade between the United States and the Middle East reached any significant levels.

The lack of trade growth between the two was due to both political and commercial factors. The Americans preferred to have few ties with any country; thus, they saw little reason to push for economic relations with the Middle East. The commercial barrier to trade relations involved a lack of products to trade. Prior to the nineteenth century, both the United States and the Middle East primarily exported raw materials and imported manufactured goods. Trade was carried on between the two, though through multilateral tradings; goods from one part of the world were shipped from the United States to another part. In 1840, United States reexports of foreign products to the eastern Mediterranean equaled American domestic exports.

The main trade center in the Middle East was Smyrna, in Turkey. Americans sold wheat, cotton, rum, coffee, refined sugar, and tobacco, and bought animal hides, raw wool, olives, figs, raisins, and opium. In 1930 the U.S. government negotiated a treaty with Turkey, giving American goods special status and American ships access to the Black Sea. Despite difficulties in navigating through the straits to the sea and high tariffs, trade with Turkey was consistant.

Trade relations with Egypt increased steadily in the 1800s. By 1848 commercial ties were important enough for the United States to establish a consulate general in Alexandria. In direct contrast to Egypt, trade with Persia was practically nonexistent until the late 1800s. The United States traded timber and wood furniture to Egypt in exchange for cotton and cotton rag.

Trade relations with the Middle East began to increase significantly after the Mexican-American War. This expansion may have been due in part to the revolution in Europe. U.S. exports now included textiles and flour; imports included wool, fruit, gums, resin, and opium.

After the American Civil War, trade relations again were on the upswing with the countries of the Middle East. Large-scale American exports of petroleum and arms reversed the U.S. balance of trade with the Ottoman Empire. Exports of industrialized products increased, namely, machinery and transportation equipment, whereas exports of raw materials and rum decreased. The United States continued to import a substantial quantity of wool and opium, while curtailing other Middle East products.

From 1860 to the late 1880s, the United States monopolized the petroleum industry. Illuminating oil was the United States' chief export to Syria and Egypt in 1868. The United States' method of shipping also changed. Foreign ships were used more and more to transport American goods. U.S. shipping never returned to the pre-Civil War level, and any attempts before World War I to initiate a shipping service were negated by the British and other competitors.

After 1890, Egypt was the United States' main trading partner in the region. Around this same time, U.S. interest in the Middle East increased substantially. Aden, Persia, and Morocco were among the Middle Eastern states with which the United States increased trade. Trade with Turkey also developed; tobacco was a major import, which was mixed with American tobacco to create "Turkish blend" cigarettes. The establishment of the American Chamber of Commerce in Constantinople in 1911 reflected the extent of United States commercial involvement in the region.

American trade basically prospered during World War I. Egypt's role as the United States' main trading partner was accented in light of the almost total elimination of trade relations with Turkey. After World War I, however, United States trade relations were limited in the Middle East by the mandate system of the League of Nations, which divided the region into spheres of British and French influence. This barrier did not halt trade growth, but slowed it down.

The United States began to export more food, food products, machinery, and transportation equipment. While petroleum was still a major export product, its volume was being cut. Crude oil discoveries in the Middle East and a growing fear among Americans that U.S. domestic supplies were running out contributed to this decrease.

World War II created no insurmountable barrier for U.S. trade. Although some U.S. imports began to decline, new products from the Middle East were imported. Fresh fruit and vegetables could now be shipped long distance because of new refrigerated transportation. The most significant U.S. import was Middle East oil. World War II marked an important change in the character, composition, and size of American exports. The United States government also took on a new role as a promoter of U.S. commercial relations. Formerly, trade deals were made by private entrepreneurs. Most export products to the Middle East were on a lend-lease financing system; they mainly consisted of ammunition and weaponry during the war.

Then, military goods and technological assistance became the chief American exports after the war to the Middle East. Also, billions of U.S. dollars were funded to this region, and this aid is still continuing. The U.S. Army Corps of Engineers has the important status of handling billions of dollars in military construction in Saudi Arabia. Iran, Israel, Egypt, Jordan, and Morocco have also received large quantities of some type of military aid. Monetary aid was not restricted to military projects; since the United States had strategic interests in the area, other help was also extended. The U.S. Agency for International Development and other American economic assistance programs have meted out over $7.7 billion in the Middle East, and eleven states in this region have been the main beneficiaries. Agricultural aid has also been extended to a number of Middle Eastern states under Public Law 480; this aid has gone mainly to Egypt, Turkey, Israel, Morocco and Tunisia.

From World War II until the Arab oil embargo in 1973-1974, the United States maintained a steady growth in trade relations with the Middle East. The most important U.S. exports were still machinery and transportation equipment, and agricultural products made up a large portion of American imports. For the first fifteen years following World War II, Turkey was the United States' largest trading partner. This

position was claimed by Israel in the 1960s. U.S. trade with
the states of the lower Arabian peninsula and with North Africa was limited by British and French influences there. Trade
with Iraq and Syria was limited in the 1970s because of their
political alliance with the USSR. By 1970, United States exports to the entire Middle East region only amounted to 4.7
percent of total U.S. exports. But oil embargo and the sharp
increases in OPEC prices had a dramatic effect on U.S.-Middle
East trade. U.S. exports to that region rose from 5.4 percent
of worldwide U.S. exports in 1973 to 10.6 percent in 1978.
Although the United States capitalized on this export growth,
in 1979, total U.S. trade in the region had an almost $12 bil-
lion deficit. Two elements are the main causes of this dramatic
change in the trade balance. U.S. import figures had risen
sharply because of rising energy resource needs and the high
price of crude oil. This increased revenue for the oil-producing states has enabled them to initiate large developmental
projects in their own countries as well as in the poorer countries of the region. The U.S. business community has played
a major role in these developments; large engineering and
construction firms hold many of the contracts for the new
projects. As of 1981, total trade between the U.S. and the
Mideast states had reached an approximate figure of $50
billion. Since then, trade has been growing, and it appears
that it will continue to grow.

Chapter eight, by Riad A. Ajami, deals with "The Multinationals and Arab Economic Development: A New Paradigm."
At present, economic growth and technological transformation
are primary concerns within the Arab community. In the
Middle East, a special sense of urgency is shared, as all Arab
policymakers anticipate with fear the day when the oil wells
run dry. The failure of most open aid programs to spur regional development has shifted the focus to trade and investment. Arab elites have since become aware that "multinational
corporate know-how and expertise, if properly harnassed,
could spell the difference between success and failure." Dr.
Ajami's chapter briefly examines some positive and negative
arguments regarding multinational investment within developing
countries, particularly those in the Middle East.

The advocates of multinational corporate investment base
their stance on the economic efficiency of such organizations
and their ability to transfer capital, technology, and managerial and organizational skills as needed. While developing
nations often lack the capability to mobilize their resources
(human, capital, and physical), multinationals are considered
to be the most effective "energizers" of such resources and
serve as "mechanisms for linking host developing countries
with the center of world finance and industry." This link, in
turn, acts to increase a state's export capacity, provides
regional employment, increases the supply of local capital, and

provides easier access to necessary foreign monetary resources.

Supporters of the multinational instrument stress the
importance of the demonstrational role models offered by prov-
en and experienced outside investors. Domestic firms may
bypass the normal learning process and acquire the skills for
operating more efficiently by emulating multinational techniques. Domestic economic efficiency improves as the real costs
of local production are lowered through the application of
greater technical and professional skills.

A number of scholarly experts question the compatibility
between multinationals and the process of economic development. Harmful aspects mentioned include excessive profits,
balance-of-payment drain upon the host economy, lack of transfer of applicable skills, and market structure distortion.

Generally speaking, the critics of multinational corporate
involvement can be divided into three broad groups. The
"nationalists" advocate national autonomy, preferring a more
limited role of participation in the world economy. Nationalists
claim that while multinational profits are extremely high, only a
small portion of the gain is reinvested within host countries.
Similarly, direct investment is concentrated in advanced-
technology industries, where profits are higher, and consequently ignores other sectors. The transfer of technology is
"minimal," nationalists persist, with the most specialized skills
being tightly guarded to ensure a condition of local dependency upon foreign talent. Finally, "the sheer size and power of
multinationals overwhelm local competitors," making such operations actually detrimental to national economic development.

The "dependencia" school of reasoning argues along slightly more radical lines, proclaiming that the activities of multinationals "make the economic performance and conditions in
the so-called periphery societies dependent on the growth,
values, and life styles of the major economies of the world.
Although the center society experiences affluent development,
the outside or periphery societies are exploited to a state of
dependent underdevelopment."

The third body of critics maintains a Marxist perspective
toward multinational investment. To them direct investment is
an outgrowth of corporate capitalism. Marxist opposition to
multinational operations is deeply founded, and is inevitable as
an offshoot of the movement's overall hostility toward capitalism
as an economic system.

Having identified the general arguments for and against
multinational intervention in developing states, Dr. Ajami di-
rects his attention to particular issues of conflict and convergence between existing multinational and nation-states
within the Arab world. According to his study, "the national
commitment in most Arab countries is . . .   one that favors
connectedness with the multinationals and substantial technology imports."

Prior to 1973, multinational corporations controlled the production, refining, and marketing of 50 to 70 percent of all Arab oil. Their power was largely founded in the ability of such transnational organizations to link the Arab oil economies with Western markets. Over time, conflicts arose between "partners" concerning such issues as managerial control and decision making. Regional tension was exacerbated by such striking events as the Mossadegh nationalization of foreign oil interest in Iran in 1951, and the U.S. government-backed restoration to power of the Shah. Such incidents "created the impression of very powerful oil firms and closely identified the multinationals in the public mind with the policies of their home governments."

A second issue of regional tension was the battle over oil revenue distribution. Oil revenues provide over 85 percent of the national income for all Arab oil-producing countries, so the felt need for governmental participation in running the oil sector was a sincere issue indeed. A natural area of conflict became apparent as multinational investors sought to ensure their indispensibilty by limiting the number of nationals holding high-level positions within the industry. As a result, the oil sector became isolated from the rest of the economy, and outside companies had tremendous difficulty projecting a favorable public image.

The year 1974 is noted as the beginning of a new era in the economic evolution of the Middle East. Arab oil producers suddenly found themselves thrusted from the periphery of the international economic order to its center. A recent survey of Arab elites' attitudes toward multinational firms has evidenced a still-favorable opinion of the impact of such bodies upon Arab economic development. Several issues of potential conflict between these two actors, however, have been predicted for the coming decade.

A primary topic of debate is whether or not the Arab oil producers should develop their own petrochemical industries. Europeans fear strict competition from the petroleum-rich Middle East, and the Arab states claim a natural right to expand in the petrochemical field. No remedy is in sight.

Second, Arab representatives have complained of a double standard in multinational contracting costs. The Saudi and Qatari governments, for instance, have charged that bid prices presented were "excessive and unreasonable" and that such prices only meant greater profits to be taken by the multinationals. The multinationals explain higher rates in terms of greater regional operation costs, such as time delays, higher repair and maintenance costs, training expenses, and the like.

Bribery on the part of multinational firms is a third area of expressed concern for the future. It is seen as "an unnecessary cost with a potential threat to sovereignty and efficient utilization of scarce economic resources." In response,

Egypt's President Sadat and Syrian President Assad have instigated regional anticorruption drives to quell this economic malady before it further taints the image of multinationals in general and deprives national economies of the implements of stable and rapid development.

Additionally, two nonmarket factors will influence the relationship between multinationals and Arab societies. The overall negative image of the Arabs in Western popular culture must change to promote more amiable cooperation, and a solution must be found for the Arab economic boycott of the state of Israel.

Dr. Ajami has brought together the opinions of numerous economic specialists and has amply presented both sides of the arguments at hand. In conclusion, he professes a generally optimistic view of future multinational operations within the Arab world. Multinational firms must adjust to the region's shifting economic needs, and the Arab states must accept the necessary costs of interoperational cooperation. Certainly, the present economic status of the Arab community would not have been possible without the multinationals, and all parties must agree to confront the future on its promise rather than relive any disturbances experienced in the past. After all, the circumstances do not dictate a zero-sum game, and barring stubborn selfishness, there is no need for a harmful conflict of interest to disrupt a positive cooperative effort.

In the final chapter of this volume, Brooks McClure assesses corporate vulnerability to the threats of political terrorism in the Middle East and elsewhere. He asserts that this form of violence is a dangerous problem which international businesses increasingly have to face. Vulnerability is a major factor that enhances a terrorist's ability to plague a corporation. Precautionary actions, however, can be taken to reduce a company's defenseless position. Company visibility is a major factor that can contribute to its vulnerability. Major symbols of capitalistic enterprises are prime targets for terrorist attacks. Low-profile international companies, although not immune to attacks, are less apt to be harassed.

Local perception of a foreign company is also important when assessing vulnerability. Locally run branches can help build the company's image and act as a deterrent to terrorists who want to emphasize the "foreign" enemy. Careful scrutiny of labor relations and health, safety, and environment impact can all have a bearing on a company's security. An assessment of the latter is particularly significant since it affects the entire surrounding region. Strong community relations are an advantage for any company; terrorist groups often seek to capitalize on local grievances, exploiting them for their own ends. The political propaganda image of a company can also have an adverse effect on its security. These image factors thus create another basis for measuring vulnerability.

In spite of these vulnerabilities, companies are not help-less in the face of a terrorist attack. Precautionary measures can be taken to reduce a company's accessibility to attack. The level of threat must be analyzed; external threats to a company can come from various sectors of society. Political violence develops along different levels, beginning with mild, nonviolent actions and ending with extreme political terrorism.

In order to assess the level of threat, a few points must be contemplated. A review should be made of all groups oper-ating in the areas and the nature of their violence. In addi-tion, it is advantageous to look at how other companies have dealt with with terrorist threats or attacks. The tactics of the terrorist group, the counter measures the company used, and the response of government authorities should all be gone over in detail. This will be helpful in determining the potential nature of a threat and what methods are effective to counter it. Moreover, learning about the availability of outside as-sistance - the police and firefighting services - is also im-portant in planning precautionary measures. Potential victims should always evaluate the effectiveness of external help, especially since the terrorists usually do.

A basic physical security profile should be made by a business. Building security, accessibility to the public and to public areas, structure characteristics, and the location of key elements of the facility should all be taken into consideration in order to reduce weaknesses. Basic security precautions, such as personnel security, avoiding concentration of important information among certain personnel, and varying the schedule of executives, should be considered as well.

"The ability to determine - and correct - weaknesses in the company's defense against terrorist attack is the greatest possible insurance that there will be no attack at all." Hence, a crisis-management group is needed to determine the extent of the problem, develop a general response or options, and then to oversee the execution of decisions that are reached. Al-though none of this guarantees that a company will be impreg-nable to terrorist attacks, it may at least help to reduce its vulnerability.

Business and the
Middle East

1 The Religious Environment in the Middle East

Roger M. Savory

HISTORICAL INTRODUCTION

Of all the great movements that have shaken the
Middle East during the last century and a half, the
Islamic movements alone are authentically Middle
Eastern in inspiration. Liberalism and fascism,
patriotism and nationalism, communism and socialism,
are all European in origin, however much adapted
and transformed by Middle Eastern disciples. The
religious orders alone spring from the native soil,
and express the passions of the submerged masses of
the population. Though they have all, so far, been
defeated, they have not yet spoken their last word.

These prophetic words, uttered by Bernard Lewis in the
course of a series of lectures delivered at Indiana University
in 1963,(1) have assumed a new significance in the light of the
continuing convulsions in Iran, the sectarian strife in Syria,
Iraq, the Lebanon, Turkey, and other parts of the Middle
East, and the growing strength of Muslim fundamentalism in
Egypt, Libya, Pakistan, and elsewhere.

Since the revolution in Iran in January and February
1979, it has been virtually impossible to pick up a newsmaga-
zine without finding in it an article on "militant Islam" or the
"resurgence of Islamic fundamentalism" or some similar topic.
The inference to be drawn from this is that the West has been
taken by surprise by the revival of Islam. This revival is ex-

---

*All diacritical marks, except those in quotes, have been
deleted from chapter 1.

1

pressed not only in religious but also in political terms, because there is no dichotomy in the Islamic tradition between religion and politics. Yet those who have a longer historical perspective than the average journalist or politician has will see recent events in the Middle East as just one more change in position in the seesaw of the power struggle between the two great rival civilizations: Islam, and what is loosely called "the West," although "the West" may for certain purposes include Japan as well as the countries of western Europe and North America, and usually includes one country which is actually in the Middle East itself, namely, Israel. A much clearer and more accurate division of the world is provided by the traditional Islamic world-view, which divides the world into dar al-islam, the 'house of Islam,' and dar al-harb, the 'house of war'; dar al-islam is "territory in which Islam is in full devotional, political and legal actuality"; dar al-harb constitutes "the areas of mankind as yet unsubdued by Islam."(2)

"From its birth, the Islamic religion was the chief contender with Christianity for the hearts of men; Islamic civilization was the nearest neighbor and deadliest rival of European Christendom."(3) For 13 and a half centuries, relations between the two religions and cultural systems have assumed the nature of cold war at best; during not inconsiderable periods of history the latent hostility between the two systems has erupted into open conflict. During the first century after the advent of Islam, Islam was in the ascendant. Victorious Muslim armies carried Islam into northern India and central Asia, and swept along the coast of North Africa, leapt the Straits of Gibraltar (711 A.D.), annexed Spain, and were not checked until they had crossed the Pyrenees and entered southern France. By the end of this period, Islam was established in its three principal aspects: religion, state and empire, and culture and civilization.

After some centuries of coexistence, the Christian counterattack was launched. In Spain, after nearly five centuries of warfare known as the Reconquista, Granada, the last Muslim stronghold, surrendered to the combined forces of Aragon and Castile, and all non-Catholics (Jews as well as Muslims) were expelled from Spain. In 1095, after Pope Urban II had declared a holy war against Islam, the crusaders carried the counterattack into the heartlands of Islam in the Middle East. In the Holy Land, the struggle between the two civilizations and faiths went on for two centuries, until the last crusaders were driven out in 1291. The crusading spirit did not die until after the conquest of Constantinople by the Turks in 1453. With that event, "the balance of power in the continuing struggle between Islamdom and Christendom had shifted once again and, as the disciplined armies of the Ottoman Turks, the most formidable Muslim fighting-machine in history, pushed further and further west to the gates of Vienna, Western Christendom was forced once more on the defensive."(4)

By the end of the 16th century, however, the tide had again begun to turn in favor of Europe, although the Ottomans themselves did not immediately realize this but mustered sufficient strength to lay siege to Vienna for a second time in 1683. The factor that above all others laid the foundations of centuries of Western domination not only of the Middle East but of many other areas of the world was the Renaissance. This rebirth of the spirit of scientific enquiry and of a belief in the power of the human intellect not only stimulated scholarship but also led to the growth of trade and economic prosperity, and this in turn ushered in the Age of Exploration. In rapid succession, the Portuguese, the English, the Dutch, and somewhat later the French sought to establish trading stations in the Middle East and the Indian Ocean, and to exploit the fabled wealth of the Indies. In the course of time, the explorer and the trader were followed by the Christian missionary and the administrator, the political officer and the colonial governor. The imperialist attitude was simple: here were people in need of good government, and the imperialist nations were able to provide people who knew how to govern. Accordingly, during the 19th century, the English shouldered the "White Man's Burden," and the French devoted themselves to their "mission civilisatrice." The subject peoples of their empires objected not so much to political domination as to the attitude of moral superiority evinced by their rulers. This feeling of moral superiority in part was the product of the Western conviction of the superiority of Christianity over Islam, and in part derived from what was by then the overwhelming technological superiority of the West which had its origin in the industrial revolution.

As the West lost its fear of the Ottoman empire, it also lost its respect for Muslims, for Islam, and for Islamic civilization. The parity of esteem between enemies, which had existed during the medieval period, no longer remained. Muslim culture was derided by writers such as Macaulay. The concept of the "exotic East," which had so titillated the imagination of 18th-century Europe, was debunked by humorists like Mark Twain and by travellers such as Ker Porter.(5) In India, Christian missionaries, secure in the protection of the British raj, attacked Islam with arguments reminiscent of the anti-Muslim polemic of the medieval period, because, as one theologian put it succinctly, "Mohammedanism is perhaps the only undisguised and formidable antagonist of Christianity."(6)

It was not to be expected that Muslims would submit meekly to this onslaught on their religion and their culture. In response to it, in many parts of the Muslim world nationalist movements developed which ultimately brought about the end of colonial rule and gave rise to independent Muslim states throughout the Middle East. At the same time, their experience of Western rule had made Muslims realize that the Islamic world had fallen far behind the West in a number of important respects. Since Islam as a faith governs every aspect of man's behavior, and since Islamic society and systems of government are the product of the basic assumptions of the Islamic faith and of the Muslim world view, any reexamination of the bases of Islamic society and systems of government necessarily meant a reexamination of the fundamentals of the faith. During the 19th century, Muslim intellectuals in Egypt, India, and elsewhere turned their attention to the basic problem: to what extent was it possible to adapt Islamic culture to changing circumstances without undermining the foundations of the Islamic faith? We shall come back to this subject later.

The point of this brief but necessary historical survey of the relations between Islam and the West is to suggest that there is no need for the West to view the present revival of militancy in the "house of Islam" in apocalyptic terms. Although Khumaini is fond of referring to the United States as "Satan," there is no need for us in the West to revert to the medieval view of Islam as the beast described in the Revelation of St. John the Divine:

> And it was given unto him to make war with the
> saints, and to overcome them: and power was given
> him over all kindreds, and tongues, and nations.(7)

The current revival of Islam should be seen rather as simply one more cyclical fluctuation in the relative power of these ancient rivals. The reason why the West has been surprised by this revival is that the period of Western ascendancy which preceded it has lasted at least since the beginning of the 19th century; that is to say, no one alive today has any personal experience of a period of Islamic ascendancy. Consequently, since few people today possess any historical perspective, the revival has tended to be seen as an unprecedented and inexplicable occurrence. In fact, the religious revival of Islam is closely associated with the marked increase in the political power of the Islamic world, which in turn originated from the sudden accession of economic power from 1973 onwards made possible by the West's dependence on Middle East oil. Petrodollars are used by Saudi Arabia and other Muslim states to finance missionary activities in the West, and are also used by revolutionary Muslim states such as Libya to train and support terrorist groups operating in nonrevolutionary Muslim states. If the West could rid itself of its dependence on Middle East oil, the process could rapidly be reversed: slowdowns in the economy of Middle East countries would exacerbate existing political and social problems in those countries which are at the moment alleviated by the great wealth accruing from oil, and the resulting decline in political stability and strength

would in turn deflate much of the crusading zeal of Islamic
militants against the West.

A second point that should be made at this stage is that
Islam is not a monolithic structure any more than is Christianity. There are at least as many sects and shades of opinion
within the Islamic tradition as there are within the Christian
tradition. Furthermore, although I have tended as far to
refer to Islam as though it were the only religious faith in the
Middle East, this is, of course, very far from the case.
There exist in many Middle Eastern countries important non-
Muslim minorities - Christians (of a variety of rites[8]), Jews,
and Zoroastrians, who were resident in the Middle East long
before the advent of Islam. Nevertheless, Islam is the dominant religion in the Middle East,(9) and has given a distinctive
coloring and identity to society throughout the whole region.
The main emphasis of this chapter will therefore be on Islam.
The modern state of Israel is in most ways atypical of the
Middle East, and constitutes a special case that requires
separate consideration.

The third and final caveat that should be entered at this
point concerns the possible assumption that "Arab" and "Muslim" are synonymous; they are not. Not all Arabs are Muslims, and hundreds of millions of Muslims are not Arabs, for
example, the Persians, Afghans, Pakistanis, and Turks. The
extraordinarily complicated ethnic, religious, and linguistic mix
that exists in the Middle East should militate against any glib
and simplistic analyses.

THE NORMATIVE ISLAMIC TRADITION

> The theologian may indulge the pleasing task of
> describing religion as she descended from heaven,
> arrayed in her native purity; a more melancholy
> duty is imposed upon the historian: - he must dis-
> cover the inevitable mixture of error and corruption
> which she contracted in a long residence upon earth
> among a weak and degenerate race of beings. [Ed-
> ward   Gibbon,   The Decline and Fall of the Roman
> Empire (New York: 1900), I, p. 505]

It is impossible to understand the violent crosscurrents which
at present wrack the Islamic world without some knowledge of
the Islamic view of the world and of the tradition of classical
Islam which has shaped and molded the thoughts and lives of
Muslims for over 13 centuries. Indeed, many of the problems
that beset the Middle East today and that complicate relations
between it and the West derive from the conflict between this
classical Islamic tradition and attempts by leaders of Muslim
states to effect policies of modernization and social reform.

Three principal aspects of Islam have contributed to the development of Islamic civilization: (1) Islam as religion and faith; (2) Islam as law and tradition; (3) Islam as state and empire. Each will be briefly discussed.

Islam as Religion and Faith

Seyyed Hossein Nasr, in his book Ideals and Realities of Islam,(10) offers the generalization that "Judaism is essentially based on the fear of God, Christianity on the love of Him and Islam on the knowledge of Him although this is only a matter of emphasis, each religion containing of necessity all these three fundamental aspects of the relation between man and God." For the Christian, God is a mystery. As St. Paul said:

> For now we see through a glass, darkly; but then face to face: now I know in part; but then shall I know even as also I am known.(11)

For the Muslim, man's knowledge of God derives from the Koran, the Word of God revealed to man through His Prophet Muhammad. The Koran is al-Furqan, the touchstone by which men can discriminate between truth and falsehood, and the Umm al-Kitab, the "Mother of Books," that is, the source of all knowledge.

According to Muslim tradition, the first revelations were communicated to Muhammad when the latter was 40 years of age, by a glorious being subsequently identified as the archangel Gabriel. For more than 20 years, Muhammad continued to receive revelations, which were memorized by his followers and may have been written down at the time, although the definitive text of the Koran was not codified until after Muhammad's death. According to Muslim tradition, the text was collected together "from pieces of papyrus, flat stones, palm leaves, shoulder blades and ribs of animals, pieces of leather and wooden boards, as well as from the hearts of men."(12) The main themes of the early Koranic revelations concerned God's goodness and power, as displayed in natural phenomena and in the creation of human beings. There is emphasis on the transitory nature of this life. Men are warned that they must return to God for judgment. Above all, there reverberates throughout the Koran a sonorous insistence on the oneness and unity of God. It is no accident that the shahada, or Muslim profession of faith, proclaims: "There is no god but God, and Muhammad is the Messenger of God."(13) Allahu akbar, "God is most great," is one of the commonest phrases uttered by Muslims. As a consequence of this uncompromising monotheism, the greatest heresy in Muslim

eyes is shirk, "associating other beings or partners with
God."   The Christian doctrine of the trinity is therefore one
of the greatest sources of misunderstanding between Muslims
and Christians.

No religion lays greater emphasis on ritual than does
Islam.   Of the principal religious duties of the Muslim, the
"congregational prayers"(14) come closest to constituting an
Islamic liturgy.(15)   "The QurᴶÄn emphasizes prayer because
"it prevents from evil" and helps man "to conquer difficulties."(16)   The other ritual and moral duties of a Muslim are
alms giving, fasting, and the pilgrimage to Mecca.   These four
ritual and moral duties, together with the shahada, constitute
the "pillars of Islam."

Islam regards itself as the final and most perfect revelation of God to man:

> This day have I perfected your religion for you and
> completed my favour unto you, and have chosen for
> you as religion Islam.(17)

"Islam" means literally "submission to the will of God."   A
"Muslim" therefore is essentially a person whose whole life
is lived in conformity to the divine will.   "It is therefore a
term which in its widest sense could be used by all monothe-
ists."(18)   Muhammad is regarded as the "Seal of the Prophets," that is, the last of a line of prophets starting from
Abraham and including Jesus.   It follows that Muslims regard
the other great monotheistic religions which originated in the
Middle East, Judaism and Christianity, as inferior and superseded.   Anyone who refused to accept Islam was branded as a
kafir, one who had shown his ingratitude to God by rejecting
the revelation brought by His Messenger Muhammad; the term
therefore came to mean "infidel," "non-Muslim."   "If Jews held
Christians to be blasphemous innovators and Christians called
Jews unbelievers and persecuted their own co-religionists for
holding divergent views about the nature of Jesus, they must
either have corrupted the original scriptures or followed
their own mischievous imaginations.   They must be brought
back to first principles - to the original truth taught by
Abraham."(19)

Islam as Law and Tradition

The Prophet Muhammad was not only the Messenger of God,
the mouthpiece of God's revelation to man, the Koran, but he
was also the leader of the first Muslim community, or umma,
and its first lawgiver and arbitrator in disputes that arose
within that community.   After Muhammad's death, the caliphs
(from the Arabic khalifa, "successor") exercised political and

administrative authority (though not, of course, the religious
authority of the Prophet), and were to a large extent the
lawgivers of the community. On what basis were they to exercise judicial authority? The first and obvious source of such
authority was the Koran, but the Koran "is primarily a book of
religious and moral principles and exhortations, and is not a
legal document."(20)   To supplement it, the early Muslims
incorporated into it the Islamic tradition the "ancient Arab idea
of sunna, precedent or normative custom."(21)   In its Islamic
guise, it assumed the form of the sunna of the prophet, the
"example" or "practice and behaviour" of the prophet. The
sunna of the prophet was handed down in the form of hadith,
an "account" of an action, utterance, or decision of Muhammad.   The authenticity of the hadith was determined by a line
(isnad) of reliable transmitters, and the task of sifting the
hadith and classifying them as either "sound" (sahih), "good"
(hasan), or "weak" (daif) gave rise to the science of hadith -
criticism.   The scholars who were specialists in this science,
the muhaddithun or "traditionists," "travelled across the
continents in search of authentication or in order to add their
own name as the last in the chain, through face-to-face contact with the immediately preceding reporter."(22)   For the
muhaddithun, the technical question of whether or not a particular hadith satisfied their scientific criteria of authenticity
tended to be more important than the inherent probability of
the content of the hadith.   "The question was not so much:
Could the Prophet have said this?   Is it reasonable and in
character? but rather: Who said that he said this?   Was that
reporter an eye witness?   Was he honest?   And who tells us
now, that he heard or saw the Prophet do or say it?   Is the
chain of attestors unbroken?   Did they all know personally the
man in front of them in the sequence going back to the first
person?"(23)

Inevitably, as the science of Islamic jurisprudence (fiqh)
evolved, differences of opinion developed among scholars on
matters of religious law, and these differences gave rise to the
four principal schools (madhhab) of Islamic law.   Individual
scholars, "when faced with a new or refined and complicated
issue, wherever the Qur'an and the Sunna gave no clear and
unequivocal decision,"(24) brought into play "considered
personal opinion" (ra y).   This use of individual reasoning,
when "directed toward achieving systematic consistency and
guided by the parallel of an existing institution,"(25) became
the third basis of the religious law of Islam and was termed
qiyas, i.e., "concluding from a given principle embodied in a
precedent that a new case falls under this principle or is
similar to this precedent on the strength of a common essential
feature called the 'reason' (illa)."(26)

The fourth and last basis of the religious law of Islam,
ijma or "consensus," came into being during the lifetime of

the companions of the prophet. As the generation of those
who had actually known the prophet passed from the scene,
"no new generation as such was thought capable of engendering new Sunna."(27) "Recourse was had, therefore, to a
fourth and much ampler source of law, namely Ijma, or consensus. Founded on the conviction that the community as such
would not long, or finally, converge on an error, Ijma in
effect entrusted the enlargement of the law to the collective
fidelity. Innovation - a concept always close to heresy in
Islam - would be saved from excess, from pretension, from
distortion, if it commended itself, in the long run, to the
whole household of the faith."(28)

By the beginning of the 10th century A.D., this whole
structure of Islamic law, known collectively as the shari a, the
"way" or "path" which, if followed by man, will lead him to
God, had been systematized in its final form. At that point,
scholars of all schools felt that on all essential questions
consensus had been reached, and henceforth "the promulgation
of new ideas on the exposition of the relevant texts of the
Koran and Hadith were as good as forbidden. . . . The right
of individual interpretation (ijtihad) was in theory (and very
largely in practice also) confined to the points on which no
general agreement had yet been reached."(29) This "closing
of the door of ijtihad', as it was called, amounted to the
demand for taklid, a term which . . . now came to mean the
unquestioning acceptance of the doctrines of established
schools and authorities."(30)

Why is the shari a so important in any consideration of
recent trends in Islam? Joseph Schacht's brilliantly succinct
statement answers this question:

> Islamic law is the epitome of Islamic thought, the
> most typical manifestation of the Islamic way of life,
> the core and kernel of Islam itself. The very term
> fikh, "knowledge," shows that early Islam regarded
> knowledge of the sacred law as the knowledge par
> excellence. Theology has never been able to achieve
> a comparable importance in Islam; only mysticism was
> strong enough to challenge the ascendancy of the
> Law over the minds of Muslims, and often proved
> victorious. But even at the present time the Law,
> including its (in the narrow sense) legal subject-
> matter, remains an important, if not the most impor-
> tant, element in the struggle which is being fought
> in Islam between traditionalism and modernism under
> the impact of western ideas. . . . it is impossible
> to understand Islam without understanding Islamic
> law.(31)

It remains only to ask how it is that a system of religious law has achieved this preeminent position in the minds of Muslims. The answer is that "at the very root of the Muslim conception of law lies the idea that law is inherently and essentially religious."(32) It is "the divinely ordained pattern of human conduct," with "its basis in the Divine Revelation,"(33) the Koran, and, as Seyyed Hossein Nasr has pointed out, in Islam it is the Koran, "being the Word of God," which "corresponds to Christ in Christianity."(34)

Islam as State and Empire

In the introduction to this chapter, it was noted that there is no separation in the Islamic tradition between religion and politics, between what is called in the Christian tradition "church" and "state," between what medieval Christendom called regnum, "the realm of the king," and sacerdotium, "the realm of the priest." As Bernard Lewis has noted, "such pairs of words as spiritual and temporal, lay and ecclesiastical, and religious and secular have no equivalents in the classical languages of the Muslim peoples."(35) Whereas Christ ex-horted his followers to "render therefore unto Caesar the things that are Caesar's; and unto God the things that are God's",(36) Islam was "involved with political power from the start."(37) "In Islam the state provides the frame within which Islam with its demands on the 'community of believers' (the umma) and on the individual Muslim must be lived."(38)

Muhammad was succeeded as head of the first Muslim community or state at Medina by a long line of caliphs who were the titular heads of the Islamic empire until the extinction of the historical caliphate by the Mongols in 1258 A.D. One of the classic formulations of the functions of the caliph was that of al-Mawardi (died (1058 A.D.):

> The defense and maintenance of religion, the deci-
> sion of legal disputes, the protection of the territory
> of Islam, the punishment of wrong-doers, the pro-
> vision of troops for guarding the frontiers, the
> waging of jihad ("hold war") against those who
> refused to accept Islam or submit to Muslim rule, the
> organization and collection of taxes, the payment of
> salaries and the administration of public funds, the
> appointment of competent officials, and lastly, per-
> sonal attention to the details of government.(39)

By the middle of the 10th century A.D., however, a century before the time that al-Mawardi was writing, practice had already departed widely from theory. Temporal rulers styling themselves amir and sultan had stripped the caliph of most of his political, military, and administrative powers, and left him little more than a symbolic function as the defender of the faith who legitimized the rule of the amirs and sultans.

With the aim of preserving the institution of the cali-phate, and thus the unity of the Islamic state, the jurists were prepared to go to great lengths to accommodate juridical theory to political reality. In order to preserve the unity of the Islamic state, the jurists were even prepared to condone the usurpation of the prerogatives of the caliph by amirs and sultans. Even tyranny, said the jurists, was preferable to anarchy. Ibn Taymiya, in his Siyasa shari a, quotes the hadith: "Sixty years of an unjust imam are better than one night without a sultan."(40) The jurists, by thus clothing the "emirate by seizure" (imarat al-istila) with the appearance of legality, eventually "saved the principle of unity (in the Islamic state) by the device of a sort of concordat, the caliph recognizing the governor's sole control of policy and adminis-tration, in return for his own dignity and right of administra-tion of religious affairs."(41) Nearly all the theoretical discussions on the locus of power in an Islamic state ultimately made reference to the key Koranic text (IV:59/62): "O ye who believe! Obey God, and obey His Messenger, and those who are in authority among you."(42) An Islamic state is therefore made up of persons whose ultimate allegiance is to God, to whom alone sovereignty belongs:

> Say, O God, Lord of Sovereignty, Thou givest so-vereignty to whomsoever Thou pleasest; and Thou takest away sovereignty from whomsoever Thou pleasest. [Koran, 3:27 part of]

In view of this, the concept of "the sovereignty of the pe-ople," enshrined in most Western democratic constitutions, is not acceptable to the Muslim. The other essential criterion of an Islamic state is that the shari a, the religious law of Islam, shall be the law of the land. Indeed, it is the first duty of an Islamic state to enforce the shari a:

> Those who do not judge by what God has revealed - those indeed are the evil-doers. [Koran, 5:47]

No legislation must contravene the Koran and the sunna:

> Whenever God and His Apostle have decided a mat-ter, it is not for a faithful man or woman to follow another course of his or her own choice. [Koran, 33:37](43)

As will be seen later, these two fundamental principles of an Islamic state have proved stumbling blocks to would-be mod-ernizers and reformers.

Schism and Esotericism in Islam

Reference was made in the introduction to this chapter that Islam is not a monolithic structure any more than is Christianity. Before closing this brief survey of the normative tradition in Islam, there are two aspects of Islam that assumed such importance within the Islamic tradition that no account of Islam would be complete without them. These are: (1) Shi ism; and (2) Sufism, or the mystical tradition in Islam.

Shi ism

The majority of Muslims, called Sunnis because they follow the sunna or practice of the Prophet, believe that Muhammad died without designating a successor, and they accept the authority of a line of caliphs or successors of the prophet chosen initially from among the leaders of the Muslim community. Shi i Muslims, however, believe that Muhammad before his death designated Ali, his cousin and son-in-law, as his successor. After the death of Muhammad in 632 A.D. and the election of Abu Bakr as the first caliph, Ali's supporters formed the Shi at Ali, the "party of Ali," and thus became known as Shi i Muslims.

The Sunni-Shi i schism had the most profound consequences for the whole of subsequent Islamic history, and the hostility between the two sects is still apparent in many parts of the Muslim world today. One need only mention the attempts by Khumaini to subvert other Muslim states in the Middle East in which power is in the hands of Sunnis; the expulsion of Shi is from Iraqi territory by the government of Iraq; and the feuds between Sunnis and Shi is in Turkey, Syria and the Lebanon. Many Muslims today, for political reasons, try to play down the antipathy between Sunni and Shi i; arguments of this type belong to the realm of apologetics and have no basis in historical fact.

Ali eventually became the fourth caliph, but Shi is continue to regard the first three caliphs, and all the caliphs who succeeded Ali, as the titular heads of the Islamic world for six centuries, as usurpers. In the Shi i view, Ali and his 11 descendants in the male line, termed Imams, are "the embodiment of the Shi i concept of the ruler. It is the imam, and only the imam, who is entitled to direct the faithful."(44) From its inception, therefore, the Shi i movement was a party in opposition to the regime in power. Instead of giving their loyalty to the ruling Sunni caliph, Shi is gave their allegiance to the Imams.

In the course of time, Shi i theologians attributed to the Imams various distinctive characteristics designed to demonstrate the superiority of the Shi i Imam over the Sunni Caliph. These characteristics have no parallel in Sunni Islam. The

most important of them are: the doctrine of   isma, the "sin-
lessness" or "infallibility" of the Imams; and the function of
the Imams as intercessors, through the redemptive nature of
the suffering and martyrdom of the Imams. To these were
added, after the year 873 A.D. when the Twelfth Imam disap-
peared from earth and went into occultation, the messianic
theory of the second coming of the Twelfth Imam, also known
as the "Hidden Imam," the "Lord of the Age," the "Imam of
the Epoch," and the "Mahdi." The second coming of the Mahdi
will be portended by various eschatological signs, and will
herald the day of judgment and the end of the world. "His
reappearance will enable human society to reach true perfection
and the full realization of spiritual life"; the Mahdi will fill
"with justice the world that has been corrupted by injustice
and iniquity."(45)

The occultation of the Twelfth Imam in 873 A.D. posed a
serious problem for the Shi i community. According to Shi i
theory, government belongs rightfully to the Imam. Who,
therefore, was to govern the Shi i community after the disap-
pearance of the Twelfth Imam? The consensus among Shi is
was that the mujtahids, that is, the most eminent Shi i jurists
of the time, should act as the representatives on earth of the
Hidden Imam. This remains the Shi i view today, and has
received emphatic endorsement by Khumaini: "In view of the
fact that the government of Islam is the government of law,
only the jurisprudent [i.e., the mujtahid], and nobody else,
should be in charge of government." Since the mujtahids are
the representatives of the Hidden Imam upon earth, they have
acquired, at least in the popular mind, the attribute of
infallibility ascribed to the Imam himself. Their authority is
therefore absolute.

> From the moment of its inception in the 7th century
> A.D., until the establishment of the Safavid dynasty
> in Iran in 1501, the Shiᶜi movement was in opposition
> to and frequently in revolt against the government
> of the day, which was a Sunni government. It was
> often a persecuted group, and acquired "to an un-
> usual degree . . . the traits so often met with in
> small and suppressed religious groups," one of which
> was "a most unpleasant aggressiveness" towards its
> opponents.(46)

As a result of persecution, Shi ism acquired martyrs.
The most celebrated of these is the Third Imam, Husayn, who
was slain at Karbala in 680 A.D. by the troops of the Sunni
caliph, Yazid. By this act, the Sunnis allowed a "fatal
weapon, sharp and double-edged"(47) to fall into the hands of
their bitter enemies. For 1,300 years since Karbala, on the
anniversary of the death of Husayn, this weapon has been

resharpened annually by the passionate commemoration of the events surrounding his martyrdom. Those who take part in the mourning processions slash themselves with knives and flagellate themselves with chains to demonstrate the overwhelming nature of their grief. During the Iranian revolution of 1979, this Shi i obsession with martyrdom was strengthened still further by the constant acquisition of new martyrs, and for a time there was a self-perpetuating cycle of 40-day periods of ritual mourning.(48) To sum up: the three primary characteristics of "Twelver" Shi ism - opposition, martyrdom, and revolt - are essentially negative. They do not constitute a basis for rational government, still less for progressive or democratic government.

As mentioned earlier, the rupture between Sunnis and Shi is constitutes the major schism in Islam. In the course of time, however, there were further schisms within the Shi i movement itself. The principal one occurred after the death of the Sixth Shi i Imam, Ja far al Sadiq, in 765 A.D. According to Shi i tradition, he was poisoned on orders from the Sunni caliph al-Mansur. Controversy arose regarding the succession to Ja far al-Sadiq because his son Isma il, who had been designated to succeed him, had predeceased him. This was a contingency that had not been provided for in Shi i theory, and the whole Shi i movement was thrown into confusion. The problem was compounded by the fact that, on the death of Isma il, most Shi is had accepted his brother Abdullah as the Imam-designate, but Abdullah had died in his turn a few weeks later. Some Shi is, however, on the death of Isma il, had hailed Musa as the Imam-designate, and this group continued to give their allegiance to a line of Imams through Musa down to the Twelfth Imam; they are therefore known as Ithna Ashari or "Twelver" Shi is. Other Shi is "believed that Isma il did not die but went into occultation, that he would appear again and be the promised Mahdi. . . . Another group believed that the true Imam was Isma il whose death meant the imamate was transferred to his son Muhammad. A third group also held that although he died during the lifetime of his father he was the Imam and that the imamate passed after him to Muhammad ibn Isma il and his descendants."(49) All those who thought that the imamate came to an end either with Isma il or with his son Muhammad, were termed Sab i or "Sevener" Shi is. The "Seveners," or Isma ilis as they came to be known, achieved political importance with the establishment of the Fatimid caliphate in Egypt, Syria, and North Africa in the tenth century A.D. Toward the end of the 11th century, a major schism occurred within the ranks of the "Sevener" Shi is, and a new branch was established in Iran whose members, because of the use of the assassination of key figures as a political weapon by the activist arm of the Isma ili organization, acquired the popular name of "Assassins." Today, the

Aga Khan is the spiritual leader of the worldwide Isma ili
community.

The Mystical Aspect of Islam: Sufism

As we have seen, Islam in its original, Sunni form is a starkly
monotheistic creed summed up in the simple and unambiguous
words of the shahada, the Muslim profession of the faith:
"There is no god but God, and Muhammad is the Messenger of
God." These words are found in the Koran, which is the
prototype of all books and the source of all knowledge.
Throughout the ages, Muslim scholars have written voluminous
works of exegesis (tafsir) on the text of the Koran. The
Koran, as we have seen, is the ultimate source of the shari a,
the divinely inspired law of Islam.
    But the scholarly expositions of the Koran commentators,
the jurisprudents, and the traditionists are not the only level
on which the Koran may be interpreted. The Koran has an
inner meaning vouchsafed only to those who are qualified to
hear and understand it. As the great 13th-century Persian
mystic, Jalal al-Din Rumi, put it:

> The Koran is a bride who does not disclose her face
> to you, for all that you draw aside the veil. . . .
> The Koran is able to show itself in whatever form it
> pleases.(50)

In other words, the Koran has an inner, esoteric meaning
(batin) as well as the obvious, exoteric one (zahir). The
process by which one arrives at this inner meaning is known
as ta wil ("hermeneutics").
    Reference has already been made to the way in which the
"Twelver" Shi i form of Islam introduced doctrines concerning
the intercessory and redemptive functions of the Imams into
the faith. In part this was an attempt by human beings to
bridge the gap between man's insignificance and the awful
majesty of the transcendent God of Sunni Islam. Islamic
mystics (known as Sufis from the garment of coarse wool (suf)
worn by the early mystics), sought to bridge this gap by
laying emphasis on the nearness rather than the remoteness of
God. Developing the doctrine of the descent of the human
soul from the godhead and its yearning to return thither,
Persian mystics of the ninth and tenth centuries A.D., trans-
ported by the fervor of the supreme mystical experience of the
reunion of the soul with God, gave vent to their ecstasy in
language that scandalized the orthodox and gave rise to a
barrage of criticism and censure from the theologians. In the
year 1095, the great Persian theologian and jurisprudent,
al-Ghazali, retired from his teaching post at the leading
theological seminary at Baghdad and devoted himself to the

task of reconciling Sufi thought with Sunni theology. As a result of his labors, Sufism, at least of the less ecstatic type, was accepted as within the pale of Islam. Al-Ghazali "succeeded in assuring the mystical or introspective attitude a place within official Islam side by side with the legalism of the lawyers and the intellectualism of the theologians."(51) As a result, the 12th century saw the rise of the great Sufi orders and the foundation of khanaqahs or "convents" in all parts of the Islamic world, and the tariqa, or Sufi way, became formalized in the manuals of the Sufi masters. Sufism, the mystical aspect of Islam, had become established as a religion within a religion, and found expression in a rich literature in Arabic, Perisan, Turkish, and Urdu. Both the divinely inspired law of Islam, the shari a, and the mystical path (tariqa) are "based on the symbolism of the way or journey. All life is a sojourn, a journey through this transient world to the Divine Presence. The Shari ah is the wider road which is meant for all men, by virtue of which they are able to attain the total possibilities of the individual human state. The Tariqah is the narrower path for the few who have the capability and profound urge to attain sanctity here and now and seek a path whose end is the full realization of the reality of Universal Man transcending the individual domain."(52) "Twelver" Shi ism, which also emphasizes the esoteric dimension of the faith, comes closer to Sufism than does Sunni Islam.

THE IMPACT OF THE WEST AND THE
BEGINNINGS OF ISLAMIC MODERNISM

For nearly nine centuries after the Sunni jurisprudents had declared early in the tenth century A.D. that the "door of independent enquiry" in matters of the religious law was closed, the orthodox theologians of Islam had striven, on the whole successfully, to maintain the legal structure of the faith intact. In this effort, they had been materially assisted by the Muslim world view discussed earlier in this chapter. Secure in the assumption of the superiority of their faith, and consequently of the civilization that was the fruits of that faith, Muslims "lived in a complacent ideologically sealed world which was simply incurious about Europe."(53) "Mediaeval Islam . . . appears to have paid Christian Europe the supreme insult of a virtually total disinterest."(54) By the end of the Middle Ages this attitude had become dangerously out of date. The breaking up of the medieval feudal order in Western Europe had unleashed tremendous political and economic energy, and the formation of nation-states provided the basis for its period of great expansion. Many of the Muslim states of the Middle East and North Africa were still part of the Ottoman

Empire, a declining military power dubbed "the sick man of Europe" by Western chancelleries.

In 1798, Napoleon invaded Egypt. The effect on the Islamic world was traumatic, and the psychological disorders that resulted from this invasion are still manifest today. Although the French occupation of Egypt was of short duration, the ease with which the French conquered the country shattered the complacent assumption of Muslim superiority to the West mentioned above. The French attack constituted the first armed invasion of the Muslim world since the Crusades, but the cause of the trauma went deeper than this. As Gustave von Grunebaum put it, "the problem of the adequacy of Islam to a given existential situation had never been raised before the 19th century."(55) During the 19th century Muslim intellectuals began to go to the West for their university education; their numbers were at first small, but as the century progressed substantial numbers found their way to France, Germany, and England. Brought for the first time into close contact with the West, these men realized that their own countries had fallen behind the West in many important respects: not simply in the arts of war and in technological expertise in general, but in matters such as political development (in particular the development of political parties and less autocratic forms of government); education; social development (particularly in regard to the emancipation of women, the abolition of slavery, and the liberation of the peasants from quasifeudal systems of land tenure), and so on. Most of these Muslim intellectuals thought that the solution was to imitate the West. In Iran, Sayyid Hasan Taqizadeh, a prominent leader of the Constitutionalist movement in that country, declared: "We must Westernize ourselves, body and soul!" Many Muslims thought, as Bernard Lewis has put it, that "by study and imitation, it might be possible to discover and apply the elusive secret of [the West's] greatness and strength, and generations of eager students and reformers toiled in the search. They may not have loved us, or even understood us, but they did admire and respect us."(56)

Within the Islamic world itself, however, the reaction was rather different. An ever-increasing area of the Islamic world was coming under the direct colonial rule of one or other of the Great Powers, for example in North and Central Africa, in India, in Egypt. Other Muslim countries, such as Iran and Afghanistan, became buffer states in the power struggle between Britain and Russia in western and central Asia. The declining Ottoman Empire, which still exercised authority over the countries of the Levant, became the object of the solicitous concern of the chancelleries of Europe, as the Western powers tried to manipulate the Sublime Porte to their own advantage. Canning's solution to the problem of the "Sick Man of Europe" was to bring it under Western tutelage and make Turkey part

of Europe. Western involvement with Muslim countries ran the
whole gamut from interference in the political and economic
affairs of supposedly sovereign states, through direct imperial
rule which brought many benefits to its subjects, to unabashed
economic exploitation.

It is possible to argue that those who were subject to
colonial government did not object so much to the fact of
political domination as to the outward show of superiority on
the part of their rulers. Whereas in medieval times the Islamic
world, convinced of its own cultural superiority, had not
bothered to concern itself with the benighted regions of the
West, so in the 19th century technological superiority produced
an unshakable conviction in the colonial powers of the moral
superiority of Western civilization. Nowhere was this attitude
more apparent than in the British Empire in India. Christian
missionaries in India, convinced that they were aiding imperial
rule by making converts to Christianity, resorted to arguments
that had the authentic ring of medieval polemic. When the
government of India declared its neutrality in religious
matters, the missionaries were scandalized. "A neutral policy," they declared, "dishonours the truth of God."(57) No
shadow of doubt entered the minds of the Christian missionaries as to the correctness of their actions: a Church Missionary Society resolution passed in 1858 stated:

> That a Christian nation entrusted with the govern-
> ment of a people ignorant of the true God, and
> suffering under the social and moral evils insepar-
> able from false religions, is bound to command the
> true religion to its subjects.(58)

Muslim reaction to the age of imperialism was on two
levels: political and religious (to use Western terminology).
Anger at political domination by the West gave rise to nationalist movements throughout the Islamic world. As these gained
in strength, they spelled the end of the age of colonialism.
The imperialist powers could either hand over power voluntar-
ily (as was the case with the British in India), or could try
and stem the tide by force (as the French did in Algeria) but
be forced to concede power to the new nationalist governments
anyway. Nationalism, of course, like all the other "-isms" -
communism, socialism, and so on - was an idea that originated
in the West; by adopting it, Muslims for the first time in the
history of Islam seriously contemplated the idea of the separation of religion and politics. But the impact of the West also
provoked a Muslim reaction of the religious plane. Many
Muslims did not share the West's belief in the innate superiority of its religion and culture. They noted that, as Western
laws, Western standards, and Western institutions were progressively imported, a "parallel process of social and cultural

disintegration" was set in train with Muslim society, and "the old patterns were destroyed, and old values derided and abandoned."(59)   In their reaction against these trends, Muslims demonstrated that their tradition of social revolt expressed in religious terms was not dead.

THE MUSLIM RELIGIOUS AND INTELLECTUAL
RESPONSE TO WESTERN IDEAS

The Fundamentalist Response

Arab nationalism, stimulated by the intrusion of the West into the Middle East, was initially both anti-Western and anti-Turkish, since the Ottoman Empire continued to embrace within its borders during the 19th century many Arab states in the heartlands of Islam.   But although the Wahhabi movement in Arabia in the 18th century, the first of the revivalist movements in the modern period, came into armed conflict with the Ottomans, it was in essence a puritanical and fundamentalist movement which aimed at purifying Islam from within.   "It rejected the corruption and laxity of the contemporary decline. It rejected too the accommodations and cultural richnesses of the mediaeval empire.   It rejected the introvert warmth and other-worldly piety of the mystic way.   It rejected also the alien intellectualism not only of philosophy but of theology.   It rejected all dissensions, even the now well-established Shi ah. It insisted solely on the Law.   The classical Law, said the Wahhabis, is the sum and substance of the faith. . . . Obey the pristine Law, fully, strictly, singly; and establish a society where that Law obtains.   This, they preached, is Islam; all else is superfluous and wrong."(60)
    The importance of the Wahhabi movement, however, lies more in its influence on other parts of the Islamic world during the 19th century.   What H.A.R. Gibb has called its "revolutionary theocratic aspect" came to the fore, and the initial thrust of its attack on what it perceived as a lax and corrupt Muslim state was transformed by the Muslim movements which adopted Wahhabi ideas in India, North Africa, the Sudan, and even as far away as Nigeria and Sumatra, into general opposition to Western powers in those areas and to Muslim governments which either failed to resist the growing influence of those powers or which actively collaborated with them.(61)
    The same two motives, the desire to reform Islam from within by a return to the fundamentals of the faith, and the aim of rousing Muslims to resist European domination, animated the outstanding Muslim activist of the 19th century, Jamal al-Din al-Afghani.   The dominant force in his life was the idea of pan-Islam, the idea of reuniting the entire Muslim world

under one leader as it had been united under the historical
caliphate. Jamal-al-Din preached his doctrine in Turkey, in
Egypt, in India, and in Iran, but his teaching perhaps had
the most lasting effect in Egypt, where he influenced a number
of young men such as Muhammad Abduh and Sa d Zaghlul,
the hero of Egyptian independence. Muhammad Abduh realized that "it was necessary to isolate the religious element in the
reform movement from the emotional influences of the revolutionary or nationalist program,"(62) but this central thrust of
his teaching was rejected by the conservatives, and "the
immediate outward consequence of his activities was the emergence of a new fundamentalist school calling themselves the
"Salafiya," the upholders of the tradition of the fathers of the
Islamic church."(63)

Islamic Modernism

In the fundamentalist response considered above, the emphasis
was on political activism and the support of nationalist
movements for independence from foreign domination. Coupled
with this was a call for the purification of the Islamic faith,
and a return to the strict letter of the shari a, the religious
law of Islam. It should be understood, however, that the call
for purification of the faith was in no sense a demand for the
reformulation or reexamination of the basic tenets of Islam.
On the contrary, it was most frequently an insistence on the
strict observance of the basic principles of Islam as interpreted in an extremely narrow and inflexible manner.
        In many Muslim countries, however, there arose during
the 19th century Muslim thinkers who saw that some degree of
modification of the normative tradition of Islam outlined earlier
in this chapter was necessary if Islam was going to adapt itself
to the modern world. Such intellectuals are usually referred
to as "Islamic modernists." Although their points of view
varied widely, they held some opinions in common. One of
these was their criticism of the legal principle of taqlid
"imitation," that is, the reliance on the teaching of an earlier
authority on the religious law. After the "closing of the door
of ijtihad" taqlid had naturally acquired disproportionate
importance in the Islamic tradition, and Islamic modernists such
as Muhammad Abduh in Egypt (1849-1905) attacked the "pas-
sive acceptance of interpretations based on blind authority,"
an attitude which, he said, "had distorted Quranic meaning
and perverted Muslim thought."(64) In India, Sayyid Amir
Ali (Ameer Ali) (1849-1928), took a similar line:

>   The present stagnation [of Islam] is principally due
>   to the notion which has fixed itself on the minds of
>   the generality of Muslims that the right to the exer-

cise of private judgement ceased with the early
legists, that its exercise in modern times is sinful.
. . . Our schoolmen and their servile followers have
made its exercise a sin and a crime. . . . Before
there can be a renovation of religious life, the mind
must first escape from the bondage which centuries
of literal interpretation and the doctrine of conformity have imposed upon it. (65)

Another basic question to which all Islamic modernists
have had to address themselves is the question of the hadith,
the traditions ascribed to the prophet, which by the time of
al-Shafi i (died 820 A.D.) had become "completely consubstan-
tial in content"(66) with the sunna of the prophet which
constituted one of the four bases of the shari a. The vast
corpus of hadith had thus become an essential underpinning of
the whole structure of the shari a. The question facing
Islamic reformists was, therefore: could any part of this hadith
foundation be removed without bringing the whole superstruc-
ture crashing to the ground? Some, like Khuda Bukhsh (died
1931) in India, took a extreme view. Khuda Bukhsh wished to
discard the corpus of hadith in toto. "Islam," he said,
"stripped of its theology, is a perfectly simple religion. Its
cardinal principle is belief in One God and belief in Muhammad
as His Apostle. The rest is mere accretion, superficial-
ity."(67) A.A.A. Fyzee (born 1899), in his book, A Modern
Approach to Islam, agreed with Khuda Bukhsh that religion
and law were essentially different and must be separated. He
recognized that this would cause upheaval and bewilderment
for Muslims, but, he said, it was becoming less and less
possible for life to be strictly controlled by the shari a.
Modern life demanded whole areas of law for which the shari a
had few if any answers: for example, international law, public
finance, insurance laws, the law of the air, the road and the
sea, and much more.(68) But such radical views did not win
majority support among Muslims, and not surprisingly, did not
find favor with the ulama, the theologians and doctors of the
religious law. The contemporary Muslim scholar Fazlur Rahman
has declared that Muslims who "wish to reject all Hadith and
rely on the Qur an" are not aware of "the issues that are at
stake. It is not clear whether they wish to deny historical or
doctrinal validity to the Hadith." "If the Hadith as a whole is
cast away," he says, "the basis for the historicity of the
Qur an is removed with one stroke."(69) The Twelver Shi i
position on the shari a is particularly uncompromising:

Shi ism believes that the Divine Law of Islam (Shari
ah), whose substance is found in the Book of God
and in the tradition (Sunnàh) of the Holy Prophet,
will remain valid to the Day of Judgement and can
never, nor will ever, be altered. (70)

It was therefore inevitable that after the establishment of the Islamic Republic in Iran in 1979, the existing codes of civil and penal law, promulgated during the reign of Riza Shah (1925-1941) and based largely on French and Belgian law, would be abolished, and the shari a reinstated. "Principle 4 of the Constitution of the Islamic Republic of Iran states:"

> All civil, penal, financial, economic, administrative, cultural, military, political, and other laws and regulations must be based on Islamic criteria (Hamid Algar's translation).

DEVELOPMENTS SINCE WORLD WAR II AND THE SITUATION TODAY

Thus Islam is once more facing the West with her back to the wall; but this time the odds are more heavily against her than they were even at the most critical moment of the Crusades, for the modern West is superior to her not only in arms but also in the technique of economic life, on which military science ultimately depends, and above all in spiritual culture – the inward force which alone creates and sustains the outward manifestations of what is called civilization.

These words, written in 1948 by the eminent British historian Arnold Toynbee,(71) have an ironical ring today. Rarely in the 14 centuries of interaction and coexistence between the "House of Islam" and the "House of War," has the pendulum swung so sharply and so dramatically. Today the West may be superior in arms, but it dare not use them for fear of igniting World War III. It is hard to assert today that the West is superior in the technique of economic life, when economists are arguing about whether or not North America is in a recession, and when North America, Europe, and Japan are subject to constant economic blackmail by the OPEC countries. As for the third ingredient in the West's overwhelming superiority to the Islamic world described by Toynbee in 1948 – namely, spiritual culture – the plain fact is that the Muslim world has, since the end of World War II, been watching a Western world that has been progressively losing its nerve and its faith in itself, its institutions, and its system of morals and beliefs.
Precisely at the same time that the West is suffering from a loss of will, "the moment of free choice has . . . arrived for the nations of the Muslim world. After a century of struggles, hopes, errors, and disappointments, full independence

from colonial rule has been won by most of the countries inhabited by Muslims."(72)   The acquisition of political independence inevitably encouraged a revival of religious fervor because of the essential blending of politics and religion in Islam.   At the same time, the inhabitants of this planet now live in a "global village," to use Marshall McLuhan's phrase, and so the "adherents of the various great religions are mingling with one another on an unprecedented scale."(73) Unfortunately, closer acquaintance with one another has not necessarily produced greater tolerance, understanding, or harmony.   On the contrary, as W. Montgomery Watt has pointed out, "because our world has become 'one world' in certain external ways, there are pressures making for the dominance of a single religion, and several religions may be said to be striving for the position of the 'one religion.' Islam is one of the contestants, a serious rival to Christianity and humanism. By the year 2000 most of Africa is likely to be under its sway, and it is growing in South-East Asia.   When it threatens our conception of our 'religion' in the world (whether that 'religion' be Christianity, humanism, Marxism or some other), and so threatens our conception of ourselves, how shall we be able to judge it objectively and assess its potentialities?"(74)

How have the countries of the "House of Islam" used this increase of political and (more recently) economic power, which in turn has given rise to the revival of a more militant form of Islam?   In many parts of the Islamic world it has led to a demand for the establishment of "Islamic states."   The view that "the organization of an Islamic state or states is an indispensable condition of Islamic life in the true sense of the world"(75) no doubt reflects the view of a majority of Muslims. The fundamental principles of an Islamic state, as formulated in 1951 by a panel of 33 accredited Ulema of Pakistan representing all the various schools of thought in Pakistan, are:

1. Ultimate Sovereignty over all Nature and all Law shall be affirmed in Allah, the Lord of the Universe, alone;
2. The Law of the land shall be based on the Qurʾ ān and the Sunnah, and no law shall be passed nor any administrative order issued in contravention of the Qurʾān and the Sunnah.

Some Muslim states, for example Iran, call themselves "Islamic republics."   It should be clearly understood that the term "republic" as used by Khumaini and others does not mean "republic" as the term is usually used in the West - that is, a state based on constitutional democracy, a state in which sovereignty is vested in the people.   In Iran, as in other Islamic "republics," sovereignty belongs to God alone.   To avoid confusion, the term "Islamic state" is used in this chapter. I will examine briefly some examples of the different ways in which Muslims have responded to the opportunity of shaping their own destinies.

Pakistan

Pakistan is a logical point of departure in any consideration of the nature of an Islamic state because in no part of the Muslim world has the debate as to exactly what is meant by "Islamic state" been fiercer. It was, of course, of paramount importance to the rulers of Pakistan that agreement be reached on this question, because Pakistan was a new state, carved out in 1947 from a preponderantly Hindu environment. If it was to survive, it had to define its identity in clear terms from the beginning. Pakistan is an affirmation of the Muslim view that "Islam can only be itself as a political expression"(76); it "embodies the Muslim assurance that Islam is a religiopolitical entity, unique, separate, distinctive."(77) Yet after three decades and more of debate, there is no consensus on what constitutes an Islamic state, beyond perhaps the fundamental principles mentioned above. All Muslim political theorists sooner or later base their concept of authority in an Islamic state on the key Koranic text:

> O ye who believe! Obey God, and obey His Messenger, and those who are in authority among you. [IV:59/62]

Apart from the fact that this text does not define "who is in authority among you," and is therefore open to different interpretations, many questions of vital importance - for example, the nature of the legislative process in an Islamic state, the status and rights of women in a Muslim society, the status and rights of non-Muslim minorities living in an Islamic state, and the whole concept of political parties and a "loyal opposition" in the political process - can only be inferred from general principles embodied in the Koran, and there is therefore much disagreement on these crucial issues.(78)

At the root of this disagreement, of course, is the vexed problem of the status of the shari a, the divinely inspired law of Islam. To repeat the words of Joseph Schacht quoted earlier in this chapter: "even at the present time the Law . . . remains an important, if not the most important element in the struggle which is being fought in Islam between traditionalism and modernism under the impact of Western ideas" (emphasis added).(79) At one extreme in the Pakistani debate stand the fundamentalist followers of Mawlana Mawdudi, the members of the Jama at-i Islami founded by Mawdudi in 1941. For Mawdudi, an Islamic state is essentially a shari a state. As E.I.J.

Rosenthal points out,(80) such an attitude does "not reveal much understanding for the real dilemma which besets devout Muslims who believe in God, but not in the immutability of Islamic law." For Mawdudi, too, Islam is "the very antithesis of secular Western democracy. The philosophical foundation of Western democracy is the sovereignty of the people."(81) At the other extreme of Pakistani thought is Ghulam Ahmad Parwez (1903-), a retired civil servant and former member of the Islamic Law Commission, who declares that the shari a is always wrong because it is based on a wrong theory of revelation; who urges Muslims to reject the whole past history of Islam, "with the exception of Muhammad and the first four Caliphs, as a period of darkness from which nothing can be learned"' who sees the religious leaders as the "basic obstacles to the creation of a new and prosperous Pakistan"; and who has earned himself the nickname of "Denier of hadith."(82) Between these two extremes are the Western-educated liberals who accept Islam as the basis of the polity of Pakistan but call for varying degrees of fresh interpretation of the shari a. Muhammad Iqbal (1875-1938) has been termed by Kenneth Cragg "the most outstanding, and exasperating, figure in twentieth-century Islam in the subcontinent."(83) Educated at Cambridge and Munich, Iqbal was strongly influenced by Bergson, Nietzsche, the neo-Hegelian McTaggart, and Freud. This seems to have laid the foundation of a love-hate relationship with the West, and to have produced an almost schizophrenic attitude toward Western ideas. "We heartily welcome the liberal movement in modern Islam," Iqbal said, "but it must also be admitted that the appearance of liberal ideas in Islam constitutes also the most critical moment in the history of Islam. Liberalism has a tendency to act as a force of disintegration."(84) As a result, Iqbal spent his life engaged in heated argument both with those who wanted no change, and also with those whom he considered to be in favor of too rapid change. As he moved increasingly into the realms of mysticism and metaphysics, he seems to have regarded an Islamic state based on nationalism as a temporary expedient, ultimately to be transcended by a process analogous to the Marxist concept of the "withering-away" of the state.(85)

Turkey

If Pakistan is the model of one polarity - namely, that of a group of Muslims consciously engaged in the task of creating an Islamic state - then Turkey represents the other polarity, that of a group of Muslims deliberately turning their backs on this Islamic heritage and setting up a secular state. Yet it need not have been so. As both Bernard Lewis and Dankwart A. Rustow have pointed out, Kemal Ataturk's nationalist move-

ment, in its early stages, "was strongly religious in character.
Its aims were to rescue 'Islamic lands' and 'Islamic populations'
from foreign - i.e., Christian - rule."(86) Ataturk was forced
into an anti-Islamic stance by the opposition to the Nationalists
of the religious authorities and the Ottoman Sultan in Istanbul.
The turning point occurred when the head of the religious
establishment, the Seyh-ul-Islam, issued the celebrated fetva
(legal opinion) of April 11, 1920 which called on true believers
to kill the Nationalists. The following month, May 1920, the
Sultan passed sentence of death on Ataturk in absentia.(87)

    The hostility of both the supreme religious authority in
the Ottoman Empire, the Seyh-ul-Islam, and of the ruler himself, the sultan, enabled Ataturk to press rapidly ahead with
the dismantling of Islamic institutions and the establishment of
a secular state. Between 1923 and 1928 the task was accomplished: the office of Seyh-ul-Islam was abolished; the seriat
(shari a) courts were closed, and a new civil code, based on
Swiss law, came into force; and the caliphate itself was
abolished.(88) "More than once in the past the ulema ('theologians') had delayed or frustrated the work of the reformers.
. . . the abolition of the Caliphate was a crushing blow to
their whole hierarchic organization."(89) On April 5, 1928 the
words "The religion of the Turkish state is Islam" were deleted
from the constitution, and Article 163 of the Criminal Code of
1926 forbade the use of religion to incite people against the
state.(90)

    By 1928 "the disestablishment of Islam was completed, and
Turkey was now, legally and constitutionally, a lay state,
secular and modern in her constitution, her laws, and her
aspirations."(91) But Islam had not been abolished; it had
merely gone underground. It remained alive among the rural
population, particularly in eastern Anatolia, the traditional
stronghold of heterodox beliefs; it remained alive among the
conservative petite bourgeoisie of traditional urban Islamic
society - the artisans, members of craft guilds, small shop-
keepers, and merchants; it was preserved by the Sufis, the
exponents of the popular Islam of "fortune-tellers, magicians,
witchdoctors, writers of amulets for the recovery of lost
property or the fulfilments of wishes"(92) - which Ataturk had
tried to suppress by draconian decrees.

    After the death of Ataturk in 1938, the first stirrings of
a religious revival could be perceived. With the formation of
the Democratic Party in 1945, the demand for a relaxation of
the ban on religious expression increased, because the Democratic Party program declared that "our party . . . rejects the
erroneous interpretation of secularism in terms of enmity
toward religion; it recognises religious freedom like the other
freedoms as a sacred right."(93) The governing party, the
People's Party, tried to preempt their rivals' position by
catering to the demand for more religion. In 1949 religious

education was reintroduced into the primary schools on a
voluntary basis. Attendance at mosques began to grow.
Religious books and pamphlets began to reappear. The pilgrimage to Mecca was resumed. The Faculty of Divinity, formerly at Istanbul, was reopened at Ankara. But these measures
came too late to save the People's Party, which was soundly
defeated in the 1950 elections. One of the first acts of the
new prime minister, Adnan Menderes, was to make religious
instruction part of the regular school curriculum. In 1951 the
Sufis, encouraged by the policies of the new government, came
out into the open and launched a violent attack on secularism.
One order, the Ticanis, demolished several statues of Ataurk
in the Ankara area, and became the object of the attentions of
the police. Members of other orders were also arrested.(94)

Since 1950, the battle between the secularists, the heirs
of the founder of modern Turkey, Ataturk, and the "clerical-
ists," has continued unabated. Few secularists today, perhaps, would echo the views of an early Turkish patriot,
Madame Halide Edib, who declared that "Islam and Turks had
never truly been compatible."(95) A majority of Turks today
probably wish Turkey to remain a Muslim country. The most
important question is whether Turkey can "discover a way in
which the deep devotion of most of her people to their religious heritage can find its due place, without retarding unduly
the social and economic changes on which the country's prosperity depends."(96)

Egypt

We have discussed, of necessity extremely briefly, examples of
diametrically opposed reactions to the impact of the West on
the Muslim world: the conscious attempt in Pakistan to create
a novo an Islamic state, and the total rejection in Turkey of
the Islamic heritage and the deliberate establishment of a
secular state. Egypt lies somewhere between these two extremes. Egypt was introduced to European ways as early as
any Arab country. After the Napoleonic invasion of 1798, the
reforms of Muhammad Ali (1769-1849) and his successors created the nucleus of an educated elite. "An embryonic national
system of education" was established, "including the first
government school for girls"; there was also established "the
first representative National Assembly in any Muslim country
which, although very limited in its powers, began to demand
more constitutional controls the deeper the country fell into
the clutches of its creditors."(97) One may speculate whether
Egypt's early acquaintance with Western ways has enabled it to
adjust to them gradually and avoid the violent conflict that has
occurred in other Muslim countries. Muhammad Abduh, for

instance, pointed out that "lifting ideas and customs wholesale from the West would only "suppress our morals, our customs, and ruin all our personality."(98)   In any case, he warned, Muslim countries could not expect to emulate the West over- night; European civilization was the end product of a long period of evolution, and had been achieved only at the price of "enormous suffering and sacrifice."(99)

The demand of Islamic modernists for a reevaluation of the Islamic tradition was also more muted in Egypt than it was, say, among Indian Muslims.   Egyptian modernists bandied words with the ulama, and, like their counterparts in India, condemned the principle of taqlid, but there was no attempt at any far-reaching theological reconstruction.   "Few, if any, of the basic theological and orthodox doctrines of Islam have been directly involved."(100)   Despite the gradualism of the Egyp- tian response to the West, however, the voice of Islamic fundamentalism has not been silent.   Founded in 1928, the Ikhwan al-Muslimin ("Muslim Brethren") movement had three basic principles; (1) there must be a single Muslim community or "House of Islam"; (2) the shari a applies to all human af- fairs; and (3) Islam is a brotherhood of all nations and classes.(101)   The more the Egyptian state moved in the direc- tion of secularization, the stronger the opposition of the Ikhwan al-Muslimin became.   The abolition of the shar i (reli- gious) courts in Egypt by Nasser violated one of their princi- ples, and they soon moved into a position of bitter hostility toward the revolutionary regime because the latter had not established the ideal Islamic state which the Brethren called for: "an absolute Islam, a pure Islamic system, the Koran as a constitution."(102)   On the status of the shari a, there is thus no difference between the views of the Ikhwan al-Muslimin in Egypt and those of the Jama at al- Ulama in Pakistan, whose president maintained in 1953 that:

> Law is complete and merely requires religious inter-
> pretation by those who are experts in it.   According
> to my belief no question can arise, the law relating
> to which cannot be discovered from the Qurʲān and
> hadith.(103)

Although between 1928 and 1936 the Ikhwan al-Muslimin con- fined themselves to religious and social activities, from 1936, when they espoused the cause of the Palestinian Arabs, they have been a good illustration of the adage that in Islam religion and politics are inseparable.   Within Egypt itself, the Ikhwan maintained clandestine military forces and awaited their chance of seizing political power.   Abroad, the Ikhwan sent volunteers to fight in the 1948 War in Palestine, and their ideology found supporters in Syria, Jordan, Iraq, and Leba- non, and even as far away as Indonesia, Malaya, and Pakistan.   After their attempted assassination of President Nasser in 1954, their organization was suppressed but was revived today as a dangerous threat to President Sadat.   As supporters of the Palestinian cause, they naturally side with the "rejectionist front" which is opposed to the policies of the present government of Egypt vis-a-vis Israel.   Their militancy may be judged from their redefinition of the "House of Islam," which in classical terms meant "territory under Muslim rule," as "any stretch of land where there is a Muslim."(104)   In their utopianism, and their readiness to resort to political terror to achieve their ideal, the Brethren have certain ideological affinities with "Twelver" Shi ism, which will be considered next.

Iran

Iran has been chosen as the fourth and final example of an Islamic state responding to the opportunity to shape its own destiny because Iran differs in one important respect from all other Muslim countries today: it is the only country in which Ithna Ashari Shi ism is the official religion of the state.   The schism between Sunni and Shi i Islam, and the basic doctrines and political theory of the Shi i form of Islam were discussed earlier in this chapter.   The fundamental Shi i doctrine is that, during the continuing occultation of the Twelfth or "Hidden" Imam, the only legitimate government in a "Twelver" Shi i state is that of his representatives on earth, namely, the mujtahids, the leading authorities on Shi i law, who of recent times have arrogated to themselves the title of ayatullah ("miraculous sign of God's power").   In the course of history, the mujtahids have acquired in the popular mind the attribute of infallibility that rightfully belongs to the Imams alone, and it is significant that some of Khumaini's supporters have not hesitated to address him as "Imam," which means, in fact, that they regard him as the Shi i messiah returned to earth.

This "Twelver" Shi i theory of government was of no particular consequence during the centuries when the Shi i movement had no political power but operated clandestinely in a predominantly Sunni environment in which Sunni rulers were by Shi i definition usurpers.   From 1501, however, when "Twelver" Shi ism became the official religion of the Iranian state, this theory of government mattered very much indeed, for the obvious reason that if the mujtahids, as representatives on earth of the Hidden Imam, constituted the only legitimate form of government, it followed that any other form of government - be it monarchy or republic (in the Western sense) - was illegitimate.   In other words, there was a built-in contradiction between the Shi i concept of government and the ancient, pre-Islamic Iranian monarchical tradition.   For more than four and a half centuries, from 1501 until the Iranian Revolution of 1979, the opposition of the religious classes to the monarchy, whether overt or covert, has been constant. In Sunni states, as we have seen, challenges developed during the 19th century to the position of the ulama, both on the part of those who thought that the ulama had betrayed their trust by being too ready to reach an accommodation with the West, and on the part of those who thought that the ulama, in part because of their fear of losing prestige or economic power, were too rigid in their opposition to new ideas and to any debate on the fundamental problems which faced Islam in a changing world. It is significant that at no time has there been any serious challenge to the position of the ulama in Iran. Their formal institutional organization has always been stronger than that of their Sunni counterparts. They have always been far more successful than the latter in "maintaining the solidarity of their organization and their independence of government control, in eliminating or weakening competitors, and in satisfying their own demands as individuals."(105) This strong political role derives from the function of their leaders as the representatives on earth of the Hidden Imam, as already noted.

Since the overthrow of the Shah in January 1979, there has been no check on the power of the mujtahids (ayatullahs) in Iran. It will be recalled that the key Koranic text on the subject of government is: "O ye who believe! Obey God, and obey His Messenger, and those who are in authority among you." In postrevolutionary Iran, the mujtahids have declared themselves to be "those who are in authority." Since the mujtahids, as the highest authorities on the shari a, are the guardians and interpreters of the religious law; and since the shari a has the status of part of the divine revelation; and since the mujtahids, as representatives on earth of the Shi i messiah, are endowed with both personal and doctrinal infallibility, their authority is necessarily absolute. In simple terms, it may be expressed as follows: obedience to the mujtahid equals obedience to the Imam equals obedience to the prophet equals obedience to God. Conversely, disobedience to the mujtahid is tantamount to disobedience to God's commands, and the mujtahid Khalkhali and others have demonstrated since the Iranian revolution that the consequence of this sin is trial without due process followed by immediate execution without the possibility of appeal. A favorite capital charge is "causing corruption in the land." In its Koranic usage, fasad fi l-ardi, "causing corruption in the land," often is simply equated with kufr, "unbelief." In its wider sense, it means "doing evil" in general, and is contrasted with ihsan, "doing good." In other words, it is a general ethical principle, not a legal charge as understood in Western law.(106) When used as the basis for a legal action, it may of course be interpreted in whatever way the prosecutor chooses, and consequently no defense against this charge is possible within the accepted and recognized international principles of law.

CONCLUSION

In the historical introduction to this chapter, a caveat was entered against the easy assumption that there exists a monolithic structure called "Islam" which could be relied upon to react in a predictable fashion in any given set of circumstances. It is hoped that the preceding brief account of the wide variation of belief and practice within the Islamic tradition, and of the way in which the impact of Western ideas such as nationalism has evoked widely differing responses from Muslim states will have dispelled this notion. In the last analysis, many of the problems confronting Islam today are similar in character to those facing Christianity and, indeed, all the major religions. All religions face the same problem of how to adapt to the technological age in which we live, and how to give their adherents the spiritual strength to deal with the psychological tensions produced by some aspects of modern life. One of the ironies of the present situation is that some people in the West have been turning to the East to find solutions to the problem of how to live a life that is spiritually as well as materially satisfying. Another caveat should, I believe, be entered at this point. To equate the West with "materialism" and the East with "the spiritual life" is both simplistic and fallacious. As Ilse Lichtenstadter has put it:

> Material benefit that resulted for the West from its rationalism, its science and its technology, roused the Muslim's desire to participate in them. He tried to achieve that end by adjusting his own life to that of the West and by adopting some of its outer forms. But he found that the change was not as beneficial as he had hoped. . . . disappointed, he began to accuse the West of "materialism" and to extol the "spirituality" of the East as superior. . . . it can no longer be accepted as an alibi for all future inadequacies either by the West or by those Muslims who earnestly think of the necessity for adjustment, change and progress. . . . The material progress in the West has nothing to do with its spiritual attitudes; the West is neither less or more "spiritual" because of its material prosperity, nor would the East be forced to give up its "spirituality" in order to improve its material standards. (107)

The majority of Muslims, however, have not yet perceived the truth of the assertion that they do not need to abandon their religious faith in order to adopt the technology that will improve their material standards. The special problem of Islam is that it is essentially a religion of the law. As a leading contemporary Islamic scholar has put it: "Islam is not technically speaking a theocracy but a nomocracy, that is, a society ruled by a Divine Law."(108) Few Muslims are prepared to accept the Western proposition that legal change corresponds to social demand. It is true that various Muslim states during the last 30 years have modified the shari a in the vexed areas of polygamy and divorce. For example, the Syrian Law of Personal Status (1953) required the consent of a court for a second marriage, and the Tunisian Law of Personal Status (1957) abolished polygamy. The Moroccan Code (1958), however, did not prohibit polygamy, and the law regarding divorce was not modified. Egypt (1960) restricted but did not abolish polygamy, and Pakistan (1961) allowed a husband to take a second wife only with the permission of an Arbitration Council.(109) The greatest step forward in the field of women's rights was the Iranian Family Protection Act of 1967, which stated that a man might take a second wife only with the consent of the first, and for the first time gave women the right to initiate divorce proceedings. But as N.J. Coulson has noted, "notwithstanding the achievements of the reform movement to date . . . it would be wholly wrong to suppose that these have met with general approval or that any Muslim government has yet a mandate to proceed full ahead along the course of what modernists would describe as social progress. There is still a deep-rooted opposition to change both in principle and in practice."(110) It is significant that one of the first acts of Ayatullah Khumaini after his accession to power was to annul the Family Protection Act of 1967.

Despite the accusation by Islamic modernists that the traditionalists are failing to understand what God requires of his community under changing circumstances, what Sheila McDonough has called "the authority of the past" still dominates Muslim thinking. Certain Muslim attitudes are unchanging: (1) there is no tradition in Islam of respect for Caesar; (2) the Muslim community is made up of persons whose ultimate allegiance is to God and not to a nation-state in the Western sense; (3) the early Muslim period is the norm for all subsequent Muslim practice (although there is no agreement among Muslims as to what constitutes the essence of this period); and (4) the worldly success of the umma, the Muslim community, is evidence of God's favor. Wordly failure implies a serious break in the community's relations with God.(111) For a thousand years, the ulama "have managed to preserve the medieval statement of Islam in all its essentials,"(112) and events of the last few years have strengthened rather than weakened their authority throughout the "House of Islam." So far, there has been no solution to the question, how or whether the fundamental principles of Islam may be reformulated without destroying its essential elements.

NOTES

1. Subsequently published; see Bernard Lewis, The Middle East and the West (London: Weidenfeld and Nicolson, 1963-1964), p. 114.

2. Kenneth Cragg, The House of Islam, (Belmont, Calif.: Dickenson Publishing Co., 1969), glossary p. 100.

3. Bernard Lewis, Islam (New York: Harper and Row, 1974), I, p. xiv.

4. R.M. Savory ed., Introduction to Islamic Civilisation (Cambridge, Eng.: Cambridge University Press, 1976), p. 129.

5. For examples, see Norman Daniel, Islam, Europe and Empire (Edinburgh: Edinburgh University Press, 1966), pp. 50-51.

6. Sir William Muir, in the Calcutta Review (1845), quoted in Daniel, Islam, Europe and Empire, p. 32.

7. The Revelation of St. John the Divine, chap. 13, verse 7 (King James version).

8. They include Nestorian Christians, Monophysites, Maronites, Jacobites, Roman Catholics, Protestants, etc.

9. "More than 98 percent of all the peoples who inhabit the Persian Gulf region profess the religion of Islam" (James E. Dougherty, "Religion and Law" in Persian Gulf States, ed. (A.J. Cottrell et al.), (Baltimore and London: The Johns Hopkins University Press, 1980), p. 305.

10. (Boston: Beacon Press, 1966), pp. 35.

11. I Corinthians, chap. 13, verse 12.

12. Bell's Introduction to the Qurʾān, completely revised and enlarged by W. Montgomery Watt (Edinburgh: Edinburgh University Press, 1970), p. 40.

13. As H.A.R. Gibb has pointed out, this profession of faith "is not found in this composite form anywhere in the Koran, but its two halves occur separately," Mohammedanism (London: Oxford University Press, 1949), p. 53.

14. For a full description of the ritual prayers in Islam, and illustrations of the postures to be adopted during them, see E.W. Lane, The Manners and Customs of the Modern Egyptians

(London and Toronto: J.M. Dent and Sons, and (New York: E.P. Dutton, 1914), pp. 77ff.

15. In its original sense of "acts of public spirit on the part of private people" (Kenneth Cragg, The House of Islam, Belmont, California: 1969, p. 57).

16. Fazlur Rahman, Islam, 2nd edition, (Chicago and London: University of Chicago Press, 1979), p. 36.

17. Koran, 5:5.

18. Alfred Guillaume, Islam (Harmondsworth, Middlesex: Penguin, 1954), p. 63.

19. Ibid.

20. Rahman, Islam, p. 37.

21. Joseph Schacht, An Introduction to Islamic Law (Oxford: Oxford University Press, 1964), p. 17.

22. Kenneth Cragg, The Call of the Minaret (New York: Oxford University Press, 1964), p. 99.

23. Ibid.

24. Rahman, Islam, p. 71.

25. Schacht, Introduction, p. 37.

26. Rahman, Islam, p. 71.

27. Rahman, p. 70.

28. Cragg, The House of Islam, p. 49.

29. Gibb, Mohammedanism, p. 97.

30. Schacht, Introduction, p. 71.

31. Schacht, Introduction, p. 1.

32. Rahman, Islam, p. 68.

33. Ibid.

34. Ideals and Realities in Islam, p. 44.

35. Lewis, Islam, I, p. xvi.

36. Matthew, 22:21; cf. Mark, 12:17 and Luke, 20:25.

37. Lewis, Islam, I, p. xvi.

38. E.I.J. Rosenthal, The Role of the State in Islam: Theory and the Medieval Practice, a paper presented to the Colloquium on Tradition and Change in the Middle East, Harvard, 1968, p. 1.

39. Encyclopaedia of Islam, new edition, Leiden: E.J. Brill, 1960, p. 884.

40. Rosenthal, The Role of the State p. 10.

41. H.A.R. Gibb, "Al-Mawardi's 'Theory of the Caliphate,'" in Studies on the Civilization of Islam, ed. Stanford J. Shaw and William R. Polk (Boston: Beacon Press, 1962), p. 162.

42. Some of the material used in this section has already appeared in my article, "The problem of sovereignty in an Ithna Ashari ('twelver') Shi i State," in Middle East Review XI 4 (1979): pp. 5-11.

43. Muhammad Asad, The Principles of State and Government in Islam (Berkeley and Los Angeles: University of California Press, 1961), p. 35.

44. Gustave von Grunebaum, Medieval Islam: A Study in Cultural Orientation, Chicago: University of Chicago Press, 1953, 2nd ed. p. 187.

45. Allamah Sayyid Muhammad Husayn Tabataba i, Shi ite Islam, trans. Seyyed Hossein Nasr (Albany: State University of New York Press, 1975), p. 212.

46. Von Grunebaum, Medieval Islam, p. 190.

47. Sir William Muir, The Caliphate: Its Rise, Decline and Fall (Edinburgh: John Grant, 1924), p. 312.

48. See Peter J. Chelkowski, "Iran: Mourning Becomes Revolution," Asia (May/June 1980), pp. 30ff.

49. Tabataba i, p. 78.

50. Arberry's translation, quoted in Seyyed Hossein Nasr, Ideals and Realities in Islam, p. 58.

51. Wensinck, La Pensée de Ghazzali, p. 111, quoted in A.J. Arberry, Sufism (London: Allen and Unwin, 1950), pp. 82-83.

52. Nasr, Ideals and Realities, p. 93.

53. J. Kritzeck, Moslem-Christian Understanding in Mediaeval Times, p. 401.

54. Ibid.

55. "Some Recent Constructions and Reconstructions of Islam," in The Conflict of Traditionalism and Modernism in the Muslim Middle East, ed. Carl Leiden (Austin: University of Texas, 1966), p. 141.

56. Bernard Lewis, The Middle East and the West (London: Weidenfeld and Nicolson, 1963-1964), p. 45.

57. Daniel, Islam, Europe and Empire, p. 261.

58. Ibid., p. 262.

59. Lewis, The Middle East and the West, p. 44.

60. Wilfred Cantwell Smith, Islam in Modern History (New York: Mentor Books, 1959), p. 49.

61. See H.A.R. Gibb, Modern Trends in Islam (Chicago: University of Chicago Press, 1947), p. 27.

62. Ibid., p. 29.

63. Ibid., p. 29.

64. Kenneth Cragg, "Counsels in Contemporary Islam," Islamic Surveys, no. 3, (Edinburgh 1965), pp. 36-7.

65. The Spirit of Islam, 1922 ed., quoted in Cragg, Counsels, pp. 52-53.

66. Rahman, Islam, p. 61.

67. Quoted in Cragg, Counsels, p. 57.

68. Quoted in Cragg, Counsels, pp. 136-137.

69. Rahman, Islam, p. 66.

70. Tabataba i, Shi ite Islam, p. 44.

71. Civilization on Trial, chap. 10: "Islam, the West and the Future," p. 187.

72. Muhammad Asad, The Principles of State and Government in Islam, p. 1.

73. W. Montgomery Watt, What is Islam? (London and Harlow: Longmans, Green and Co., 1968), p. 5.

74. Ibid.

75. Muhammad Asad, Principles, p. 4.

76. Cragg, Counsels, p. 24.

77. Cragg, Counsels, p. 15.

78. For fuller details of the debates on these questions in Pakistan, see particularly E.I.J. Rosenthal, Islam in the Modern National State (Cambridge University Press, 1965).

79. See above, p. 9.

80. Rosenthal, Islam in the Modern National State, p. 141.

81. Mawdudi, quoted in Rosenthal, p. 138.

82. Sheila McDonough, The Authority of the Past (Chambersburgh, Penn.: American Academy of Religion, 1970), pp. 36-38.

83. Cragg, Counsels, p. 59.

84. Quoted in McDonough, The Authority of the Past, pp. 21-22.

85.   Cragg, Counsels, p. 64.

86.   Bernard Lewis, The Emergence of Modern Turkey (London: Oxford University Press, 1961), p. 396.

87.   See Dankwart A. Rustow "Politics and Islam in Turkey 1920-1955," in Islam and the West, ed. R.N. Frye (The Hague: Mouton and Co., 1957), pp. 75ff.

88.   The Ottoman sultans had a tenuous claim to the historic office of caliph.   After the destruction of the Abbasid caliphate at Baghdad by the Mongols in 1258 A.D., survivors of the Abbasid family were granted asylum at Cairo, where they and their descendants became state pensioners of the Mamluk Sultans, to whose rule their presence added a certain prestige.   When the Ottomans conquered Egypt in 1517 and overthrew the Mamluk regime, they inherited this shadowy ghost of the historical caliphate.   The Ottoman sultans themselves never attached much importance to this function, but during the 19th century, when the pan-Islamic movement aroused dreams of the reunification of the Islamic world under one leader, the Ottoman sultan, as the head of the most powerful Muslim state at that time, was an obvious candidate for the post.   Muslims in India gave particular support to this idea, and founded the Khilafat ("Caliphate") movement there.

89.   Lewis, Emergence of Modern Turkey, p. 260.

90.   Ibid., p. 271, 406.

91.   Ibid., p. 271.

92.   Ibid., p. 405, quoting Jäschke.

93.   Rustow, Politics and Islam in Turkey, p. 91.

94.   Ibid., p. 97.

95.   Cragg, Counsels, p. 147.

96.   Eleazar Birnbaum, "Turkey from Cosmopolitan Empire to Nation State," in Introduction to Islamic Civilisation, ed. R.M. Savory (London: Cambridge University Press, 1976), p. 188.

97.   L.M. Kenny, "The Modern Arab World, in Savory Introduction to Islamic Civilisation, p. 151.

98.   Osman Amin, "The Modernist Movement in Egypt," in R.N. Frye (ed.), Islam and the West, ed. R.N. Frye (The Hague: Mouton and Co., 1957), p. 168.

99.   Ibid., p. 168.

100.   Kenneth Cragg, "The Modernist Movement in Egypt," in Frye, Islam and the West, (The Hague: Mouton and Co., 1957), p. 151.

101.   Kenneth Cragg, Counsels, p. 117.

102. I.M. Husaini, The Moslem Brethren. The Greatest of
Modern Islamic Movements (Beirut: 1956), p. 47, quoted by
Gustave von Grunebaum, "Some Recent Constructions and
Reconstructions of Islam," in The Conflict of Traditionalism
and Modernism in the Muslim Middle East, ed. Carl Leiden
(Austin: University of Texas, 1966), p. 146.

103. Quoted in Cragg, Counsels, p. 76.

104. I.M. Husaini, quoted in von Grunebaum, Some Recent
Constructions, p. 147.

105. Leonard Binder, "The Proofs of Islam: Religion and
Politics in Iran," in Arabic and Islamic Studies in Honor of
H.A.R. Gibb, Cambridge,Mass: Harvard University Press, ed.
Makdisi, Jurj (1965), p. 121.

106. Readers interested in pursuing this concept further are
referred to Toshiko Izutsu's excellent work, Ethico-Religious
Concepts in the Qurʾān, (Montreal: McGill University, 1966),
pp. 211-213, and other references listed in the index of this
book.

107. Islam and the Modern Age (New York: Brookman Associates, 1958), pp. 196-197.

108. Seyyed Hossein Nasr, Ideals and Realities, p. 107.

109. These details of modernist legislation are taken from
M.K. Nawaz, "Some Aspects of Modernization of Islamic Law,"
in Leiden, The Conflict of Traditionalism and Modernism in
the Muslim East, p. 75.

110. N.J. Coulson, Conflicts and Tensions in Islamic Jurisprudence (Chicago: University of Chicago Press, 1969), p.
112.

111. Sheila McDonough, The Authority of the Past, pp. 50-
51.

112. Leonard Binder, The Proofs of Islam, p. 119.

2 The Middle East: Political and Security Assessment—An Overview

Waldo H. Dubberstein

The term "Middle East" has come increasingly to be used to designate Iran, Turkey, Cyprus, Israel, and the Arab states, including those of North Africa. In this study the emphasis is on the Arab states and Iran. A political and security assessment of this area requires a recognition of its complex historical background as well as an identification of the deep roots of the Arab-Israeli conflict. Israel's role in the modern Middle East is of special importance and is treated as such in this chapter. The Egyptian-Israeli peace effort adds to the complexities of the scene. The unique position of the Palestinians is next treated. Arab disunity is also an important element in any political and security assessment of the area, and the Lebanese tragedy must be recognized, as well. The Iraqi-Iranian war underscores the basic conflicts that exist. Finally, a political and security assessment of the Middle East must recognize the overhanging Soviet threat.

BACKGROUND

Historians have often called the Middle East "the crossroads" of Europe, Asia, and Africa. Geographically, these three continents are linked by the physical land connections that exist in the Middle East. This area thus was subjected from prehistoric times to continuing movements of people from the three continents. When peoples migrate there often is conflict and war, and the Middle East was involved from prehistoric times with both movement and conflict.

Both Arabs and Israelis are Semites. As such they share the Middle East as their homeland where they had a common linguistic and ethnic origin. The earliest records, some 3,200 years ago, dealing with the Hebrews (Jews, Israelis) reveal them as Semitic desert tribesmen invading and conquering Palestine (now Israel and the West Bank). The records also identify an assemblage of peoples, some Semite, some of other racial origins, living in Palestine at the time of the Hebrew conquest.

The Arabs are identified in historical records for the first time about 2,600 years ago. They, too, were Semitic desert tribesmen invading the Tigris-Euphrates river valley (now Iraq) in which various peoples, including other Semites, were living. Thus, as the Hebrews and the Arabs first appear on the pages of history they are both nomadic, Semitic tribesmen seeking the better life through conquest of fertile areas.

Hebrew national culture was developed in Palestine in a turbulent period of over a thousand years. Frequent local warfare, and conquests by major powers - Assyria, Babylonia, Greece, Rome - finally left the Jewish people some 1,900 years ago shattered and dispersed but cherishing the hope of returning to Jerusalem and to the land they viewed as their own. The Arabs after centuries of obscurity achieved their place in history about 1,300 years ago when their leader Mohammed gave them religion, and political and military motivation. Palestine became Arab in the seventh century A.D. and Moslem tradition has Mohammed visiting Jerusalem. Thus, Palestine assumed unique importance for Moslems, and Arabs came to view Palestine as their land and Jerusalem as a holy shrine city.

Centuries of persecution and discrimination in many parts of Europe encouraged Jewish interest in returning to Palestine where small numbers of Jews had always remained. During World War I Britain sought Arab support and promised to help them create an Arab state after the end of the war. Britain also sought and received Jewish support in World War I and promised to support Jewish interest in a homeland in Palestine. The patterns of assured conflict were thus laid down. And when Britain finally after World War II, and after many years of frustration, relinquished its mandate over Palestine on May 14, 1948, Israel was immediately born and the first Arab-Israeli war began.

The above summary of 3,000 years of history highlights the complexity of Arab-Israeli relations. It also helps to explain why a resolution of differences and a negotiated peace has not been obtained.

Virtually all parts of the Middle East have long and complex histories. Nearly all other areas had mixtures of diverse peoples and extensive conflicts. An occasional effort has been made to identify and define a "pure" Arab or a "pure" Turk or a "pure" something else; such an effort is an exercise in futility. The racial mixtures began in prehistoric times and continue.

Aside from Israel, which will be treated in more depth shortly, two non-Arab states in the Middle East deserve recognition here. These two states, Turkey and Iran, are also uniquely complex in their historical, ethnic, and cultural developments.

Turkey's ethnic background is intricately linked to the earliest history of the area. Written records of 4,000 years ago reveal a mixture of warring peoples with diverse European and Asian origins living in what is now Turkey. Peoples identified as Turkish arrived in this area about a thousand years ago. Turkish tribesmen out of central Asia moved in in great numbers and overran areas that are now part of modern Iran, Iraq, and Turkey. This latter country received its name and much of its culture from these invaders. The Turkish tribes became converts to Islam and then slowly destroyed the Greek Byzantine Empire as they established their own rule. Ottoman, a distinguished Turkish leader, gave his name to the Turkish Empire which reached its peak in the 16th century and thereafter declined.

Modern Turkey was created by the great Turkish leader Mustafa Kemal Ataturk who took power in 1920. He gave direction and dynamism to present-day Turkey. In recent years, however, Turkey has been increasingly beset with major political and economic problems that it has not been able to resolve. Street violence, urban terrorism, and rural disorders have plagued Turkey as ineffective political figures failed to maintain order or to solve its other problems. In early September 1980 the top military commanders acting under the general chief of staff removed the civil government, established firm military order, and began to tackle their problems. It will be a tough job to bring Turkey back.

Iran, a non-Arab, Moslem, Middle East state has a long and complex history with periods of unique greatness and periods of collapse. Man began living there in prehistoric times. The Achaemenid Empire which was established more than 2,500 years ago came to be the most powerful military assemblage created up to that time. Its culture was the cumulative experience of the various small states and tribal groupings that had preceded it. Its Zoroastrian religion was an impressive formulation. After the Achaemenids were destroyed by Alexander the Great of Greece, Iran, like other Middle East countries, experienced centuries of conflict as dynasties rose and fell. Like the rest of the Middle East, Iran became converted to the Moslem faith by the middle of the seventh century A.D. Thereafter there were Iranian Moslem dynasties in Iran.

Iran entered the modern world with the advent of Colonel Reza Khan who became minister of war in 1921, prime minister in 1923, and shah in 1925. He took over an impoverished and weak state, and began the process of building an independent

absolute monarchy. During World War II, in September 1941,
Reza Khan, who was not cooperating with Britain and the
USSR, was forced to abdicate in favor of his son Mohammed
Reza who became Shah Reza Pahlavi and for the next 37 years
gave increasingly absolute rule to Iran. The shah departed
from Iran in January 1979 and Ayatollah Khomeini took over.
A very complex new era had begun in which a revolutionary
Shia Moslem state was created.

ISRAEL ON THE SCENE

Possibly the most significant political development for the
present-day Middle East was the creation of the state of Israel
on May 14, 1948. Not only did Israel bring into being a
dynamic, democratic state that immediately received the hostile
attention of its Arab neighbors, but its very existence stimulated wide reaction and change in those Aab quarters. The
creation of Israel gave the Soviet Union the opportunity to
insert itself into the Middle East. In view of the obvious
importance of these developments it is essential that some basic
data on Israel be reviewed.

Israel established itself in the first war with the Arabs
which was fought in 1948 immediately after Israel proclaimed
itself a sovereign state. But after that war Israel had
continuing difficulties, notably with the Palestinian refugees
who mounted raids from Jordan, from the West Bank (which
joined Jordan in 1950), from Syria and from Gaza. Israel
retaliated as it saw fit and tensions mounted.

A development of great significance and one which also
promoted rising tensions was Egyptian President Abdel Gamal
Nasser's arms agreement of August 1955 which brought
"Czech" (read Soviet) military equipment to Egypt. Thus the
Soviets came into the middle of the Arab-Israeli dispute on the
Arab side. Israel could only view this as an increased threat.
This Soviet involvement was in part the cause of the second
Arab-Israeli war, although the immediate occasion derived from
the British and French determination to retake control of the
Suez Canal which Egyptian President Nasser had nationalized
in July 1956.

On Octber 29, 1956 Israel, having a secret pact with
Britain and France, struck into the Sinai and drove rapidly
toward the Suez Canal. Subsequently the British and French
issued an ultimatum to both sides to withdraw 20 miles from
the canal. Egypt refused; Israel, in line with its new allies,
was ready to comply. British-French troops then joined their
Israeli allies and invaded the canal area. Subsequently, the
United Nations with American and Soviet support induced Israeli, British, and French withdrawal.

The USSR, which in August 1955 had begun to furnish arms to Egypt, increased its military aid in the years that followed and in 1958 agreed to finance and manage the building of the Aswan High Dam in upper Egypt. The Soviet connection with Egypt came to be a major matter of increasing concern to Israel. Arab guerrilla activity against Israel continued to increase across the frontiers with Egypt, Jordan, and Syria. The Syrian government in 1966 formally proclaimed its support for a recently created Palestinian guerrilla organization. This organization was Fatah under the direction of Yasir Arafat.

By early 1967 Egypt, Jordan, and Syria were mobilizing and President Nasser threatened Israel with activating the Egyptian-Syrian Defense Agreement. When, in May 1967, President Nasser ordered the closing of the Strait of Tiran - the entry to the Red Sea and thus to the Gulf of Aqaba - to Israeli shipping it was virtually certain that there would be a third war between the Arabs and Israelis. Israel brought in a new "national" government. Included as defense minister was General Moshe Dayan, the victor in the 1956 war.

On June 5, 1967 Israel made a preemptive ground strike into Egyptian Sinai and by air also struck airfields in Egypt, Jordan, Syria, and Iraq. Within six days Israel had defeated Egypt, Jordan, and Syria and had conquered the Egyptian Sinai, Gaza, the Jordanian West Bank, and the Syrian Golan Heights. Another war had been won but no peace settlement was in sight.

Five months later on November 22, 1967 the United Nations Security Council passed its now famous and much quoted Resolution 242 which stated that the establishment of a just and lasting peace in the Middle East should include the application of the following principles:

> (1) Withdrawal of Israeli armed forces from territories occupied in the recent conflict and (2) termination of all claims or states of belligerency and respect for an acknowledgement of the sovereignty, territorial integrity, and political independence of every state in the area, and their right to live in peace within secure and recognized boundaries free from threats or acts of force. The Council affirmed also the necessity for (a) guaranteeing freedom of navigation through international waterways in the area, and (b) achieving a just settlement of the refugee problem.

The text lends itself to various interpretations. For example, the phrase "from territories occupied" is translated in the French "les territoires." The Israelis have insisted it means "from some of the territories."

Israel's brilliant victory brought with it an increasing Arab determination to revenge their humiliating defeat. It brought to Israel "occupied territories" with a million Palestinian Arabs and it brought continuing Arab guerrilla activity. The 1967 victory ultimately also brought to Israel another war, the Yom Kippur War, or the October 1973 war, a surprise attack by the Arabs which began on October 6, 1973 and achieved considerable Arab success in the first days. Then the Israeli response began to be effective. The Syrian thrusts were halted and the Israelis broke through the Egyptian lines, recrossed the canal, and threatened the Egyptian Third Army at Port Suez. On October 25 a precarious ceasefire was negotiated and the weary process of ending the war began once again.

This time there was no clear victor and, of course, there was no peace. For the Israelis the war was most disturbing. The Arabs had been able to pull off a surprise attack - Israel had been deceived - its intelligence had failed. The Arabs had also demonstrated some military capabilities. The Egyptians had crossed the Suez Canal and had overrun the Israeli defenses, the Bar-Lev line. The Syrians had driven forward and then had held their new lines with determination. The Arabs had used modern Soviet equipment effectively and they had fought well. This could augur evil for the future.

Israel had heavy casualties; some 2,500 had died in action and several hundred were missing. Popular Israeli confidence in its military establishment seemed to be shaken. People were unsure. Some thought a negotiated peace should be sought; most believed there was no solution except a strong, alert defense establishment.

The Arabs in turn insisted that they had finally won a victory. Details of Egyptian and Syrian accomplishments were carefully noted and cherished. The Suez Canal crossing became a heroic achievement, as was the breaching of the Bar-Lev line. The Syrian push foward was detailed. But when it was all over the Israelis were still in possession of the West Bank, the Sinai, Gaza, and the Golan Heights. And many Arabs continued to doubt their own military abilities.

In November 1974 the Arab summit meeting at Rabat, Morocco formally recognized the Palestine Liberation Organization, headed by Yasir Arafat, as the "sole representative of the Palestinian people." This frustrated Jordan's King Hussein, who had maintained a relationship with the West Bank Palestinians and had hopes that someday the West Bank would return to a special relationship with Jordan.

Israel too had a host of problems following the October 1973 war. Prime Minister Yitshak Rabin faced serious economic problems, much postwar criticism, and finally he himself came under fire because of an illegal bank account.

When the election smoke of May 1977 cleared, Menachim Begin's hard-line Likud party had won 43 seats (out of 120), a plurality. It was then able to form a coalition government. The Labor Party which had governed Israel since 1949 was out. Israel faced a troubled future.

EGYPTIAN-ISRAELI PEACE

Then the unbelievable happened. Again the patterns of the Middle East were recut. In November 1977 President Sadat flew into Jerusalem, addressed the Israeli Knesset, and began peace talks. Despite worldwide enthusiasm for peace it became obvious that peace would not be achieved easily or quickly. It also became apparent that a major sticking point would be the Palestinian problem. If there were to be peace and settlements in the Middle East the Palestinians must be brought into the process. The West Bank-Gaza Arabs must attain some kind of autonomy. It became clear that Begin would grant some kind of administrative autonomy to the West Bank but the Palestinians wanted a politically independent Palestinian state.

In September 1978 the Egyptians and Israelis, under the prodding of U.S. President Jimmy Carter, signed an agreement that there would be a five-year time period during which the West Bank-Gaza would obtain full autonomy and self-government. In addition, Egypt and Israel would sign a peace treaty within three months. The signing was delayed over arguments as to whether the two provisions, autonomy and the peace treaty, were to be linked together.

On March 27, 1979 the peace treaty was finally signed. It provided the return of all of Sinai to Egypt within three years. The autonomy issue was handled in a separate letter which provided that within one month after ratification of the treaty the two sides would begin negotiations for the autonomy of the West Bank-Gaza and that these negotiations would be completed within one year. There would then be elections of Palestinians to West Bank councils and a five-year transitional period would follow, during which time the final status of the West Bank-Gaza would be established.

This is the background and the basis on which autonomy negotiations began on May 26, 1979 among representatives from Egypt, Israel, and the United States. When May 26, 1980 had passed without any significant progress on an agreement for West Bank-Gaza autonomy, this situation was widely viewed as a serious failure in the peace process.

Meanwhile, the Begin government maintained a firm line to the effect that the West Bank was part of ancient Israel and thus it remained part of the "land of Israel" today. Accordingly, even while negotiations for the autonomy of the West

Bank-Gaza were being conducted, Israelis were creating new Israeli settlements in the West Bank.

This settlement activity resulted in a series of developments in the West Bank in late spring and early summer 1980 which added to the tensions in the area and set back the peace process.   Arab terrorists killed four new Jewish settlers at Hebron.   Two West Bank Arab mayors were deported by the Israeli government.   Later two other Palestinian Arab mayors were severely maimed in terrorist bombing of automobiles. Many Arabs view these bombings as the work of Jewish terrorists and believe that the Israeli government condoned this type of illegal action.   And, of course, the Arab terrorists at Hebron vanished, presumably sheltered by local Arabs.

This is obviously a difficult situation, and one that could deteriorate quickly.   There is behind it, however, the determined policy of the Begin government.   Begin will not relinquish the claim to the "land of Israel, ancient Judea and Samaria."   In line with this position Israel will continue to insist that it has the right to create Israeli settlements in the West Bank-Gaza.   Israel will not relinquish claim to Jerusalem - any of it - including East (Arab) Jerusalem (where important Arab shrines are located) and which was acquired by Israel in the June War of 1967.

The Arabs, the United Nations, the United States, and many of the Western European states disapprove of current Israeli policy of creating new Israeli settlements in the West Bank-Gaza.   This is a serious problem which to some extent blocks the search for peace in the Middle East.

In any assessment of the Middle East it must be concluded that in some way the most important, the militarily most powerful state, is Israel.   It is hated, and feared, and respected.   But it has not achieved one of the things it wants most - acceptance by its neighbors.   It is truly physically isolated.   It has not achieved the other thing it desperately wants and needs - real security.   Its neighbors are dedicated to the destruction of Israel.   This is not a happy environment even though there is no doubt that Israel has the military capacity to survive.

THE PALESTINIANS

Another serious problem in the search for peace in the Middle East is the Palestinians, specifically those associated with the Palestine Liberation Organization, the umbrella created in 1964, headed by Yasir Arafat whose own organization Fatah (founded in 1956) is the largest of the several that are gathered together to form the PLO.   Fatah - the Palestine National Liberation Movement - is often but probably erroneously labeled the most moderate of the PLO groups. It includes so-called moderates (Arafat is often considered a moderate) but also has hard-core activists who have helped to create such dedicated terrorists as "Black September" and "Black June."

Well known as a hard-line Marxist group is the Popular Front for the Liberation of Palestine (PFLP) headed by the well-known Dr. George Habbash, a Palestinian who is a graduate of the Medical School of the American University in Beirut, and a Christian.

Other Palestinian groups active in the PLO are the Popular Front for the Liberation of Palestine, General Command, a splinter from Habbash's organization. The Democratic Front for the Liberation of Palestine is another small but determined group under Marxist influence. Saiqa (Vanguard of the Popular Liberation War) is a Syrian-backed operation. The Arab Liberation Front and Palestine Liberation Front are two Iraq-supported groups. There are other Palestinian organizations, such as the Popular Struggle Front, that also belong to the PLO.

The PLO has offices and representatives in every Arab country and in a host of other states including the United States, the Soviet Union, China, Britain, and Switzerland. The PLO is a member of the Arab League and has permanent observer status at the United Nations General Assembly. The PLO has an elaborate apparatus which includes an army - the Palestine Liberation Army - a national council, an executive committee, trade unions, Red Crescent (Cross), and various other bodies such as medical, architect, writer, and teacher organizations. The PLO has its national charter and a political program. Its position is bitter and unyielding on all matters concerning Israel. It has of course condemned the Camp David accords and the Egyptian-Israeli peace.

The PLO and its various members seem to be receiving an increasingly large flow of money. The PLO receives into its Palestine National Fund 3 to 6 percent of the income of all Palestinians regardless of where they are. Other friendly Arabs also contribute to this fund. More importantly, the PLO as well as specific fronts receive large sums of money directly - tens of millions of dollars - from oil-producing Arab states. Large contributors are Libya, Iraq, Saudi Arabia, Kuwait, and the United Arab Emirates. Most observers of the Arab scene have the impression that the Palestinians have all the weapons and money they can use.

An aspect of the Palestinian activity about which not much is known is the Moscow connection. It is known that Yasir Arafat has received some Soviet equipment and that he has often visited the Soviet Union. The impression widely held is that his relations with Moscow have expanded in recent years. But Arafat is discreet. He knows that some of his benefactors, notably Saudi Arabia, do not care for a Soviet connection; that part of his activity is therefore deemphasized and hidden.

If one looks at the Palestinians as part of the Middle East equation it becomes apparent that this relatively small group of Arabs - some four to five million - have an inordinate amount of influence in the Middle East. After Israel, the Palestinians may be exerting the most influence in the area and may be driving the Arab world into many of the positions that are held.

The basic Arab positions on Israel and Palestine are in the first place formulated by the PLO. It has a formal Palestine Research Center and a Palestine Planning Center. It maintains departments of information and national guidance, of culture and education, of political and international relations. The PLO, as noted above, maintains a Palestine Writers' Organization, and a Palestine Teachers' Organization. It operates several radio stations, identified as the "Voice of Palestine." It has its own "Palestine News Agency" and issues several newspapers.

The most precise statement on the Palestine problem, as the Arabs see it, may be the 33-article PLO "Palestine National Charter," which begins: "Palestine is the homeland of the Palestinian Arab people; it is an indivisible part of the Arab homeland, and the Palestinian people are an integral part of the Arab nation."

There is almost universal agreement that the Palestinians are among the most talented, the best educated, and the most competent of the Arabs. They are now scattered widely over the Middle East where they are often in positions of trust and influence.

The Palestinians in Jordan are an important part of every phase of Jordanian life. In Lebanon, the Palestinians are a major block to any political settlement there. In Syria, they are increasingly important in the national work force, especially in the skilled labor and in the professional arenas. Elsewhere in the Arab world they furnish an incredible amount of talent. There are, for example, nearly half a million Palestinians in Kuwait and possibly a hundred thousand in Saudi Arabia. Most Palestinians, wherever they are, maintain a Palestinian awareness and loyalty. They are propagandists for their cause even though they may never go "back home."

The Palestinians are highly important in another arena of activity - terrorism. Arab terrorism was actively practiced against the British, civilians and military, and Jews in the 1930s when the Arabs opposed the British policies on the immigration of Jews into Palestine. After the state of Israel was created, the frustrated Arabs, notably the Palestinians, who had left their homes in Israel began to resort to terrorism once again. For over 30 years the terrorism of the Palestinians has been operative. While Israel is the obvious primary target, the Palestinians quickly recognized that targets of opportunity and targets of cooperation (with other terrorist organizations) also accomplished in part the publicity they wanted to achieve. Thus, any state, any organization, or any individual who cooperates with Israel or the United States is considered a legitimate target.

Under this definition it was appropriate for Palestinians to blow up a Swiss airliner, to kidnap OPEC officials, to murder, and to cooperate with the various fronts.

As noted earlier in this chapter the PLO and its various terrorist membership groups are well financed. The Palestinians have been able to help kindred groups such as the Iranians who operated against the shah, the Eritrean Liberation Front, the Japanese Red Army, the Irish terrorists, the Moros terrorists of the Philippines, and various similar organizations.

The Middle East Palestinians have had a large assemblage of training camps. The best and the most extensive probably are located in Libya where Colonel Muammar Qadhafi has put together a sophisticated number of camps staffed in some cases with adept, internationally known terrorists. Other camps have functioned in Algeria, Iraq, Jordan, Lebanon, and South Yemen. Some training facilities are general, others are highly specialized and prepare the trainees for special missions in sabotage, infiltration, hijacking, guerrilla fighting, assassination, and radio operations.

It is impossible to assemble accurate data on the number of Palestinians trained in the various camps. Thousands have certainly received some training and many hundreds have received specialized indoctrination.

After the training is completed, the graduate Palestinians have received back-up support such as false documentation, specialized equipment, explosives, arms, financing, and contacts. Since the 1973 war there has been an increasing Palestinian determination to infiltrate sabotage experts into Israel and to create terror and confusion inside Israel. Most of these operations have not been successful; the terrorists were either apprehended or they never got into Israel, but enough got through to make the Palestinians feel that the operations are worthwhile.

There is a belief among those who have studied Palestinian terrorism that there are periods of heavy activity when there appears to be extensive coordination. There are periods when the activity is greatly reduced.

Finally, it is necessary to note that aside from Palestinian-directed terrorism there is a great deal of intra-Arab terrorism. Syria, Iraq, Libya, and the PLO have all engaged in such intra-Arab activity. Some of this activity has been extremely bloody and has often occurred outside the Middle East. When a shootout or a bombing takes place in a European capital, innocent locals are sometimes among the victims. And when a massive explosion takes place in a high rise building, as it has, the death count is certain to be heavy.

ARAB DISUNITY

Arab disunity and conflict is a factor of major importance in the present Middle East scene. Ever since Mohammad, the unity of Islam has been a major theme and a major objective which, however, has not been achieved. The creation of Israel gave a new modern-day impetus to the unity quest. For the past 30 years the Arab world repeatedly achieved a kind of synthetic unity whenever military action against Israel took place. But that unity was most imperfect, very ineffective, and certainly ephemeral.

Instead of moving toward unity, the Arab world over the past 30 years has been developing increasingly into an Arab world of disunity and hostility. It had long been recognized that there were deep cultural, regional, and religious differences between various parts of the Arab world. Certainly the Moroccan culture and patterns had very little to do with the lifestyle of Oman. And Beirut, Lebanon was quite unrelated in style and manner to Khartoum, Sudan. Shia Iran has little in common with conservative, Sunni Saudi Arabia.

There came to be a deep cleft between the traditional pattern of Arab kingship or paramount tribal rule and the new democratic, socialistic, military dictatorships that developed in the Moslem world. In the 1940s and thereafter the Arab world came increasingly to depart from traditional patterns of power. The colonial powers such as Britain and France withdrew and other forms of government took over. Military dictators or juntas, socialistic or semidemocratic formats were developed. Algeria, Libya, Egypt, Syria, Iraq, and Yemen, all experienced developments. In Libya, Egypt, Iraq, Iran and Yemen, kings, imans, and emires vanished. But kings or their equivalents have remained in Morocco, Jordan, Oman, and in the smaller Arab states of the Persian Gulf.

Over the past 30 years there has developed increasing tension in one way or another between the "royal" states and others. Egyptian President Nasser reportedly made direct efforts to assassinate the rulers of Saudi Arabia, and Colonel Qadhafi of Libya has reportedly made similar attempts. The departure of the shah from Iran has sent stress signals throughout the Arab conservative states. The obvious question is who will be next.

The development of the Baath Party, the Arab Socialist Resurrection Party in Syria, Lebanon, and Iraq has brought a new element into Middle East politics. The Baath Party is the creation of three men, Michael Aflaq, a Christian; and two

Moslems, Saleh el Bitar and Akram Hourani. Aflaq and Bitar, as students in France, became acquainted with socialism, communism, Western democracy, and Western philosophy. This was added to their awareness of Arab philosophy, history, and the Moslem religion. The Baath Party reflects some of all these elements. It quickly came into conflict with the rulers of Syria, the home of Aflaq and Bitar, but was not given much of a reception elsewhere in the Arab world.

Today Syria and Iraq are both dedicated Baathist states. The two states are also, however, fiercely antagonistic and each has its own version of the true Baath political philosophy. The rest of the Arab world remains deeply suspicious of Baathism.

In Libya, Colonel Qadhafi, the powerful dictator of the state, has developed his own peculiar philosophy of government which he labels "Arab Socialism." He is strongly opposed to kingship which automatically brings him into conflict with the kings and rulers in the Arab world. His "Arab Socialism" has not been sold to other Arabs, but Qadhafi has had a profoundly disturbing effect on the Middle East with his terrorist apparatus and his oil revenues which he uses continuously to promote his ends. Many experienced observers view Qadhafi as a very dangerous individual.

THE LEBANESE SITUATION

In some ways Lebanon is the epitome of the Middle East. It sits astride the coastal roads that lead from Europe through Turkey to ancient Palestine, Egypt, and Africa. Lebanon was also "the road" that led from the areas of the ancient cultures of Babylonia and Assyria in the fertile valley of the Tigris and Euphrates rivers to Egypt and beyond.

Lebanon was part of the history of earliest man in the Middle East, of the Babylonians, the Assyrians, the Hittites, the Egyptians, the Phonecians, the Persians, the Greeks, and the Romans. Thereafter came the people with the Christian faith and then the Arabs with their Moslem religion. All took root and flourished in Lebanon. In the 11th century the Christian crusaders from Europe settled in, and then came the Ottoman Turks. Finally the French took over as a mandate power in 1920 and in 1941 the Free French declared Lebanon independent.

Lebanon with its long and complex history obviously has a complex population mix. Some 60 percent of the population is Moslem - Sunni, Shia, and smaller heretical groups such as the Druze. Nearly 40 percent are Christian Maronite, Roman Catholic, Greek Orthodox, Armenian, and Protestant Christians.

All these Lebanese factions had by the early 1950s agreed to a delicately balanced state in which Sunnis and Shias, Maronites and Greek Orthodox, Druzes and small Christian groupings all had their percentages of representatives. The president was always to be a Christian, the prime minister was always to be a Sunni Moslem, the speaker of the Chamber of Deputies was always to be a Shia Moslem. And the protocol continued in this manner. The cards were stacked slightly in favor of the Christians, but it was an agreed upon stacking and it appeared to work.

But the creation of Israel disturbed this fine balance, especially after the Palestinian refugees began to move into Lebanon in numbers and began to use it as an operational base against Israel, notably after 1970. The arrival of these Palestinians also disturbed the fine balance of the various groupings inside Lebanon who began to react with hostility against each other.

Since 1975 Lebanon has been embroiled in an incredibly complex war which includes not only all the elements delineated above, but also involves Syria, Israel, and various Arab states. By the summer of 1976 more than 30,000 Syrian troops were trying to keep the peace in Lebanon. The Arab League also became entangled in a peace-keeping operation during the latter part of 1976, and the Arab world generally struggled in vain to find a solution.

In 1977, fighting in Lebanon began to expand to southern Lebanon and soon reached the Israeli border. In early 1978 a large Palestinian raid into Israel resulted in an Israeli invasion of Lebanon. After a United Nations Interim Force in Lebanon (UNIFIL), some 5,000 strong, appeared in southern Lebanon in June 1978, Israel withdrew but left its surrogate behind in the form of a Christian militia under the leadership of Major Saad Haddad. The conflict has continued and Israel gives full and unabashed support to Haddad's forces.

Meanwhile, the area around Beirut saw continuing bitter and deadly conflict among the various parties, notably the Christian militias and the Syrian army. It is widely rumored that the Israelis have given and are giving various kinds of support, including military equipment, to the three Christian groupings: Phalange (Jumayyil), National Liberal Party (Chamoun), and Zgharta Front (Franjiyah). These groupings have become increasingly powerful with their own seaports and heavy armor.

There are still close to 30,000 Syrian troops in Lebanon and thousands of well-armed Palestinians. There are, of course, also thousands of well-armed Lebanese Christians, and there are the armed forces of the Lebanese government under President Elias Sarkis trying somehow to develop strength so that they can take over. Finally, there are in the southern part of Lebanon the UNIFIL troops who are bedeviled by the Palestinians and the Christian forces of Major Haddad.

A Beirut newspaper described the plight of Lebanon thus: " - here we are with three armies, two police forces, 22 militias, 42 parties, 9 Palestinian organizations, four radio stations, and two television stations." And it is appropriate to add that after five years of conflict, possibly as many as 100,000 are dead and that the once beautiful city of Beirut is reduced in large extent to rubble with billions of dollars worth of destruction.

Mirages of peace have repeatedly appeared on the Lebanese horizon, but chaos and bloodshed continue. As of now there seems to be no real hope that settlements and an end to the fighting can be achieved. The possibility of partition, of Christian enclaves detaching themselves, continues to be very real. And the threat of ever more conflict is very real.

CURRENT DEVELOPMENTS

The Middle East has a way of being ever kaleidoscopic. Some overpowering changes have occurred over the past two years. The shah's departure from Iran in January 1979 has not only sent shockwaves all over the Middle East but indeed all over the world. The erratic government of Ayatollah Khomeini has added to the fears and uncertainities in the world which is concerned that the flow of oil from the Iranian, Iraqi, and Persian Gulf area continue. The world is also worried about "what after Khomeini." Many students of the Middle East believe the next turn of the wheel will bring a communist regime to power with direct Soviet backing. Most of the Arab states are worried about the Islamic Shia Republic of Khomeini. The smaller gulf states are frightened and Saudi Arabia is concerned over the Shia preaching of revolution.

In mid-September, President Saddam Hussein Takriti of Iraq launched an attack on Iran. As of Fall 1981 that war continues with no indication of a ceasefire or a negotiated settlement. President Saddam has issued a number of statements on the reasons why he went to war. It would appear that the primary cause for Saddam's attack was his conviction that the revolutionary Shia state of Iran with its religious pronouncements directly threatened his own state. More than 50 percent of Iraq's population are adherents of the Shia faith. Saddam and most of the rulers of Iraq are Sunni Moslems and all of them are Baath Party members. Saddam apparently fears a Shia uprising. Thus, it becomes a question of Saddam or Khomeini.

High on the agenda of Saddam's objectives is the restoration of Iraqi control and hegemony over the Shatt al-Arab, the confluence of the Tigris and Euphrates Rivers, which debouches into the Persian Gulf. This is, of course the route to the sea from the port of Basra, Iraq and other Iraqi port facilities. For Iran the Shatt is the exist to the Persian Gulf for the products of the oil refinery of Abadan and the entry to the important Iranian port of Khorramshar.

In 1975, the shah "forced" a treaty with Iraq - signed by Saddam - which placed the international boundary in the middle of the Shatt. Saddam now wishes to reclaim full control of this waterway as well as some of the land he relinquished at that time. Iraq also insists that at this point it requires Iranian assurances that it will not interfere in the internal affairs of Iraq; this would seem to reflect Iraqi concern over Shia preachings of revolution.

Saddam also demands that Iran return to the rulers of the United Arab Emirates the three islands - Abu Musa, and the Greater and Lesser Tunbs - which guard the entrance to the Persian Gulf. The shah occupied these islands as Britain withdrew from the positions it held in the Gulf.

Finally, and highly important, the Iraqi president has let it be known in various ways that he would support the creation of an independent state of Arabistan (Khuzistan). The Iranian province of Khuzistan is adjacent to the Shatt al-Arab and contains most of the oil installations and the oil fields of Iran. Khuzistan's population includes a large percentage - possibly close to 50 percent - of ethnic Arabs. Its detachment from the rest of Iran would destroy that country as a modern state by depriving it of more than 90 percent of its income.

Thus, if Saddam has his way the Middle East will be subjected to yet another major change. At this point Iraq has broken relations with Libya and Syria which it charges are supporting Iran. Jordan has firmly backed Iraq. Presumably the Jordanian motivation for this position is in part the large subsidies Baghdad has furnished Amman as well as the basic antagonism that exists between Jordan and the Khomeini government. Most other Arab states, notably the gulf states, are anxiously trying to avoid involvement in this dispute. They were directly threatened by former Iranian President Bani Sadr. Egypt, which has its own problems in the Arab world, gives basic support to Iraq but chiefly because of its unfriendly relations with Iran.

For Israel, the Iraqi-Iranian war continues the never-ending problems created by the Arabs. For Israel it would in theory be good if Iran and Iraq exhausted each other in a destructive war. This would, however, create oil problems for Israel as it would for the world generally. The support given by Jordan to Iraq is bothersome for Israel, which sees Soviet shipping moving into Aqaba only a few miles from its own port of Eilat. It also considers it possible that Iraq might move into close military support of Jordan and that a new, combined Arab drive against Israel might then take place.

Israel also notes with concern the friendship treaty signed on October 9, 1980 in Moscow between Syria and the USSR. After resisting Moscow's invitations to sign such a treaty for a decade or more, Damascus finally capitulated. Israel thus asks what this means. Is there a secret protocol that brings Soviet troops into Syria? Most observers do not as yet see an uniquely sinister motivation in this treaty but Israel is concerned.

For Israel and the Middle East generally all the old problems remain. Egypt is still largely isolated and outside the Arab camp, and has serious internal domestic stresses. At the same time, Egypt is frustrated with Israel over the autonomy talks. Only strong Washington pressure brings the two states back to the conference table and there are still grave doubts about the likelihood that anything can be achieved.

The Libyan-Syrian union is not of major concern to Israel nor would it seem to be a significant power development in the Middle East. It must be considered a worrisome development, however. It appears to be an opportunistic move on both sides by two leaders who first of all feel isolated. Now they have each other. Syria expects to get massive financial support from the oil of Libya. In turn, Libya, which always feels threatened by Egypt, and Colonel Qadhafi who always feels threatened by assassins, expect to get military support from Syria. In theory, when and if somewhere in the future there is a new conflict between Israel and Syria, Libya will give full support to Syria against Israel. From an Israeli angle there must then also be added the assumption that there will be general Arab support for any war against Israel.

THE SOVIET UNION AND THE MIDDLE EAST

The final element in this current political and security assessment of the Middle East appropriately is the Soviet Union. Russia's interest in the Middle East and specifically in Turkey and Iran predates the Soviet Union. Several dates are noteworthy in the history of Soviet activity in the Middle East. With the opening of World War II the Soviets and Britain dictated the removal of Reza Shah in Iran and the insertion of his son who they assumed would be more pliable. When WW II ended the Soviets tried unsuccessfully to dismember Iran by creating an independent Azerbaijan and an independent Kurdish republic. American determination blocked this.

Another notable date is the summer of 1955 when the Soviets made their first arms deal in the Middle East. Egypt, under President Nasser, received Soviet arms. Other Arab states also began to get Soviet arms. In a series of actions beginning in July 1972 Egyptian President Anwar Sadat

expelled the Soviets from Egypt. Yet another notable date is
December 1979 when Moscow found it necessary to launch a
massive invasion of Afghanistan which has had extensive
worldwide repercussions.

An inspection of Soviet activity in the Middle East over
the past three and a half decades permits a few simple conclusions. The Soviet Union is determined to expand its influence
in the Middle East and reduce that of the United States. To
achieve this it uses a variety of means and tactics including
massive military aid, propaganda, military maneuvers, and
diplomacy.

Recent developments in the Middle East raise obvious
questions as to what the Soviet Union is prepared to do in the
immediate future in this arena. There has been and is intense
interest in such questions as: will the USSR depart from
Afghanistan? Will the USSR move into Pakistan or into Iran?
Will the USSR move into a position to exert influence on Middle
East oil? Will the Soviet Union move to exert a determining
influence in the Iraq-Iran war?

It would appear that as of now the USSR has no intention
of leaving Afghanistan until it has a subservient local puppet
government firmly in place. Moscow does not appear interested at present in moving into Pakistan. As for Iran the Soviet
Union is capable of moving in with massive military force, but
is probably is willing to wait and see if it cannot achieve its
objectives by default or by invitation. As of now the Soviet
Union probably will not move in abruptly to exert control in
the oil arena, but its longer-range objectives are certainly in
this direction. As of now the USSR is not happy to see the
Iraqi-Iranian conflict expanding. Its objectives appear to be
to do business with both sides.

Moscow, however, is capable of exerting strong military
power in the area if it decides to do so. Its forces are
organized and poised on the border of the Middle East and it
maintains an impressive naval force in the Indian Ocean.

In October 1980 the Middle East appears to be in a tense
and perilous condition. If past patterns prevail the present
situations will be somewhat resolved, and there will be temporary accommodations in the months ahead, but there will be no
definitive solutions.

3 Egypt: Strategic, Economic and Political Assessment

Ibrahim M. Oweiss

An assessment of Egypt's strategic, economic, and political dimensions is an important prerequisite to understanding and analyzing the most current domestic and international trends pertaining to Egypt. It is the relationship between these three variables that gives Egypt its unique set of assets and liabilities and make it the focus of major international interest and concern.

STRATEGIC ASSESSMENT

The background against which all current economic and political events should be analyzed is Egypt's strategic position. Egypt is a country whose regional and global strategic importance is indisputable. With a geographic location that connects Africa with the states of the fertile crescent and the Arabian Gulf, Egypt has historically enjoyed a central position in the Arab world. Further, bordering the Mediterranean on the north and the Gulf of Suez, Gulf of Aqaba, and the Red Sea on the east, Egypt has traditionally been the crossroads for trade and culture in the region. The Suez Canal, opened over a century ago, has been the source of sporadic conflicts, but only because of its strategic importance as a vital waterway linking the Mediterranean and Red Seas. A population of over 44 million people today reinforces Egypt's key geographic location by producing the main literary and artistic works upon

*My research on recent developments in the Egyptian economy since the mid-1970s was made possible by a grant from the Ford Foundation.

which the Arab world's culture depends. As the most populated country in the Middle East, Egypt has played a pivotal
role in regional events since the dawn of history. The combination of geography, population, and culture, then, has
resulted in a long history in which Egypt's centrality to the
region remains unquestioned.

Perhaps one important strategic consideration for Egypt is
its role in the Arab-Israeli conflict. Although the status of
this role has changed dramatically since President Sadat's visit
to Jerusalem in 1977, Egypt is still the major "front-line state"
in dealings with Israel. Any Arab military action that has
been taken in the past with Israel and any such action in the
future, unlikely as it may seem at present, must include the
participation of Egypt. Without the support of Egypt's vast
military establishment, especially its military manpower, the
other Arabs party to the conflict - Syria, Jordan and Palestine
- recognize the futility of military confrontation.

Since Sadat's peace initiative, Egypt has fallen out of
favor with its Arab neighbors. In the immediacy and severity
of the reaction by the Arab states to Sadat's visit to Jerusalem
and the subsequent signing of the Camp David Accords, however, one can read yet another example of Egypt's importance
to the Arab world. Sadat's initiative effectively moved Egypt
temporarily out of the Arab fold and resulted in a sense of
resentment and betrayal on the part of radical and moderate
Arab regimes alike to the realization that Egypt could move
independently of them. That little substantive retaliation has
been forthcoming after the initial statement of condemnation in
Baghdad in 1977 indicates that Egypt's Arab neighbors are
relatively powerless to act against the traditional center of
their community. It will only be a matter of time before
Egypt's relationship with the other Arab countries will be
gradually normalized.

At the same time that Egypt remains the principal Arab
actor in the Arab-Israeli situation, other factors on the
regional level have emerged in recent years that suggest that
Egypt may be losing some of its traditional regional importance. Specifically, the 1973 quadrupling of the price of oil
by the Organization of Petroleum Exporting Countries (OPEC)
has led to a shift in regional power and influence toward the
Arab oil-exporting countries, especially Saudi Arabia. The
accumulation of vast amounts of petrodollars has given Saudi
Arabia a financial strength that weighs heavily in the region.
With respect to Egypt, this strength has manifested itself in
an increasing dependence on Saudi financing to help its economy stay on track with development objectives. Again, Sadat's
peace initiative has led to a discontinuation of Saudi aid, at
least temporarily.

If Egypt has played a pivotal role in the Middle East as a
regional power, it has also drawn the attention of the super-

powers over the years in their contest for global strategic dominance. United States interests in the Middle East have focused on three broad objectives: resolution of the Arab-Israeli conflict, containment of Soviet influence in the region, and assured access to Middle East oil. In the pursuit of the first two of these objectives, friendly relations with Egypt are not only desirable but necessary. Throughout the 1950s and 1960s, under the socialist influence of President Nasser, Egypt looked to the Soviet Union as its major source of military and development assistance. The United States had narrowly identified its strategic interests in terms of its special relationship with Israel. In addition, other strategic interests were defined in terms of the "two-pillar system" - Iran and Saudi Arabia, which were counted on for their moderation and friendliness toward the West. Of course, underlying the "two-pillar system" was U.S. concern for the third national objective mentioned above, namely, access to Middle East oil. It was not until Sadat became president and had time to develop his own diplomatic style and strategy, that Egypt-United States relations blossomed. Particularly since the October 1973 war, the United States has perceived its interests in the region as linked to a moderate, pro-Western regime in Egypt. With the Soviet Union sponsoring the more radical Arab regimes in opposition to anything short of a comprehensive solution to the Arab-Israeli conflict, a strong U.S. influence in Egypt seemed all the more important. Sadat's Jerusalem visit signaled a shift in initiative for the resolution of the conflict away from the United States and to the parties of the conflict themselves. Even with the initiative now coming from Egypt and Israel, the United States has no alternative, given the continued rejectionist front of the more radical Arab regimes, but to support Cairo's strategy.

Egypt's strategic importance to the United States is not limited to concern for regional stability out of a resolution to the Arab-Israeli conflict. Recent events throughout the region attest to the fact that the United States' traditional "two-pillar system" is presently a one-pillar system at best. The revolution in Iran and the loss of the shah as a valuable ally have caused a reevaluation of American strategy toward the Middle East. While the shah's loss of power does not necessarily mean a gain of Soviet influence in Iran (especially given anti-communist sentiments voiced by Iranian religious leaders), the recent military intervention in Afghanistan increases American concerns over Soviet objectives in the region and therefore the importance of maintaining the Egyptian alliance. In fact, Washington's attempt to replace Iran as a strategic friend in the Middle East has resulted in a rapidly growing commitment in Egypt; U.S. military assistance continues to expand and the U.S. economic aid program to Egypt, the largest in the world, is entering its eighth year.

In addition to speculation about Soviet expansionist
motives, the United States must be concerned with a loss of a
critical supply of oil as a result of the revolution in Iran.
This concern naturally leads to a similar concern over Saudi
Arabia where conditions not unlike those in Iran exist for
national aspirations and sentiments. The possibility that the
Saudi royal family would act in a way inconsistent with American interests cannot be dismissed out of hand if the American
foreign policy disregards its own interests by neglecting the
national objectives of Saudi Arabia.

Other developments in the region give further significance
to Egyptian-American strategic relations. Afghanistan, as has
been mentioned, is currently under direct Soviet control with
no end to the occupation in sight. A pro-Soviet regime has
been in power in South Yemen since 1978, causing concern in
the more conservative gulf states as well as their Western
allies. The Mengistu regime is able to remain in power in
Ethiopia with Soviet and Cuban assistance and to maintain a
check on the separatist movement in Eritrea. Even in Egypt's
neighboring state, Libya, Soviet arms are being supplied in
quantities that far exceed what could be used by the Libyan
armed forces. With Soviet activity so clearly molding events in
the Arab world, a staunch, pro-Western ally in Egypt gains a
fundamental importance for the United States, one that is
unlikely to lose significance in the future.

ECONOMIC ASSESSMENT

Since the adoption of Egypt's open-door policy in 1974 considerable progress - after a long period of stagnation - has been
made. For example, the Egyptian economy has witnessed a
substantial growth rate since 1975 ranging from 8 to 9 percent
in real terms per year, with an average annual real growth
rate of close to 9 percent over the last five years. Although
this growth has not been even across all sectors, the overall
performance of the economy has improved remarkably since
1975 despite many adverse factors.

The high real growth rate of gross domestic products has
been attributed to the performance of the industrial (including
mining) and petroleum sectors. Within the industrial sector,
there has been a marked growth in textiles, foodstuffs, engineering, metallurgical products, and others such as the shoe
industry. Output performance in these areas improved mainly
due to increased capacity utilization made possible by increased
foreign capital inflows in the form of intermediate and maintenance inputs. Crude petroleum production has increased by
more than 30 percent over the 1976 level. With the return of
the Sinai oil fields in November 1979, oil production has in-

creased by approximately 10 percent. Oil revenues, which will
be discussed below, have increased by a much higher percentage than the increase in oil production owing mainly to the
increase in the price of oil, particularly since mid-1979.
Furthermore, the construction sector has performed well in
recent years, experiencing a rate of growth of about 12 percent per annum which reflects growing investment in this
sector. Demand for housing, however, is still far in excess of
supply. Agriculture did not match the performance of the
above-mentioned sectors. Even though this sector represents
a significant percentage of Egypt's GDP (about one-fourth)
and employs about one-half of the labor force, its relative
contribution has been decreasing owing on the one hand to an
upsurge of other sectors and on the other hand to a host of
government policies that serve as economic and social disincentives to increased production.

The other producing and service sectors have performed
well since 1975. An overall rate of growth in these sectors is
estimated at about 10 percent per annum. The most significant
rates of growth occurred in the transport and communications
sector as well as in those service sectors related to tourism
and banking. Growing production and investment expenditures
combined with more active tourism are the main reasons cited
for the high rates of growth. Expenditures in the tourism
subsector, for example, are estimated to have increased by
over 45 percent in 1977 alone. Even with the decline in the
number of Arab tourists after the signing of the Egyptian-
Israeli accord in March 1979, the revenue from tourism has
increased to an estimated level of almost three-quarters of a
billion dollars in 1979. Tourist revenues lost owing to the
decline in number of Arab tourists were more than matched by
revenues generated by American and European tourists in
1979.

The overall aggregate investment spending has been
steadily increasing since 1975. It is significant to note,
however, that nearly one-fifth of this increase was in the
private sector - a fact that reflects the success of the
government's policy of promoting private investment. To
attract Arab and foreign capital for investment opportunities in
Egypt, Law No. 43 of 1974 concerning the Investment of Arab
and Foreign Funds and the Free Zones was enacted. Law 43
was later amended by Law No. 32 of 1977. Under Law 43,
investments may be made in the following areas: industry,
mining, energy, tourism, transportation, animal and land
development, and "other fields." Provisions also exist for
investment in the field of banking and include investment
companies, merchant banks, and reinsurance companies dealing
in Egypt must be established jointly with public or private
sector Egyptian participation; the law does not impose strict
percentage requirements for this local participation. The law

also stipulates that special priority will be given to "those projects which are designed to generate exports, encourage tourism, or reduce the need to import basic commodities as well as to projects which require advance technical expertise."

Many incentives and protections are included in the law to make investment opportunities more attractive to foreign firms. Projects, whether located in an inland or free-zone area, are guaranteed protection against nationalization, confiscation, or sequestration of the assets by judicial procedure. Further, a five-year exemption for approved projects from taxes on commercial and industrial profits, revenue on movable capital, general income tax, and proportional stamp duty is granted. As concerns repatriation of profits, projects that are self-sufficient in their foreign-exchange needs may transfer their net annual profits within the limits of their foreign exchange bank balance. Projects can also import without a license or government approval whatever machinery, equipment, or other material is needed for installation and operation of the project. Similarly, projects can export their products without a license.

Within the context of Law 43, the general authority for investment and free zones carries the responsibility for coordinating and approving potential projects with a view to avoiding bureaucratic slowdown as much as possible.

One last and significant point relating to the investment law is an important amendment made under Law 32 of 1977 in the area of foreign-exchange regulations. Projects can now maintain foreign-exchange accounts in Egyptian banks in which they can deposit their foreign-exchange capital, foreign loans, the proceeds of visible and invisible exports, and foreign exchange purchased from local banks "at the highest rate prevailing and declared for free foreign currency," in other words, at a parallel rather than a fixed exchange rate.

These incentives have contributed to an expansion of investment activities in Egypt. What appeared as initially slow growth in investment activity following the enactment of Law 43 has been accelerating noticeably in recent years. From 1974 through the end of 1979, the government approved 1,079 foreign investment projects valued at approximately $8 billion. Of the total approved, 455 projects involving investments of $1.6 billion are already in production and 329 projects worth $3.9 billion are under construction (see Appendix 3.A). If these figures are evaluated in terms of Egypt's gross national product of $17 billion, the substantial amount of investment present in Egypt is easily appreciated. A positive reflection of this level of investment can be seen in the size of industrial production which increased by 12.5 percent in 1977 over 1976, or by slightly over half a billion dollars. Also important is the fact that more than 50 percent of capital investment under this "open-door" legislation is carried out by Egyptian nationals in the private sector.(1)

Another policy move related to the investment field is the revival of the Egyptian stock exchange system. With the passing of a new set of regulations on August 7, 1977 securities registered and denominated in U.S. dollars, British sterling, and other currencies are now allowed to be traded. Furthermore, the Ministry of Economy and Economic Cooperation, in collaboration with the International Bank for Reconstruction and Development and Morgan Stanley International, has recently studied means of transforming the local securities exchange markets in Cairo and Alexandria so that in due time they can be linked to such world money-market centers as London, Zurich, New York and Tokyo. Several concrete steps have already been taken to revitalize the system which was founded in 1882, developed to the point where it traded actively with many European countries by the 1920s, but has lain dormant under Nasser's regime. The Egyptian government appointed a high-ranking official at the ministerial level to coordinate necessary reforms undertaken by the relevant ministries in order to facilitate the development of the money market.(2)

As much as progress is being made in the private sector, the government's activities in the public sector continue to play a major role in the Egyptian economy. The government budget is in deficit despite the increased receipts from taxes on international trade which almost doubled in a single year from $1.4 billion in 1976 to $2.8 billion in 1977. On the expenditure side of the budget, the increase was due mainly to increased subsidies and public sector deficits. Other factors that added to the burden of increased public expenditures include a devaluation of the parallel market exchange rate, the imports of subsidized commodities (such as wheat, fava beans, tea, and sugar), and the need to maintain domestic distributive prices at a constant level. The total deficit of the government budget increased from $1.8 billion in 1977 to $2.9 billion in 1978.

To consider inflation, it is important to differentiate between the actual rate of inflation for which there is no official assessment and the governmental rate of inflation. According to the official statistics, the consumer retail price index increased from 100 percent in 1975 to 138 percent in 1978, which means an annual rate of inflation of about 11.5 percent. This figure, however, does not reflect the actual rate of inflation because it is downwardly affected by a number of subsidized consumer items as well as expenditures of a price-controlled nature (rents, for example). A fair estimate of the actual rate of inflation is in the neighborhood of 23 percent per annum.(3)

Prices have been mainly affected by rapid increases in the money supply, an increase in credit, the government deficit, a decline in production of major agricultural crops, and the new purchasing power of Egyptians earning their income abroad. (This last factor will be considered below.) The supply of money which includes near money (or quasimoney) increased by about 25 percent from 1977 to 1978. Domestic credit increased by almost the same percentage for the same period. Furthermore, nearly half of the government deficit was borrowed from the banking system; twice as much of the financing for the total deficit came from domestic as from external sources in 1977 and 1978. Domestic financing in 1978 amounted to slightly less than $2 billion while external financing amounted to about $.9 billion.

Despite the high rate of inflation, accelerated economic activity has been enjoyed in sectors. The Ministry of Planning estimated that aggregate employment increased by about 8 percent per annum since 1977. This is due largely to the increase in employment in distributive sectors such as transportation and communication, storage, trade, and finance. The government has announced its intention to reduce the disguised unemployment in the public sector by slowing down the policy of automatic employment of all university graduates in public agencies.

It is clear that despite several positive developments in the Egyptian economy, there remain monumental problems to overcome. The Five-Year Plan, 1978-1982, has identified these major problems as: inflation, a large balance-of-payments deficit, inadequate supply of internal savings to meet requirements for investment expenditures, traditional habits that inhibit development efforts, rapid increase in population, and a shortage of managerial talents at all levels.(4) The list is by no means exhaustive. Other problems can be added, such as the negative impact of Egypt's widespread subsidy program on economic allocation of resources, government's failure thus far to remove certain impediments to growth in the construction industry, its reluctance to change specific laws and regulations that obstruct efficient utilization of manpower and other resources, and a high rate of disguised unemployment.

No matter how one classifies these problems, they all need serious attention. They must first be clearly identified and singularly evaluated. Next, policy options and future strategies must be presented according to some sort of a cost-benefit criterion. At this point, an analysis of the interrelationships among these major problems is essential - before any attempt is made to devise a reform program. Finally, a ranking of the problems whenever possible would provide policy makers with a list of priorities that would be useful in structuring a meaningful development plan.

One of the most crucial problems facing Egypt which deserves top priority is the rapid rate of population growth. In November 1981 it was officially announced that the total had reached the 44 million mark, following an increase of one

million persons in only ten months.(5)   This is equal to an
increase in population of 100,000 persons per month, 3,333
persons per day, or one person every 26 seconds. It should
be noted that additions to population by the million's have
been occurring in narrower intervals in recent years. If this
trend continues into the future, the next million will be added
to the population in less than ten months.

It is important to note that the increase in population is
measured by the difference between birth and death rates.
On the average, Egypt faces one birth every 18 seconds.
This increase, along with other factors, has led to overcrowding in urban centers and unbearable congestion in certain
areas. For example, the metropolitan city of Cairo which was
meant to accommodate three to four million people, now has a
population of 9.5 million, or 21.6 percent of Egypt's total
population. If this trend continues, by the year 2000, Egypt's
population may reach the 66 million mark; Cairo's population
would be approximately 15 million, the size of the population of
the entire country in 1935.

Alternative population projections based on some plausible
assumptions were estimated. At an upper limit Egypt's population will reach 71 million by the year 2000 if the growth rates
declined from 2.7 percent in the 1980s to 2.4 percent in the
1990s.   At mid-range, the forecast calls for 65 million with
growth rates declining from 2.6 percent to 1.9 percent consecutively for the same two decades.   At the low limit, the
population of Egypt may reach 60 million by the year 2000 if
rates of growth decline from 2.6 in the 1980s to 1.4 percent in
the 1990s.(6)

Consequences of this rapid increase in population have
been many, especially in a country that has limited agricultural
land. One result therefore has been a drastic reduction in the
per capita area of farm land. This has led to a fall in land
productivity and subsequently to an increase in wheat imports
and a steady decline in the quantity of exported traditional
agricultural crops.   Another consequence has been the rapid
expansion of enrollment in learning institutions without
adequate facilities and drastic shortage of qualified teachers.
Quality of education has necessarily been adversely affected.
Given a positive correlation between the quality of education
and the level of productivity, the latter has therefore been
declining. Although more than half of all Egyptians are still
illiterate, there has been a substantial increase in the number
of students enrolled in universities.(7)   In the course of the
last 25 years, the number of universities in Egypt has tripled
from four to twelve.(8) In the period 1973 - 1978, given the
number of graduates in almost all fields in comparison to real
job opportunities and investment capabilities, Egypt has been
unable efficiently to absorb the ever-increasing supply of its
university graduates.   The resulting unemployment, disguised

or not, can be viewed as an abundant factor for production
(i.e. labor) or, in other words, as an export capital item in
the form of migrating labor. The inflow of remittances from
Egyptian nationals working abroad can then be regarded as an
ameliorating factor in the country's balance of payments in the
same way as the return on capital invested abroad.

If there is a relative abundance in any one factor of
production so that it cannot be adequately absorbed in the
production process, it becomes economically meaningful to use
that excess factor more effectively elsewhere. Otherwise, the
marginal productivity of the excess factor may fall to zero,
or, in certain cases, become negative. With the advent of
petrodollar surpluses since 1973 in sparsely populated Arab
oil-exporting countries, there has been a sharp increase in
demand for a wide variety of skilled and unskilled Egyptians.
The number of Egyptian migrant workers was estimated in 1974
between one-half and one million individuals.(9) By 1978, this
figure had reached 1.75 million and by 1980 it was estimated at
almost three million. This migration may temporarily be re-
lieving strains on the economy caused by population pressures.
This pattern, however, only serves as a short-term release
valve and should not be mistaken for a long-term solution to
Egypt's population and consequent unemployment problems.

Since this recent phenomenon of Egyptian migration has
far-reaching economic, political, and social implications, it is
worth examining its origin, costs, and benefits. Traditionally,
Egyptian workers have migrated to neighboring Libya and
Sudan. Since 1973, as mentioned, the migration has flowed
increasingly toward Saudi Arabia, Kuwait, United Arab Emirates, Qatar, and Iraq. Although Egyptian migrant workers in
Libya were skilled, there has recently been an increase in the
flow of unskilled labor as well.

By and large Egyptian immigration to Arab oil-exporting
countries is not of a permanent nature. Two reasons can be
cited. First, the legal structures in the receiving countries
are designed to discourage and in some cases officially to
refuse permanent residency to migrant workers, and second,
there is an intrinsic desire on the part of the immigrant to
return to his home country after satisfying certain economic
needs. On the average, an Egyptian migrates for a period of
three to four years. The economic phenomenon of the "backward bending supply curve" is very much applicable to Egyptian immigrants. As soon as they have earned enough to
achieve their basic economic objectives, their desire to
terminate their work abroad becomes evident.

The initiation of the "open-door" economic policy in 1974
has, among other things, streamlined the exit procedures for
workers who wish to work abroad. While there is no official
Egyptian migration policy, the government implicitly encourages

migration by eliminating customs complications, minimizing
taxation of remittances, and in effect allowing the laws of
supply and demand to take their course.

The motives for such a policy are obvious. Even if it
appears to encourage a "brain drain," the outflow of labor
reduces unemployment and prevents further growth of the
bureaucracy. Moreover, it rids the country of a potentially
explosive situation in the form of discontented, unemployed,
or underemployed university graduates. The salaries that
migrants earn in oil-rich countries, which generally exceed
what could be earned in Egypt for comparable labor, are often
remitted to the migrants' families at home, thereby aiding the
unhealthy balance-of-payments situation. Their remittances,
both direct money transfers and imports to Egypt of goods
purchased abroad, increased by 85 percent between 1976 and
1977. As recently as 1974, for example, remittances amounted
to $220 million and by 1977 they had reached $1.53 billion.
The estimated figures for 1978 and 1979 are $1.18 billion and
$2.0 billion, respectively.(10) Without entering into a lengthy
analysis, it is safe to say that the dramatic amelioration in
Egypt's balance-of-payments deficit which was drastically
reduced from $2.48 billion in 1975 to $1.56 in 1977 can be
attributed in part to the rapid increase in the level of
worker's remittances. A final reason for encouraging migration
is that the presence of Egyptians workers, especially in
management and other skill positions, formalizes channels of
cooperation between Egypt and its oil-exporting neighbors.
Both its cultural similarity to the other Arab states and its
traditional role as mediator between technology and Arab
technical requirements makes the available supply of Egyptian
labor a valuable asset for Egypt and the Arab world.

The Egyptian government is certainly justified in seeing
benefits to encouraging labor migration. Yet, an analysis
would not be complete without examining the costs of migration
to Egyptian society. In this regard, it is useful to note the
distinction between supply of labor and supply of human capital. With respect to Egypt, although there is certainly a labor
surplus, it may turn out to be that there is a shortage of
human capital. In other words, Egyptian migrant workers may
be those individuals who possess valuable skills that could be
put to productive, much-needed economic and social use at
home yet who prefer to work abroad for the higher salaries
and better standard of living they can enjoy. In this case,
the human capital element is drained from the country under
the guise of oversupply of labor.

In recent literature, Lawrence Hadley has examined this
aspect of the Egyptian migration issue by attempting to build a
cost-benefit model that quantitatively evaluates the export of
Egyptian human capital.(11) His study is undertaken from two
perspectives: 1) that of maximization of income of all Egyp-

tians, and 2) that of maximization of national product within Egypt. Hadley's attempt to estimate an internal rate of return to Egypt from migration is useful in many ways, yet it fails to take into account certain factors that cannot be measured quantitatively. In addition, despite the assumption in the study that a migrant attempts to maximize his income, it appears that most Egyptian migrants are more interested in increasing their welfare function. If a migrant were primarily interested in maximizing his income, he would evaluate the job market in every oil-exporting country and then try to migrate to the country where he could earn the maximum income. After attaining this goal, he would likely stay in the host country until retirement. In studying the case of Egyptians working in the Arab oil-exporting countries one does not find this pattern of behavior. On the contrary, one observes that an Egyptian seeking a job abroad will accept work without any study of the job market. Even if he is given the choice among countries, he may prefer a less-paying job if, for example, he is offered better working conditions, an area with better climatic conditions, or the opportunity to be near relatives or acquaintances who are already established in the area. He may also prefer a location within close proximity of his area of permanent residency at home.

This pattern of behavior suggests, then, that an Egyptian seeking a job in an Arab oil-exporting country does not intend to maximize his income but rather to upgrade his standard of living to a certain level after which he would prefer to return to his country. In other words, he seeks to increase his welfare function by improving his economic status until he is able to achieve some modest goal as purchase of a residency, car, household electrical equipment, and the like.

No cost-benefit analysis is complete unless it takes into account all relevant direct and indirect costs and benefits, even those that cannot be measured in monetary terms. In this regard, one can cite several indirect, nonquantifiable costs and benefits of Egyptian migration. The benefits include:

1. Positive contribution of migration to expanding interregional communications is seen as a sociopolitical benefit.
2. Increased interdependence in the Arab world which may lend credibility to the goal of Arab unity and that benefit the entire region economically and politically.
3. Deepened individual identity through true exposure to common problems and challenges facing the Arab world.
4. Revenue in the form of net total taxes collected from customs duties imposed on goods imported into Egypt by its citizens working in Arab oil-exporting countries.
5. Net profits to Egypt's air and sea lines derived from expanded use of these services by Egyptians working abroad as well as their families, goods, and belongings.

There are also numerous indirect costs associated with
Egyptian migration to Arab oil-exporting countries. Owing to
serious shortages in housing, services, infrastructure, and
overall production, any additional income earned abroad is
tantamount to an increase in the supply of money that has a
direct effect on the already high rate of inflation. This in
turn has severe economic consequences in a country where the
majority of wage earners already suffer from low, fixed-money
income. High rates of inflation aggravate maldistribution of
income and contribute to economic and political instability.

Income generated from jobs abroad has also contributed to
an increase in the purchasing price of dwellings and a sky-
rocketing of "key prices" for apartments by creating new
demand for housing. It has been a common practice in Egypt
for a tenant to give up his apartment - and its key - to
another for a "price" without regard to or consent of the
property owner. Although this practice is illegal, it has
proved impossible to crack down on such cases, especially in a
country like Egypt which suffers from enormous shortages of
housing units. For all practical purposes, the "key-price"
practice is accepted in virtually all crowded urban centers.

There is also a cost associated with depletion and maintenance costs of an overexhausted infrastructure which result
from imports of automobiles by Egyptians working abroad.
With almost no increase or widening of roads, the influx of
these vehicles has led to more congestion in the overcrowded
urban centers in the form of traffic delays, increased fuel
consumption, environmental hazards, and other external dis-
economies.

A cost-benefit analysis of Egyptian migration may show it
to be a net gain to Egyptian society eventually. It is too
early, however, to draw any definite conclusions concerning
this relatively new pattern of migration.(12) What is certain
at this point is that the government is depending on worker
remittances to increase revenues in order to pursue the high-
growth strategy called for in the 1978-1982 plan. The strategy aims at alleviating the fundamental short-term problems
facing the economy and paving the way for sustained long-term
growth. At the same time, it emphasizes the importance of
economic and social equity and does not lose touch with the
concept of Arab socialism. Gross national product is expected
to grow at an annual compound rate of 12 percent in real
terms over the plan period. By 1982, it is estimated that
the gross national product will be around $24 billion compared
to about $17 billion in 1979 (see Appendix 3.B). This would
mean a per capita GNP of $550 in 1982 (measured in 1979
prices) and assumes an average population growth rate of 2.3
percent per annum.

To meet these objectives, the plan assumes that economic
growth can depend on increasing revenues not only from work-

er remittances but also from crude oil sales and the Suez Canal. It also assumes a higher rate of public savings than in the past so that investment in productive areas will increase. The assurance of continued foreign aid flows will also be necessary. It has been pointed out that these assumptions are overoptimistic and will not permit the high rate of GDP growth predicted by the planners. The foreign-financed component of the huge investment program, for example, is estimated at nearly $8 billion over the five-year period. The plan has been called "soft" in that it does not provide an integrated strategy or set priorities that account for sectoral sacrifices; instead each sector is scheduled to receive all the investments it could conceivably absorb.(13)

Finally, to complete the picture of the Egyptian economy it is important to analyze the foreign sector. Cotton has traditionally been the key export item, and while it remains an important source of foreign exchange, textile manufactures and petroleum have become increasingly important in recent years. In the service sector, revenues from the Suez Canal, tourism, and workers' remittances from abroad constitute the major foreign-exchange earners. Despite the revenue earned in these areas, Egypt remains a net importer with a deficit of $1,254 million in 1977 and $1,275 in 1978 in its current account balance. Unable to keep agricultural productivity apace with the rapid rate of population growth, foodstuffs form the bulk of imports. Other key imports fall in the categories of intermediate goods, machinery, and equipment.

The most recent trade data on Egypt indicate a consistent improvement in the balance-of-payments situation since 1975. In 1977, for example, exports increased by about 31 percent over the previous year. Although this was due in part to an increase in export prices (about 7 percent), the real increase was nonetheless quite substantial. The export volume of petroleum doubled while that of cotton and rice increased by approximately 59 percent and 76 percent, respectively. It should be noted, however, that the exports of rice and cotton were largely from stocks and do not indicate increased export capacity. Export volumes of textiles and other manufactures decreased because trade with the East European countries fell. Exports of nonfactor services (mainly Suez Canal and tourism revenues) increased about 18 percent in real terms. Factor services (workers' remittances both directly and in the form of financing imports) increased by about 85 percent.

Despite the improvements in exports, imports increased by a slightly higher rate of 32 percent. The bulk of the increase was in the form of intermediate goods (including imports of light crude) which increased by about 80 percent and capital goods which increased by about 31 percent. Agricultural goods (mainly foodstuffs) increased by about 16 percent while other manufactured goods decreased by about 20 percent. Nonfactor services increased about 63 percent owing primarily to higher volumes of commission charges and technical assistance costs (the result of rising investment expenditures). Factor services, largely in the form of interest payments, increased by about 22 percent. The average rate of price increase was about 7 percent, or about the same as for exports. Therefore, the terms of trade were unchanged from 1976 to 1977.

In an attempt to correct major distortions in the economy, the Egyptian government incrementally devalued the parallel market rate from its dollar parity LE 0.58/US$1 in February 1976 to the rate of LE 0.70/US$1 in early 1978. This was equivalent to a 79 percent devaluation in terms of the official parity. Transactions through the parallel market have been expanded so that 45 percent of the convertible currency earnings and 70 percent of convertible payments were channelled through this market by early 1978. Since March 1977, an open license system has been established whereby certain commodities have been freed from all exchange controls. In addition, access to the parallel market for payments of "invisibles" was liberalized in 1976. On January 1, 1979 the conversion of Egyptian pounds to U.S. dollars is carried out at a unified exchange rate of $1.43 per Egyptian pound. On July 26, 1981, the rate was reduced to $1.19.

A fundamental part of total external assistance to Egypt has been aid in liquid form. Financial assistance from the Gulf Organization for the Development of Egypt (GODE) has been crucial in this regard. GODE, which was created with a capital of $2 billion, committed almost its entire share capital in 1977. Included in this assistance was a $250 million guarantee of a Eurodollar loan to Egypt (disbursed), a $1,075 million cash loan to Egypt for elimination of arrears (disbursed), and $650 million for imports of commodities and repayment of short-term debt (committed, of which $150 million was disbursed in 1977). As a result of deteriorating relations with the Eastern European countries, especially the Soviet Union, net capital movements from the bilateral account countries changed from a positive net flow of about $10 million in 1976 to a net outflow of approximately $135 million in 1977. More positively, OECD members' economic assistance, particularly from the United States, and aid from multilateral organizations to Egypt have increased and become more and more important in terms of commitments that will ensure a flow of aid for future years. The European community has provided Egypt with increasing amounts of food aid as well as commitments for $70 million in grants and $119 million in concessional loans over a five-year period.

The short-term debt situation in Egypt appears to be improving. Repayments outstanding (including undisbursed) year-end 1976. Still, the volume of short-term debt remains a major burden on Egypt's external liquidity. Egypt's nonmilitary medium- and long-term debt (outstanding and disbursed) a-mounted to $8,107 million at year-end 1977 compared to $5,858 million at year-end 1976. A structural shift from short-term debt to medium- and long-term debt accounts for much of this increase. Debt service on medium- and long-term debt in 1977 was $1,067 million. The debt-service ratio was about 20.8 percent compared to 25.0 percent in 1976, but will continue to be in the neighborhood of 22 percent in the eighties (see Table 3.1). Table 3.2 shows an estimated foreign public debt of Egypt for 1979-1984.

POLITICAL ASSESSMENT

An appreciation of the factors affecting economic development in Egypt cannot be achieved without looking at the social and political factors in the country. The most fundamental problem facing Egypt in the social as well as economic sphere is its large population which puts a serious strain on almost all aspects of Egyptian life. From overuse of an already depleted infrastructure, to overcrowding in its major cities, to the inability to feed its own people, Egypt faces serious challenges in dealing with this problem.

Given the severity of the population problem, and the stress it places on Egyptian society, political stability in Egypt is remarkably high. After succeeding Gamal Abdel Nasser to the presidency in 1970, Anwar Sadat modified domestic poli-cies, both political and economic, in the direction of greater freedom. Security controls were relaxed and individual and press freedoms were improved. Political opposition has been heard more frequently in this more liberal political environ-ment.

Economic dissatisfaction is the primary cause of unrest in Egypt, as witnessed in January 1977 when Egyptians took to the streets to protest the government decision to remove subsidies on key consumer items. While these demonstrations do occur among university students and urban workers, the Sadat regime maintains tight control over internal unrest with the help of the military. During the spring and summer of 1977, the press was brought under tighter control and editor-ial staffs loyal to the president were appointed.

Mubarak's control of the country takes place within the framework of a governmental system characterized by an elect-ed president who serves as head of state and chief executive, an extensive cabinet, presidential bureau and agency system and supporting civil service, an elected legislature called the People's Assembly, an independent secular judiciary, and a

Table 3.1.
Official Foreign Aid Flows and External Debt
(US$ millions)

	1979	1980	1981	1982	1983	1984
Aid Commitments						
1. Starting Pipeline	4,300	5,155	5,750	5,990	6,580	7,380
(of which, project)	(3,000)	(3,305)	(3,370)	(3,575)	(4,125)	(4,775)
2. New Commitments	2,015	2,245	2,500	3,575	4,000	4,500
(of which, project)	(860)	(985)	(1,285)	(2,350)	(2,650)	(3,380)
Aid Disbursements	1,160	1,650	2,260	2,985	3,200	3,600
(project)	(555)	(920)	(1,110)	(1,770)	(2,000)	(2,300)
(Ratio of Pipeline)*		31%	34%	54%	56%	56%
(non-project)	(605)	(730)	(1,150)	(1,215)	(1,200)	(1,300)
Amortization	938	970	1,150	1,560	1,970	2,050
Interest Payments	415	430	448	480	540	600
Debt-Service Ratios	20.6%	18.4%	18.5%	21.2%	23.6%	22.6%
Net Inflow						
Aid Disbursements less Debt Service	-193	250	672	945	690	950

*Project Disbursement as related to previous year's pipeline.

Source: Ministry of Planning, Egypt's Development Strategy, Economic Management and Growth Objectives, 1980-1984 (Cairo, Egypt: October 29, 1979), p. 12.

Table 3.2.
Estimated Foreign Public Debt of Egypt
for the Period 1979-1984
(in Millions of U. S. Dollars)

	1979	1980	1981	1982	1983	1984
Debt Service	2,443.8	1,052.3	1,183.4	1,310.3	1,258.0	1,151.6
Special Loans	542.4	406.0	320.4	270.5	224.9	145.0
Multilateral Loans	122.4	176.9	192.1	463.6	459.0	447.0
Bilateral Loans	1,779.0	469.4	670.9	576.2	574.1	559.6
Installments Paid	2,007.4	677.6	810.3	952.4	937.6	873.0
Interest	436.4	374.6	373.1	357.9	320.4	278.6

Source: Unpublished report, Central Bank of Egypt (Cairo, Egypt) 1980.

system of law derived from Islamic and French codes. The constitution of 1971 describes the country as a democratic socialist state and part of the larger Arab nation. Islam is the religion of the state and Arabic the official language. In actuality, the three branches of the government are subject to extensive executive control and implementation. With the cooperation of a vice president, prime minister, deputy prime ministers, and a cabinet, the President supervises all activities of the government as chief executive.

Until quite recently, Egypt had a single-party system, the Arab Socialist Union (ASU). In November 1976, open parliamentary elections were held for the first time in 25 years. The left, center, and right platforms of the ASU became the Progressive Assembly, the Egypt Party, and the Liberal Socialist Party, respectively. The government's Egypt Party occupied the majority of seats in the People's Assembly while the other two parties formed small minorities. The experiment in open elections had barely gotten underway when the January 1977 food riots broke out. The Left, including the progressives, was directly implicated in the disturbances and Sadat took advantage of the situation to claim a state of emergency and take measures that included a strict prohibition on meetings and other activities that would disrupt public order. Measures were taken to censure a well-known member of Parliament, Kamal Hussein, and to revoke his membership after he openly suggested that incompetence on the part of the Sadat regime had caused the riots. Thereafter, criticism of the regime by all groups decreased significantly.

The Neo-Wafdist Party (a reestablishment of the Wafd Party which dominated Egyptian politics from 1919 to 1952) emerged as a source of opposition to the Sadat regime by appealing to unsatisfied elements in the private sector as advocates of protective measures against foreign investment and higher tariff walls. The Wafdists were a force to be taken seriously since they claimed a legitimate popular base of support. In January 1978, the group gathered the necessary 20 signatures, drew up its program and requested authorization as a party. A clever move by Sadat, however, left the leaders of the Neo-Wafdist Party in a position where it was extremely difficult to operate and they opted to dissolve their political organization.

In order to have even more control over the legislative branch, President Sadat formed his own party, dissolved parliament after the signing and ratification of the Egyptian-Israeli Accord, and called for elections in June 1979. Sadat's National Democratic Party won the vast majority of the seats in the new People's Assembly, thereby leaving no room for strong opposition.

Since the signing of the Camp David accords, only a few narrow groups on Egypt's far left and right have voiced much

discontent. On the left, the main group is the Progressive
Unionist Party organized by educated leftists who oppose
Sadat's separate peace with Israel out of conviction to the
pan-Arab principle of the late President Nasser. The official
opposition party on the left, the Socialist Labor Party, has
avoided taking a strong position against the peace treaty
probably because of its weak position within the government.
Opposition on the right is voiced by Islamic fundamentalist
groups that oppose the existence of Israel on the grounds of
Moslem solidarity. The most prominent such group, the Moslem
Brotherhood, is tolerated in Egypt but strictly controlled.
The strength of opposition on the right is hard to gauge
because their threat to the regime lies more in their ability to
rouse the masses than in any formal party membership. Most
observers agree that the Islamic rightists could pose a serious
threat to Sadat's peace with Israel and friendship with the
West only if they attached their platforms to a wave of economic frustration in mass protests. "Islamic Groups," for
example, are being organized and spreading quickly in all
universities in Egypt. Further, they are finding sympathy
from many new quarters in both rural and urban areas. In
spite of the grass-root nature of this movement, it has remained politically ineffective owing to a lack of national cohesion
and organizational structure.

     The current regime is aware of this growing Islamic
sentiment and is taking measures to demonstrate its understanding of the situation. A national referendum held on May
22, 1980 proposing several constitutional amendments stipulates
that according to Article 2 of the Constitution, Sharia - the
Islamic legal code - be the principle source of legislation
rather than one of several sources of law as has been the case
in the past. In his speech before the People's Assembly a few
days before the referendum, President Sadat reiterated his
position in this regard by announcing that Egypt is a Moslem
country, ruled by a Moslem president, with Sharia as its
principle source of law. As much as he recognizes the significance of the emerging Islamic groups, President Sadat hopes to
limit their activities to religious matters only. Toward this
end, he has made it illegal for such groups to organize political associations. The same strategy is now pursued by President Mubarak.

     One result of the spread of Islamic fundamentalism in
Egypt is a resurfacing of an existing polarization between
Moslems and Christian Copts, the largest minority in Egypt.
Because of great sensitivity to religion, many vested groups
have tried to take advantage of this tension in the past. In
1919, for example, the British attempted such a strategy but
failed in the rising tide of Egyptian nationalism that swept the
country during a revolution under the leadership of Saad
Zaghoul. Even though Egyptian Copts have significantly con-

tributed to Egyptian society and are well integrated culturally,
the feeling of persecution as a minority persists. This longstanding attitude between Moslems and Copts means that even
a minor clash - whether internally or externally instigated -
may lead to another outbreak of hostilities between the groups.
Yet, the common aspirations of all Egyptians have always
reversed seemingly dangerous tensions between Moslems and
Copts. This round should be no exception.

Other recent developments suggest the concern for en-
suring long-term internal stability in Egypt. One major
constitutional change that received overwhelming support
according to the voting in the May 22, 1980 national referendum was one that allowed President Sadat to remain in office
for life. The Constitution stipulated that the president of
Egypt may not run for more than two successive six-year
terms. Another current development was the cancellation of
marshall law by President Sadat during a speech before the
People's Assembly on May 14, 1980. Yet another was a constitutional change that would make the establishment of a multiparty political system official in Egypt.

Political stability at home will also be affected by how the
President conducts Egyptian foreign policy. Egypt's position
of relative isolation from its Arab neighbors since the signing
of the Camp David accords has been discussed above. One
possible outcome of the movement to isolate Egypt could be
expulsion of migrant workers from the Arab oil-exporting
countries. This would have serious repercussions at home -
the return of large numbers of dissatisfied workers and the
loss of foreign exchange resulting from such a move would act
as a major source of instability for the present regime. It
appears highly unlikely, however, that this will occur. No
matter what the political situation between the governments of
Egypt and the Arab oil-exporting countries, there is general
understanding that no punitive measures will be directed
against Egyptian nationals. And in a more practical vein, the
difficulty of replacing Egyptian workers, given such valuable
traits as cultural similarity and much-needed skills, is
significant. Another aspect of foreign policy to keep in mind
is the political vulnerability of the present regime created by
its close identification with the United States. It is too early
to evaluate the implications of such a policy but it seems that
President Sadat has strongly committed Egypt to move in this
direction. It is almost certain that President Mubarak will
moderately pursue Sadat's policy.

OVERALL ASSESSMENT

The economic and political variables discussed in this chapter
allow one to draw several conclusions and to make some projec-

tions about Egypt's future.   In terms of the economic situation, the overall picture has been rather impressive since
1975.   It seems that further amelioration will take place in key
segments of the economy in the coming years.   First, oil
revenues, as mentioned above, have increased both in terms of
quantity of oil produced and amount of revenue earned.   The
increase in production has been due primarily to the return of
the Sinai oilfields following the Camp David accords.   Oil
revenues have increased by even more than production levels
because of rising world prices for oil.   Outside of OPEC,
Egypt is considered the second largest exporter of oil (Mexico
is first).   The policy adopted by the Ministry of Petroleum
aimed at selling oil on the spot market has brought a particularly high price per barrel of oil.   Oil revenues have increased
from close to $600 million in 1977 to nearly $1 billion in 1979.

A second important source of foreign exchange that has
contributed to the stability of the Egyptian economy is worker
remittances.   The figure for 1979 was as high as $2 billion and
constitutes a direct benefit to the economy from Egyptian
laborers, technicians, and highly trained professionals working
abroad.   It contributes as well, however, to a shortage of
trained Egyptians at home and price increases in the service
sector as a limited supply of trained workers in Egypt find
themselves in great demand.   This in turn has aggravated
domestic price levels in recent years.

The boom in the construction industry in urban areas
following the relaxation of regulations governing rents of
luxury apartments is still another positive factor.   It would
be less accurate, however, to overlook the serious problem
of adequate housing facilities for poor and middle-class
Egyptians.

Another healthy indicator in the Egyptian economy is the
consistent increase in private-sector activity.   In fact, more
than 50 percent of total capital outlays invested in Egypt as a
result of the "open-door" policy have been due to the high
rate of return enjoyed on projects for which there had been a
dormant demand for years prior to implementation of this
policy.

The U.S. AID program constitutes an important fact of
economic development in Egypt as well.   Egypt is the recipient
of over $1 billion from the United States in 1981 in economic
assistance.   This flow of financial and technical assistance is
crucial in alleviating short-term economic problems and allowing
longer-term objectives to be pursued.   In light of Egypt's
strategic importance to the United States, this assistance can
be expected to continue into the foreseeable future.

Among negative factors that will continue to affect the
course of economic development in Egypt are the following:
lack of adequate housing, the recent downward trend in agricultural productivity, inefficiency in the public sector, the

balance-of-payments deficit and the government's subsidy policy.

In spite of the boom in the construction industry since 1975, there has been a severe housing shortage in Egypt to the extent that some graveyards on the outskirts of Cairo have been used by the poor for shelter. The government is concerned about this problem and is therefore devoting a significant amount of time and energy to finding a solution in as short a period of time as possible. Given the extensive nature of the housing shortage, however, it is realistic to say that it will continue to be a source of discontent and instability for quite some time.

In the agricultural sector, it has been observed that the continuous migration from rural to urban areas had taken its toll on productivity. In addition to adding to the burden of inadequate living facilities in the cities, the low agricultural productivity places further pressure on Egypt's balance-of-payments situation since increases in imports of foodstuffs will be necessary to compensate for short supply of domestic production. The situation is only aggravated by a population increase of about one million persons every ten months with narrowing intervals, if the same birth rate continues. Some possibilities for improving agricultural productivity do exist. The New Valley and the region east of the Suez Canal offer potential new lands for reclamation and cultivation. The government is taking measures to create incentives for investment in agricultural projects. While foreign investors have been slow to seize these opportunities, the Egyptian private sector has taken advantage of new opportunities to expand agricultural lands. The fruits of these projects should begin to be seen in about five to ten years.

The public sector, as noted above, has been a net burden on the government's budget. Many companies that were nationalized by Nasser in 1961 are now operating at a loss or at less than full capacity. President Sadat does not hide his displeasure with the public sector and has made it one of his top priorities. Especially since the signing of the Camp David accords, one can expect that considerable attention will be given to improving efficiency in the public sector. The Ministry of Economy has recently announced that no further government expenditures will be made to help the ailing public sector. Already, the recapitalization of some public-sector companies is being financed through shares owned by private citizens. So long as public-sector activities represent the major portion of Egyptian industrial output, there will be a net burden on the Egyptian economy that will have negative consequences for overall economic stability.

The balance-of-payments deficit will continue to be a major concern to the economy in the years ahead, even with the positive contribution of certain foreign-exchange earners discussed above. It seems that this chronic problem may last at least until the turn of the century.

One other major negative factor haunting the economy is the question of subsidies. Beginning with small amounts of the budget being allocated to subsidize basic consumer goods such as bread, sugar, and tea during the Nasser years, subsidization has grown to unmanageable proportions in recent years. Economists insist that such subsidization creates distortions in the allocative system or limited resources, yet policy makers seem unable to face the hard reality of removing them, especially since the lesson learned during the January 1977 food riots. The government policy is to attempt a phase-out of the subsidy within the limits imposed by public reaction to increase in the price of basic commodities.

One possible negative side effect of the recent gains in the Egyptian economy relates to the widening disparities in income between rich and poor. There has been no assessment of recent trends in income distribution in Egypt nor has there been any serious study that addresses itself to the economic, social, and political repercussions of such income disparities. Still, it is widely believed that there are several hundred millionaires reaping a significant portion of the new wealth in Egypt. This phenomenon creates a potential source of instability, particularly among the bulk of employees and workers in both government agencies and public-sector companies who suffer a relatively low and fixed income and are faced with a high rate of inflation that further erodes the purchasing power of their inadequate pay. With their earnings reaching near subsistence level, President Sadat ordered a monetary increase in 1978 to all employees of the government and public-sector companies. In mid-1980, the government increased the minimum-wage rate by 25 percent and raised the subsidies on a number of commodities. The result has been at least a temporary public satisfaction among Egyptians even though inflation has been eroding any pay increase.

The general framework of Egypt's current economic situation provides an understanding of the factors affecting its trade policies. As outlined above, one of these factors is balance-of-payments chronic deficit which resulted in an excess demand for foreign exchange.

In spite of an accumulated fund in British sterling since World War II, Egypt has been faced with a shortage in hard currencies ever since. Unable to pay off its debts after the war, including what it owed to Egypt, Britain froze them. It took long-winded negotiations to free those frozen sterling assets gradually. Nevertheless, the quest for more imports and industrialization caused by an increase in population, a rise in the per capita income, and the unquestionable pattern of constant shift from traditional rural to urban centers and to modernity exacerbated the balance-of-payments problems.

Such a chronic and increasing deficit in its foreign sector lead Egypt to pursue a policy of foreign-exchange controls. They resulted in a wide variety of laws, rules, and regulations that were designed to ration the limited supply of hard currencies through a bureaucratic and a complicated structure of import licensing and a system of multiple exchange rates. Furthermore, during Nasser's regime, Egyptians were banned from holding accounts in banks denominated in foreign currencies. Even travel abroad necessitated an exit visa that was not easily obtained from the Department of Passports and Naturalization, a division of Egypt's Ministry of the Interior. Foreign travel was therefore drastically curtailed unless it was for medical reasons, education, or business.

After Nasser's death in September 1970 a gradual policy of liberalization was adopted. Exit visas were cancelled and Egyptians were therefore allowed to work abroad more freely. With the advent of the open-door policy in 1974, it was necessary to change or at least to modify a host of restrictive rules. We have already alluded to several reforms such as a unification of the exchange rate and the liberalization policy of inviting foreign capital for investment in Egypt.

Furthermore, Law 97 regulating foreign-exchange operations was promulgated in 1976. According to this law, Egyptians, whether individuals or companies, can now hold accounts denominated in foreign currencies except the proceeds from exports or tourism. Under the provisions of the law, transfer of funds from such accounts is allowable.

Given the prevailing political and social relative stability, it seems that liberalization policies as witnessed in such laws will start to show even more positive effects on the Egyptian economy than thus far has been realized.

For example, it is obvious from Appendix 3.A that half of the projects approved by the General Authority for Investments and Free Zones have not yet started production. Moreover, projects requiring less capital outlays started earlier than projects requiring larger capital expenditures. Until the end of 1979, the total investment of the 455 projects already in operation amounted to $1.6 billion whereas the total investment of the 329 projects under implementation amount to $3.9 billion and for the 295 projects that are still on the drawing board, capital outlays are estimated at $2.5 billion.

With such an expanded investment activities, the foreign-trade sector of Egypt is bound to increase particularly at a time when the foreign-exchange earnings have continued to grow to reach $6.6 billion in 1979 and an estimated figure of $7.6 billion in 1980. These earnings in foreign exchange represent a sizable portion of Egypt's gross national product, 38 percent and 39 percent consecutively in 1979 and 1980.

Moreover, the increase in population by one million persons every ten months or less in the future, together with

an even faster rate of urbanization will generate further demand for imported goods at a time when local consumption will
divert some items such as cotton textiles from the export
market.

Because of an apparent conflict between Egypt's desire to
increase exports and the current trends, it is expected that in
the coming decade or two there will be a significant change in
the composition and the flows of Egypt's trade. Traditional
exports of cotton and cotton textiles are no longer Egypt's
first earners of foreign exchange. Oil exports and remittances
of Egyptians working abroad will continue to play a more
significant role in the export market for the forseeable future.
Furthermore, most of Egypt's trade is with both East and West
Europe. Almost three-quarters of Egyptian exports flow to
Europe while two-thirds of the imports flow in the opposite
direction.(14) It seems, however, that Egypt's trade with the
United States will increase in relative and absolute terms
pending the ability of American manufacturers to compete with
their European counterparts, on the continuation of American
commitment to Egypt, and of course on a more favorable political environment than the current stalemate.

CONCLUDING REMARKS

Although he will have to contend with many serious problems such as those just outlined, it appears that President
Mubarak's political future is relatively secure. The Egyptian-
Israeli accord has both positive and negative elements. It will
benefit Egypt by allowing military appropriations to be redi-
rected into more productive economic activities. Effectively
implemented, this should improve domestic conditions and ensure Mubarak's domestic security. The liability of the accord,
however, resides in the fact that it has effectively isolated
Egypt from the rest of the Arab world. Economically, this
isolation has resulted in the discontinuation of financial aid to
Egypt from several Arab funds, the loss of which is only
compensated for by other sources of revenues such as sales of
oil, Suez Canal earnings, and tourism. If Egypt can ride out
the tide of isolation from the Arab world with the help of its
allies, especially the United States, there will probably be a
cosmetic amelioration within its boundaries. An optimistic view
of Egypt's future will only be possible when its deep-rooted
historical and cultural relations with the Arab countries are
once again normalized as it gradually resumes its position of
leadership in the Arab world.

NOTES

1. Ibrahim M. Oweiss, "Some Positive Aspects of the Egyptian Economy," CCAS Reports, Center for Contemporary Arab Studies, Georgetown University, October 1978.

2. Minister Fouad Kamal Hussein is the first minister to be appointed in charge of the development of the money market in Egypt.

3. Based on unpublished research by the author for the period 1975-1979.

4. Ministry of Planning, The Five Year Plan, 1978-1982, Vol. 1: The General Strategy for Social and Economic Development, (Cairo: 1977).

5. Central Agency for Public Mobilization and Statistics, Cairo, Egypt.

6. Ministry of Planning, "Egypt's Development Strategy, Economic Management and Growth Objectives (Cairo: October 29, 1979), p. 4.

7. The oldest universities in Egypt are Al-Azhar, Cairo, Alexandria, and Ein Shams. The newer ones include Asiut, Tanta, El-Mansoura, El-Zagazig, Helwan, Canl, El-Menia, and El-Menufia.

8. Central Agency for Public Mobilization and Statistics, Statistical Yearbook (Cairo: July 1979), pp. 149-185.

9. Nazli Choucri, Migration and Employment in the Construction Sector: Critical Factors in Egyptian Development (Cairo University/ MIT), p. 127. See also Fred Halliday, "Migration and the Labor Force in the Oil Producing States of the Middle East." Development and Change 8(1977):277.

10. Based on unpublished reports from the Central Bank of Egypt and the Chase Manhattan Bank.

11. Lawrence Hadley, "The Migration of Egyptian Human Capital to the Arab Oil-Producing States: A Cost-Benefit Analysis," International Migration Review 11 (1977):285ff.

12. Ibrahim M. Oweiss, Migration of Egyptians, Economic Commission for Western Asia, Seminar on Arab Brain Drain, February 4-8, 1980, Beirut, Lebanon.

13. John Waterbury, Egypt: Burdens of the Past, Options for the Future (Bloomington and London: Indiana University Press, 1978).

14. Central Agency for Public Mobilization and Statistics, Monthly Bulletin of Foreign Trade (Cairo, Egypt: April 1979), p. 130.

APPENDIX 3.A. FOREIGN INVESTMENTS IN EGYPT
(Figures in Thousands of Egyptian Pounds)

Approved Inland, Public and Private Free Zones Projects
(31/12/1979)

		Number	Capital Local C.	Capital Foreign C.	Total	(Value in L.E. 1000) Total Investment
A.	**Inland Projects:**					
1.	Investment Companies........	87	199 129	255 947	455 076	501 046
2.	Banks & Banking Institutions.	43	72 465	120 835	193 300	193 300
3.	Touristic Projects	96	195 962	209 326	405 288	716 979
4.	Housing Projects	43	59 131	100 762	159 893	234 569
5.	Transportation Projects	12	3 086	29 615	32 701	78 347
6.	Health Projects	17	16 987	21 435	38 422	51 275
7.	Agriculture Projects	38	59 379	56 860	116 239	275 684
8.	Contracting Projects	72	21 948	38 399	60 347	105 419
9.	Consultation Projects	20	2 849	4 596	7 445	8 600
10.	Services Projects	22	24 871	131 031	155 902	199 743
11.	Textile Projects	38	66 530	55 645	122 175	652 400
12.	Food and Beverages Projects..	53	33 063	34 157	67 220	172 509
13.	Chemical Projects	91	76 521	93 953	170 474	282 809
14.	Wood Products Projects	12	3 610	12 242	15 912	26 046
15.	Engineering Projects	42	43 148	62 953	106 101	280 690
16.	Building Materials Projects ..	37	70 749	39 518	110 267	292 473
17.	Metallurgical Projects	25	13 346	20 448	33 794	46 062
18.	Pharmaceutical Projects	9	3 831	6 062	9 893	16 731
19.	Mining & Petroleum Projects ..	9	3 026	14 176	17 202	34 658
	Total	766	969 691	130 796	2 277 651	4 188 918
B.	**Public Free Zones**					
1.	Cairo Public Free Zone	41	816	40 012	40 828	53 016
2.	Alexandria Public Free Zone ..	52	1 456	37 725	39 181	129 642
3.	Suez Public Free Zone........	43	535	16 301	16 836	20 599
4.	Port Said Public Free Zone ...	113	3 068	90 965	94 033	114 174
	Total	249	5 875	185 003	190 878	317 431
C.	**Private Free Zones Projects**					
1.	Cairo Private Free Zones	24	2 939	42 018	44 957	106 885
2.	Alexandria Private Free Zones	32	1 497	132 035	133 532	865 226
3.	Suez Private Free Zones	5	197	28 753	28 950	31 467
4.	Port Said Private Free Zones .	3	60	515	575	954
	Total	64	4 693	203 321	208 014	1 004 532
	Grand Total	1 079	980 259	519 120	2 676 543	5 510 881

(continued)

APPENDIX 3.A. (cont.)

Inland, Public and Private Free Zones Projects
(31/12/1979)

	Number	Capital		(Value in L.E. 1000)	
		Local C.	Foreign C.	Total	Total Investment
A. Inland Projects:					
1. Investment Companies........	36	130 919	126 763	257 682	267 352
2. Banks & Banking Institutions.	31	31 510	73 690	105 200	105 200
3. Touristic Projects	21	11 939	20 080	32 019	62 030
4. Housing Projects	3	188	385	573	658
5. Transportation Projects	4	1 803	18 762	20 565	32 065
6. Health Projects	1	200	35	235	390
7. Agricultural Projects	10	28 959	22 182	51 141	119 154
8. Contracting Projects	26	6 883	10 576	17 459	33 060
9. Consultation Projects	11	1 158	1 787	2 945	3 100
10. Services Projects	10	1 259	2 961	4 220	5 307
11. Textile Projects	20	1 839	11 260	13 099	16 342
12. Food and Beverages Projects.	14	10 107	9 039	19 146	40 113
13. Chemical Projects	41	10 577	21 938	32 515	36 921
14. Wood Products Projects......	4	404	737	1 141	1 263
15. Engineering Projects	17	7 031	10 269	17 300	25 048
16. Building Materials Projects .	9	2 498	5 761	8 259	9 702
17. Metallurgical Projects	15	9 112	13 110	22 222	29 031
18. Pharmaceutical Projects	2	72	1 826	1 898	2 285
19. Mining & Petroleum Projects .	5	2 366	4 468	6 834	15 204
Total	280	258 824	355 629	614 453	804 225
B. Public Free Zones					
1. Cairo Public Free Zone	11	163	12 167	12 330	14 119
2. Alexandria Public Free Zone .	29	1 346	16 385	17 731	97 098
3. Suez Public Free Zone.......	15	130	5 303	5 433	7 506
4. Port Said Public Free Zone ..	82	1 798	57 807	59 605	66 654
Total	137	3 437	91 662	95 099	185 377
C. Private Free Zones Projects					
1. Cairo Private Free Zones	19	2 439	21 420	23 859	32 687
2. Alexandria Private Free Zones	16	322	47 959	48 281	52 047
3. Suez Private Free Zones.....	1	--	26 034	26 034	26 034
4. Port Said Private Free Zones.	2	60	375	435	639
Total	38	2 821	95 788	98 609	111 407
Grand Total	455	265 082	543 079	808 161	1 101 009

(continued)

APPENDIX 3.A. (cont.)

Inland, Public and Private Free Zones Projects
(31/12/1979)

| | Number | Capital | | | (Value in L.E. 1000) |
		Local C.	Foreign C.	Total	Total Investment
A. Inland Projects:					
1. Investment Companies.........	23	32 738	50 556	83 294	89 594
2. Banks & Banking Institutions.	6	30 140	24 860	55 000	55 000
3. Touristic Projects	55	62 898	153 245	216 143	398 713
4. Housing Projects	31	56 355	80 906	137 261	196 325
5. Transportation Projects	4	1 061	9 024	10 085	42 215
6. Health Projects	12	14 522	20 457	34 979	60 609
7. Agricultural Projects	17	19 660	25 969	45 629	87 996
8. Contracting Projects	15	3 567	7 849	11 416	24 277
9. Consultation Projects	3	225	225	450	450
10. Services Projects	5	615	3 237	3 852	10 041
11. Textile Projects	12	60 427	40 625	101 052	615 164
12. Food and Beverages Projects..	18	8 416	10 741	19 157	61 879
13. Chemical Projects	23	6 814	28 933	35 747	65 567
14. Wood Products Projects	6	2 796	5 265	8 061	13 973
15. Engineering Projects	10	6 014	11 373	17 387	59 895
16. Building Materials Projects ..	17	56 906	20 744	77 650	226 267
17. Metallurgical Projects	9	3 984	7 338	11 322	16 596
18. Pharmaceutical Projects	4	1 810	2 215	4 025	6 334
19. Mining & Petroleum Projects ..	3	660	958	1 618	1 954
Total	273	369 608	504 520	874 128	2 032 849
B. Public Free Zones					
1. Cairo Public Free Zone	10	178	6 884	7 062	14 007
2. Alexandria Public Free Zone ..	6	--	10 028	10 028	18 078
3. Suez Public Free Zone........	11	345	1 254	1 599	2 232
4. Port Said Public Free Zone ...	18	1 270	18 527	19 797	26 939
Total	45	1 793	36 693	38 486	61 256
C. Private Free Zones Projects					
1. Cairo Private Free Zones	2	--	1 575	1 575	2 175
2. Alexandria Private Free Zones	9	720	9 633	10 353	624 078
3. Suez Private Free Zones......	--	--	--	--	--
4. Port Said Private Free Zones .	--	--	--	--	--
Total	11	720	11 208	11 928	626 253
Grand Total	329	372 121	552 421	924 542	2 720 358

Source: The General Authority for Investment and Free Zones,
Facts and Figures, VI (Cairo, Egypt, December 1979).

APPENDIX 3.B.   EGYPT'S FIVE-YEAR PLAN (1980-1984)

The General Equilibrium of the Five-Year Plan
1980-1984
(At constant 1979 Prices)
(In millions of Egyptian Pounds)*

Uses of National Income	1979	1980	1981	1982	1983	1984
Household Consumption	7372	7807				
Plus Subsidies	1200	1600				
Total Value of Household Consumption	8522	9407	10110	10925	11805	12805
Government Consumption	2060	2390	2700	2985	3270	3580
Gross Investment	2720	3450	3710	4040	4525	5030
of which: Public Sector	2140	2965	3170	3420	3765	4100
Private Sector	380	385	430	500	620	730
Changes in Stocks	200	100	110	120	140	200
Exports	2920	3550	4029	4467	4917	5415
of which: Agriculture	400	417	425	447	460	482
Industry	452	510	565	630	710	800
Oil and Products	868	1154	1270	1417	1575	1735
Oil Companies' Share	220	365	409	480	527	593
Suez Canal	400	504	760	813	870	920
Tourism and Other	580	600	600	680	774	885
(-) Imports	4350	5250	5545	5960	6460	7020
of which: Consumption Goods	1300	1430	1508	1601	1704	1800
Intermediate Goods	1700	1980	2113	2259	2426	2605
Capital Goods	1150	1590	1634	1780	1990	2265
Non-Factor Services	200	250	290	320	340	350
(+) Net Factor Income	625	685	661	640	683	687
Gross National Expenditure	12497	14232	15665	17097	18740	20497

*   The Egyptian Pound is approximately equal to $1.4.

APPENDIX 3.B. (cont.)

Gross Output	1979	1980	1981	1982	1983	1984
Agriculture	3500	3620	3719	3836	3964	4114
Industry and Mining	5667	6120	6640	7253	8098	9096
Petroleum and Products	1660	2282	2587	2934	3282	3658
Electricity	132	148	165	185	204	221
Construction	1210	1400	1500	1630	1820	2057
Transportation and Communication	698	775	860	957	1070	1203
Suez Canal	412	517	776	830	889	955
Trade and Finance	1376	1500	1660	1830	2025	2248
Housing	178	195	216	242	272	310
Public Utilities	48	53	59	66	74	84
Other Services	2700	3118	3480	3847	4211	4620
Total	17581	19718	21662	23010	25909	28566
Annual Growth Rate %	-	13.3	9.8	9.0	9.7	10.3
Total Production Inputs	7721	8461	9183	9933	10902	12091
of which Commodity Imports	1700	1980	2113	2259	2426	2605
Total Inputs as a Ratio of Gross Outputs %	43.9	42.9	42.4	42.1	42.1	42.3
Value Added at Factor Cost	9860	11257	12479	13677	15007	16475
Annual Rate of Growth %	-	16.1	10.8	9.6	9.7	9.8
Net Factor Receipts	625	685	661	640	683	687
Indirect Taxes	2012	2290	2525	2780	3050	3335
Gross National Product	12497	14232	15665	17097	18760	20497

*The Egyptian Pound is approximately equal to $1.4.

Source: Ministry of Planning, Egypt's Development Strategy, Economic Management and Growth Objectives, 1980-1984 (Cairo, Egypt: October 29, 1979), p. 36.

FURTHER READING

Abdel-Fadil, Mahmoud. Development, Income Distribution and Social Change in Rural Egypt (1952-1970): A Study in the Political Economy of Agrarian Transition. Cambridge, England: Cambridge University Press, 1975.

Ahmad, Ysuf J. Absorbtive Capacity of the Egyptian Economy: An Examination of Problems and Prospects. Paris: Development Centre of the Organization for Economic Cooperation and Development, 1976.

Baer, Gabriel. A History of Landownership in Modern Egypt, 1800-1950. London and New York: Oxford University Press, 1962.

Barbour, K.M. The Growth, Location and Structure of Industry in Egypt. New York: Praeger, 1972.

Crouchley, Arthur Edwin. The Economic Development of Modern Egypt. London: Longmans, 1938.

Drewry, H.P. The Suez Canal and its Impact on Tanker Trades and Economics. London: H.P. Drewry, 1978.

El-Barawi, Rashid. Economic Development in the United Arab Republic. Cairo: The Anglo-Egyptian Bookshop, 1972.

El-Kammash, Magdi M. Economic Development and Planning in Egypt. New York: Praeger, 1968.

Hansen, Bent. Economic Development in Egypt. Santa Monica, Calif.: Rand Corporation, 1969.

Hansen, Bent and Girgis A. Marzouk. Development and Economic Policy in the UAR (Egypt). Amsterdam: North Holland Pub. Co., 1965.

Hansen, Bent and K. Hashishibi. Egypt: Foreign Trade Regimes and Economic Development. Vol. 4. New York: National Bureau of Economic Research, 1975.

Issawi, Charles Phillip. Egypt in Revolution, An Economic Analysis. London and New York: Oxford University Press, 1963.

Kanovsky, Eliyahu. The Economic Impact of the Six Day War; Israel, The Occupied Territories, Egypt, Jordan. New York: Praeger, 1970.

Kardouche, George K. The Flow of Financial Resources: The United Arab Republic: Case Study of Aid through Trade and Repayment of Debts in Goods and Local Currencies. Geneva: UNCTAD, 1968.

Kerr, Malcolm H. The United Arab Republic: The Domestic and Economic Background of Foreign Policy. RM-5967. Santa Monica, Calif.: Rand, 1969.

Landes, Davis S. Bankers and Pashas; International Finance and Imperialism in Egypt. London: Heinemann, 1958.

Mabro, Robert. The Egyptian Economy, 1952-1972. Oxford: Clarendon Press, 1974.

Mabro, Robert and Samir Radwan. The Industrialization of Egypt, 1939-1973. London: Oxford University Press, 1976.

Mead, Donald C. Growth and Structural Change in the Egyptian Economy. Homewood, Ill.: R.D. Irwin, 1967.

Nagi, Mustafa H. Labor Force and Employment in Egypt: A Demographic and Socio-Economic Analysis. New York: Praeger, 1971.

O'Brien, Patrick Karl. The Revolution in Egypt's Economic System: From Private Enterprise to Socialism, 1952-1965. London: Royal Institute of International Affairs, 1972.

Radwan, Samir. Capital Formation in Egyptian Industry and Agriculture 1882-1967. London: Ithaca Press, 1974.

Saab, Garbiel S. The Egyptian Agrarian Reform: 1952-1962. London and New York: Oxford University Press, 1967.

4 The Arab States of the Gulf: A Political and Security Assessment

Malcolm C. Peck

In the course of just over one year, three major events or series of events have profoundly affected political realities and security concerns on the Arab side of the Persian Gulf. The resulting situation holds serious implications for American interests and policy in that region.

The Camp David discussions and the Egyptian-Israeli peace treaty that issued from them reinforced and intensified the dynamics of the relationship between the Arab-Israeli conflict, especially the Palestinian issue at its core, and the internal and external politics of the Arab states of the gulf. It could no longer be credibly suggested that the conflict and the gulf were separable in formulating American policy toward the latter, although perception of this lagged.

At the outset of 1979 the fall of the shah removed the principal "pillar" on which the United States had relied for protecting its interests in the gulf area. The Khomeini revolution had a deeply unsettling effect on the other side of the gulf, dramatized by internal disturbances in Saudi Arabia and some of the smaller Arab states, lending further uncertainty to the future of the American relationship with them.

Finally, the Soviet invasion of Afghanistan, raising the spectre of a subsequent drive to accomplish the old Russian dream of direct access to the gulf, spurred a sharp, perhaps precipitate, American response. This took the form of the "Carter Doctrine," asserting the intention to apply American military power directly to defend the Persian Gulf-Indian Ocean area against external threat. There followed an attempt to secure military facilities in the area for the use of American forces.

In the early part of 1980 little was certain. With a hostile and enigmatic Iran still holding 50 American embassy personnel hostage, with numerous Americans, including gov-

ernment officials, departed from Arab countries of the gulf in
the wake of hostile demonstrations spawned by those in Iran,
with apparent strains affecting the longstanding close relations
of Saudi Arabia and the United States, with the price of oil
soaring to unanticipated heights and its availability in adequate
amount in continuing doubt, and with the heightened possibility of superpower confrontation in the region, it was clear
only that significant dangers lay ahead and that a major test
of the efficacy of American policy was in store.

This chapter will examine briefly the major political and
security issues of the seven Arab states of the gulf (stretch-
ing the definition a bit to include Oman), with particular
reference to their regional concerns and their relations with
the United States. The smaller states, which tend broadly to
share a common outlook, will be considered first. The two
major Arab countries of the gulf, Iraq and Saudi Arabia, are
then examined. Last, American policy toward this part of the
Middle East, the challenges it faces, and the response offered
will be assayed.

Kuwait, Bahrain, Qatar, the United Arab Emirates, and
Oman all pursue policies that derive from an acute awareness
that their neighbors are much larger and far stronger militarily than they are. Most (Oman was a particular exception)
feared the shah's Iran, which seized the Arab islands of Abu
Musa and the Tunbs in 1971. They all fear Khomeini's Iran -
Bahrain because of the intimated revival of irredentist claims
to its territory, and with the others, because of Iranian
efforts to foment unrest among their Shia communities. (Bahrain is about half Shia, while Oman, Qatar and the UAE have
large Shia minorities). Such efforts had already produced
some degree of unrest in several of these states by fall 1979
and a tense atmosphere in all of them. Moreover, the populist
rising that toppled the shah's regime represents a potential
model for emulation by those who may chafe under the paternalistic rule of hereditary rulers, though disaffection is
generally not widespread. At his inauguration, former President Abol Hassan Bani-Sadr reaffirmed export of the Iranian
revolution to do away with remaining monarchical regimes.(1)

These small states have sought to protect themselves
largely by pursuing policies designed to accommodate, or, in
any event, not offend their large neighbors. They have been
inclined to look to Saudi Arabia for support - financial/military
in the case of Oman and political in the cases of Bahrain and
Qatar - and tend (especially in the case of the latter two) to
follow the Saudi lead in regional and inter-Arab politics. From
early 1979, in response to events in Iran, and perhaps taking
a cue from the Saudis and their renewed discussion concerning
a consultative council, there have been indications of an
impending move to increased democratization of the political
systems, especially in Kuwait, Bahrain, and the UAE.(2)

There has been some interest in the formation of a loose security community, with discussions taking place periodically over the past several years. Traditional jealousies and rivalries and differing perceptions of the principal source of external threat, however, have precluded real action. More in evidence are recent indications of an increased reliance on the acquisition of national military defense capabilities.

Kuwait, with the largest population and greatest wealth among the smaller states and, excepting Oman, with the longest experience of political independence, has endeavored to preserve a precarious position among the gulf's powers and between the attentions of the two superpowers. In one observer's apt, piscine image, "Kuwait might be compared to a small fish in a large pond - not only must it be wary of large and hungry fellow fish; it must also avoid being hooked on lines cast into the pond from outside."(3) The country has maintained a relatively stable existence owing to an enlightened welfare policy that distributes the benefits of oil wealth to its citizens, a relative degree of political liberalization, and the promotion of a socially and intellectually tolerant and cosmopolitan atmosphere. There are limits as to how outspoken the National Assembly is permitted to be. In August 1976 the government dissolved the Assembly, even though the majority of its members have not been disposed to question the rule of the Sabah family. Currently a committee is revising the constitution (one revision being a provision for female suffrage), originally drawn up in 1962, and a new Assembly will be elected in the coming months.(4) This reaffirmation of Kuwait's democratic tradition should help to sustain its stability.

This stability and enlightened secularization, the perceived legitimacy of the Sabah family and the small size of Kuwait's Shia minority help buffer the impact of the Khomeini revolution.(5) Generally, good relations are maintained with the other small states of the gulf, although a certain sense of superiority can produce acerbity in dealings with the lower gulf states, which are perceived as less developed and sophisticated. Kuwait's political system has served as a model for them and the Kuwait Fund for Arab Development, providing financial assistance to Arab and non-Arab states, has been emulated by Abu Dhabi in the UAE and, indeed, by Saudi Arabia.

Relations with the Saudis are generally good. Demarcation of the two countries' offshore boundary awaits settlement. The Saudi view of the whole Arabian Peninsula as its proper sphere of influence can lead to exertion of some political pressure and attempts to make Kuwaitis conform more closely to austere Saudi norms of Islamic rectitude, provoking a degree of resentment. Kuwait does, on occasion, take actions not designed to please the Saudis, as when the latter raised their per barrel price of oil by $2.00 to bring it in line with the former's price and Kuwait then responded with a $2.00 increase that appeared as a leapfrogging maneuver.(6) The relationship, however, is a positive and close one, whatever the occasional divergences on particular issues.

The source of real menace for Kuwait has been Iraq, whose threatened invasion at the time of Kuwaiti independence in 1961 was checked by the dispatch of British and later by Arab League forces. Iraqi seizure of border posts in 1973 and incursion in 1976 were responses to Kuwaiti refusals to relinquish or share sovereignty over the islands of Warba and Bubiyan, which command the entrance to Iraq's port of Umm Qasr.(7) The recent moderation of Iraqi policy toward its conservative Arab neighbors in the gulf may push the threat to Kuwait into the background for the time, but its derivation from geostrategic realities suggest that it will persist.

Kuwait's reliance on a policy of accommodation to preserve its security has kept its armed forces small, with just over 11,000 men in the army, air force and (very small) navy. From the mid-1970s, however, an expansion program has been undertaken with an attempt to phase out non-Kuwaitis, who have included British, Pakistani, Jordanian, and Egyptian officers. Its main arms suppliers have been Western countries, with the United States inaugurating a military relationship following a 1972 Department of Defense survey of Kuwait's military requirements. Equipment delivered included A-4 Skyhawk aircraft and Hawk, Sidewinder, and TOW missiles.(8) Kuwait felt a certain unease with the closeness of this relationship, jeopardizing its precarious neutral position in inter-Arab policies. It made modest arms purchases from the Soviet Union with which Kuwait maintains diplomatic relations, the only Arabian Peninsula country, other than the Yemens, to do so. At the same time, the Kuwaitis were careful to exclude Soviet technicians from Kuwait, which reflects their deep suspicion of Soviet intentions.(9) In 1979 and early 1980 Kuwait extended this pattern of diversification with the purchase of sophisticated Soviet surface-to-surface missiles.(10)

Bahrain, though less modern and secularized than Kuwait, is generally considered the most advanced among the lower gulf states. The discovery of modest oil deposits in 1932 led to early development of a modern economic sector. In recent years Bahrain has sought to promote itself as the international commercial and communications center of the gulf. While most of the population is indigenous, by contrast with the other small gulf states (Oman excepted) where nonnatives are in the majority, it is about equally divided between Sunnis and Shia. Of the Shia, those of Iranian origin comprise about 10 percent of the total population. These, together with Indians and Pakistanis, play a role in the commercial sector out of proportion to their numbers and contribute a flavor of urbanity and middle-class pragmatism to the life of the country.(11) At the same time, the sectarian split, the substantial Iranian presence and the history of Iranian claims to Bahrain, revived, if ambiguously, since the fall of the shah, create a special concern over events across the gulf.

Unrest in the fall of 1979, tied to the visit of Khomeini's representative, Hujjat-al-Islam Sayyed Hadi al-Modarresi, seemed to lend special credence to the sectarian threat from Iran. The demonstrations, however, were apparently provoked by economic and political grievances put forward by petitioners who appealed to more than religious fundamentalists.(12) This fits a well-established pattern of radical ferment in Bahrain. While the Khomeini revolution may intensify that ferment, it arises from the lack of popular representation and tight control of the Khalifa family over a restive press and bourgeois class.(13)

Internal and external threats help promote very close relations with Saudi Arabia, symbolized by the projected causeway that the Saudis are committed to constructing to link their eastern province with Bahrain. Differences from contrasting levels of social development and Shia resistance to the Saudi fundamentalist Sunni influence set limits to the relationship, but Saudi self-interest dictates a solicitous concern for Bahrain. The causeway project is intended to help solidify the two countries' economic relationship and guarantee sufficient prosperity in Bahrain to check an upsurge of political unrest.(14)

Bahrain's armed forces are tiny, amounting, in effect, to a police force suitable for control of smuggling and illegal immigration. Its security rests on the close Saudi tie, generally friendly relations with its Arab neighbors, including, currently, Iraq and the presence of a U.S. naval command, MIDEASTFOR. This small force (consisting of five small vessels) shared base facilities at Jufair from 1949 with a British naval force until the British East-of-Suez military withdrawal in 1971. In that year of Bahrain's independence an agreement was reached with the new government for continued American use of the Jufair facilities. It was cancelled in 1973 following the October war, renewed in 1974, and extended in 1977, but with limitations on the use of the facilities.(15)

MIDEASTFOR, as a military and political demonstration of American concern for the stability and security of the area, with access to Bahrain commercial port facilities, provides a measure of psychological security. At the same time it is a prime target for Bahrain leftists and a source of embarrassment in the Arab world at times of strain in Arab-American relations. Bahrain's dilemma in this regard reflects the general ambivalence of the conservative Arab states of the gulf concerning tangible manifestations of the American security umbrella.

Qatar is still a tribal society and adheres to the same conservative interpretation of Sunni Islam as its immediate neighbor, Saudi Arabia. While some modernization of the political structure has occurred, political power remains in the hands of the hereditary ruling family, the Al Thani. Of a population of about a quarter-million, of which perhaps only some 60,000 are indigenous, 10 percent are of Iranian extraction.(16) There has not, however, been indication of significant sectarian or political tension. In general, there is certainly none of the spirited opposition and radical ferment of Bahrain and, to an extent, of Kuwait.

As in the case of Bahrain, the military forces are very small and defense against possible external threat is secured through a low-profiled external policy, good relations with neighbors, and very close ties with Saudi Arabia. Indeed, the Qatari position on Arab and international issues is essentially a carbon copy of the Saudi.(17) Like the Saudis, they have sought to diversify their international economic relations, welcoming European contractors and balancing Western and Middle Eastern expatriates with East Asians. In the short run Qatar's security seems reasonably well assured. In the long run it will depend on the ruler's capacity to adapt the old sociopolitical order so as to deal adequately with changed circumstances.

As with its small neighbors to the north, the federation of the United Arab Emirates disposes of military, political, and demographic resources quite incommensurate with the economic wealth and strategic location which make it important to the outside world. Nevertheless, like Kuwait, the UAE has undertaken an upgrading of its military forces, which consisted at independence of the British-created Trucial Oman Scouts and the Abu Dhabi Defense Force. In 1979 defense expenditures were $750 million and the armed forces numbered over 21,000. Most of the UAE's arms, including advanced jet fighters, have come from France and Great Britain.(18) Clearly the armed forces are more than just an internal security force. Beyond providing prestige and a symbol of national unity, however, their mission is uncertain.(19) It is clear that security against external threat must still rest largely on the nature of relations with Arab neighbors and Iran and on the success of domestic policies designed to promote the transformation of formerly separate, traditional shaikhdoms into a unified, modernizing nation.

The Iranian threat has not appeared to have a major unsettling impact. Like the other small states, the UAE is attempting to control the results of Khomeini's revolutionary appeal, while not giving unnecessary offense, thus far succeeding. The indigenous population and its strong, genuine Arabism provide a buffer. Cultivation of good relations with the Arab world at large (excepting the PDRY, and until very recently Iraq) and emulation of Kuwait's generous economic assistance to Arab and other Islamic states have helped to preserve its integrity. With earlier territorial disputes settled or shelved, foreign policy is now closely aligned with that of Saudi Arabia.

Perhaps what has been most significant in promoting the security of the UAE and stability of the lower gulf is the enlightened role of the Shaikh Zayid ibn Sultan al-Nihyan, as president of the federation, preserving and consolidating its unity despite the confident predictions of the breakup from many observers when it was formed in 1971. While continuing to rely on the traditional legitimacy of the seven shaikhly rulers, creation of a modern administrative-political structure has been initiated. Abu Dhabi has been generous in providing economic assistance to the four non-oil-producing members of the federation. Federal institutions, including a federal defense force, have been created and the traditional sharp rivalry among the UAE's two principal members, Abu Dhabi and Dubai, seems to have been significantly moderated if not ended with the latter's ruler, Shaikh Rashid ibn Sa'id al-Maktum, who accepted Shaikh Zayid's offer to become prime minister and form a new government in mid-1979.(20)

Yet, despite the maintenance of political stability and accommodation of the social strains attendant upon rapid economic development, the principal threat to the survival of the UAE and the other small states of the gulf is their massive dependence on expatriates for provision of services from unskilled labor to political and military advisory roles at the highest levels. This is especially true in the UAE, whose indigenous population is probably less than a fourth of the total, and in Kuwait and Qatar, where expatriates are also in a large majority.(21) Large numbers of South Asians perform unskilled and semiskilled labor, while thousands of middle-class Egyptian, Palestinian, and other Arab professionals are teachers, businessmen, and government employees. In addition, the role of Jordanian military officers in the small gulf states is a very important one.(22) The impact of more cosmopolitan (and politically more radical) values on these states is pronounced and feared, though subversive threats have been contained and the influence of new perspectives within traditional societies has probably been, on balance, positive. At the same time, there is a danger of growing disaffection among those who have made their careers there (especially the stateless Palestinians), and who are excluded from citizenship and its privileges.

In the long term the principal danger will be failure to create the indigenous human infrastructure necessary to maintain viable, modern economic and political systems and defense establishments. The need for dependence on expatriates, created by an irreversible commitment to rapid economic devel-

opment, will make this very hard to accomplish. The rulers of
these states are aware of the danger of internal subversion
but do not give evidence of sufficiently realizing the latter
problem. As one scholar, in looking at Qatar, has remarked:
"The influx of vast numbers of foreign personnel . . . has
resulted in repercussions for Qatari authorities. The government, faced with the fast pace of modernization, has lacked
the time to assess and deal with current and future problems
of a large expatriate population."(23)

Oman presents a contrast to the other Arab states of the
Persian Gulf, deriving largely from its relative physical
isolation (only a few miles of coastline of the detached
Musandam Peninsula territory of Oman actually border the
gulf). This helped over the centuries to preserve a quite
distinctive cultural difference, reinforced by the sectarian
anomaly of the Ibadhis in the interior. In the recent past
extension of Omani rule into East Africa and into territory
which is now part of Iran and Pakistan reinforced its different
orientation and perspective. Further, while avoiding the
colonial relationship experienced by the other small gulf states,
Oman has had longstanding and close ties with Great Britain.

Oman's ruler, Sultan Qaboos bin Said, also offers a
contrast to the rulers of the other states. While very much a
traditional Arab ruler, he is a Sandhurst graduate with a
European orientation, which gives him a dual outlook. Oman is
the least developed of these states in terms of political
institutions. Expatriates also play a significantly slighter role,
though Britons in the government and military and Jordanians
in the latter have taken on important functions. Intensive
efforts have been undertaken to replace foreigners in military
command positions with Omanis in the near future.(24) A
greater internal problem relating to the country's security is
the fact that there is no designated successor to Qaboos (his
marriage is thus far childless). Two other potential problems
are possible resentment in the interior of Oman at the disproportionate expenditure of revenue in the capital of Muscat and
in Dhofar Province (the latter reflecting the socioeconomic
aspect of the pacification effort in the south) and potential
future middle-class chafing under rule by a narrowly based
elite. These are not present threats and the beginning of a
move toward delegating and institutionalizing political authority
has been made while the local merchant community is prosper-
ing. Qaboos, moreover, enjoys genuine popularity.(25)

The greater security threat, again in contrast to the
situation of the other small gulf states, is external. This
threat took the form of a guerrilla war in Dhofar, indigenous
in its origins but promoted and broadened by the People's
Democratic Republic of the Yemen (South Yemen), and therefore, indirectly supported by the Soviet Union as well as
abetted by Iraq. Hence, Oman displays strong fear and hos-

tility toward those governments as well as the successors of its former ally, the shah, whose military assistance was crucial in bringing the Dhofar rebellion under control. A history of border disputes with the UAE and resentment of Kuwaiti aid to the PDRY during the rebellion have soured Oman's attitude toward those two states and relations with Bahrain and Qatar have been slight. With Saudi Arabia, despite some assistance in combatting the Dhofar rebellion, relations have not been cordial, reflecting historical suspicions from Saudi expansionism and border problems as well as a certain Saudi hauteur in bilateral dealings. (26)

Relations with the West, especially Great Britain and the United States, are contrastingly good, as they are with Jordan, whose military officers on loan have been an important contribution to Omani security, and Egypt, with which ties are close. American concern with Omani security has been substantial since the British East-of-Suez military phase-out in 1971. Yet Omani eagerness to establish a military relationship met generally with coolness on the American side until the enunciation of the "Carter Doctrine" in the president's state-of-the-nation address, following the Soviet invasion of Afghanistan. (27) Increased American access to military facilities in Oman and an agreement for storing fuels and equipment there for emergency use, key elements in the contemplated bolstering of the American military presence in the Persian Gulf-Indian Ocean area, were granted in return for increases in American military aid. (28) That aid will further strengthen armed forces of nearly 20,000 on which Oman currently spends about a fourth of its Gross National Product. These include a small navy, largely officered by British on loan or contract, and an airforce with 35 combat aircraft. (29)

In September 1979 an American military mission reviewed Oman's defense needs in connection with American concerns about the perception of the industrial world's vulnerability in the Strait of Hormuz. At that same time Oman put forward a "Protection of the Waters" plan, proposing that $100 million be provided by the states of the gulf, the United States, and other oil importers to strengthen the Oman navy for ensuring the security of the strait. Under its provisions, American, British, and European experts would also be involved to operate sophisticated electronic equipment, while gulf states would contribute troops. Iraq promptly rejected the plan, with Kuwait, Saudi Arabia, and other gulf states following suit. (30) It is interesting to note that since the cessation of patrols by the shah's expensive and sophisticated navy, the tiny force of very modest Omani vessels has overseen traffic through the critical passage without incident.

Immediately after rejection of the Omani plan, Iraq set forth a plan of its own, incorporating an offer of military assistance to Kuwait and Bahrain in the event of internal or

external threats. The Iraqi proposal went further than the
other, calling for the following elements: negotiation of a
collective security pact among the Arab states of the gulf,
conclusion of bilateral defense agreements with any state ob-
jecting to a collective arrangement, and creation of a joint
military command, with autonomous states, in charge of the
envisaged gulf security force.(31) The offer made to Kuwait,
if correctly reported, would be in dramatic contrast to earlier
policy toward that country and the initiative to take the lead
in organizing gulf security suggests a dramatic turn from
previous policy in the area as a whole. Since this ambitious
new departure currently has the most powerful indigenous
military apparatus in the Gulf region behind it, with very
considerable expansion - especially in its naval forces - now in
progress and, because both external and internal developments
have given the country's leadership a new sense of self-
confidence about its ability to play a major role, Iraq needs to
be regarded much more seriously than it has been.

Iraq evinced little interest in the gulf until after the 1958
overthrow of the monarchy. As noted above, Iraq's interest
then took the tangible form of an attempted takeover of Kuwait
in 1961. Thwarted in that attempt, Iraq resumed active involvement in the gulf only following the Ba'th's return to
power in 1968. British withdrawal from the gulf in 1971, the
demonstration of oil's growing importance in 1973, and, nega-
tively, the feud with the Syrian Ba'thi government that
thwarted projection of Iraqi influence into the Fertile Crescent
all served to focus attention on the gulf. Failure of a policy
to achieve a unified Arab position against Iranian territorial
claims and the United States-backed Iranian assertion of a gulf
policeman's role gave away to an ideological confrontation with
Iran and the conservative Arab states and support of radical
political forces in the gulf. From 1975 another shift brought
settlement of outstanding differences with Iran, agreement on
division of the Iraqi-Saudi neutral zone and pursuit of an
overall gulf policy more generally oriented toward detente and
rapprochement. Subsequently, the successful convening of
conferences in Baghdad to produce a very nearly unanimous
Arab stand against Camp David and the Egyptian-Israeli treaty
and the February 1979 agreement with Saudi Arabia on cooperation on border security and other issues, together with the
disarray of Iran's military forces in the wake of the Khomeini
revolution, have left Iraq in a position to embark on a major
new effort to take a leading role in the gulf.(32) The earlier
American tendency to overlook Iraq as a major factor in the
gulf - deriving from courtship of the shah, perception of
longstanding Iraqi internal instability, that country's own
slighter past interest in the gulf, and the hostility generated
between the United States and Iraq over the Arab-Israeli
conflict - may dangerously persist, obscuring both Iraq's new

orientation in the gulf and the assets it brings to promotion of a changed policy.

The Islamic conference of foreign ministers in late January 1980 in Islamabad, called to consider action on the Soviet invasion of Afghanistan, dramatically suggested how great the shift in Iraqi policy has been. Iraq's erstwhile radical Arab allies, Algeria, Libya, the PDRY, and Syria, boycotted the meeting while Iraq joined with Saudi Arabia in pushing through a condemnation of the Soviets' invasion and a demand that their troops be withdrawn.(33) Closer rapprochement with the Saudis and other conservative regimes in the gulf has thus been solidified and dramatized.

It is not suggested that Iraq has abandoned its revolutionary, Ba'thi principles, but that it is now prepared to countenance and work with a variety of Arab regimes, including those it was recently trying to subvert, in order to play a mediating and enabling role aimed at achieving common Arab goals. Further, without going so far as to claim a break with the Soviets, to whom they remain tied by the 15-year Treaty of Friendship and Cooperation signed in 1972, it is clear that the Iraqis are prepared forcefully to criticize and condemn Soviet actions that they view as inimical to their interests in the Middle East. Indeed, as Claudia Wright points out in a recent article in Foreign Affairs, the Iraqis, in line with their determination to prevent intervention by either superpower in the region, have warned the Soviets to stay out of the gulf, Saudi territory, and the Red Sea.(34) At the same time, she suggests, Iraq is trying through its present more subtle and friendly approach to wean Saudi Arabia away from the American embrace.(35)

The departure in regional policy to a more flexible, accommodationist approach may, in part, be aimed at enhancing internal stability, but it would seem to be the effect as well as the cause of a greater measure of confidence emanating from a new access of oil wealth, abatement (if not settlement) of the Kurdish problem, disintegration of Iran's military threat and Saddam Hussein's full assumption of the country's leadership. While stability could be threatened by renewed Kurdish opposition and intensified Shiite resentment, at present the regime would appear to enjoy fairly broad support.(36)

Iraq is not only relieved of a military threat on its eastern border, but, in contrast to the other Arab states of the gulf and in spite of its own Shiite majority, it does not fear Iran as a source of subversive threat. This reflects the secular basis of Iraq's government as well as the significantly greater secularism of much of the population. Fear in Iran is more indirect - that events in that country could bring superpower intervention, thwarting Iraq's own aim of regional leadership.(37)

Iraq has now clearly inherited Iran's position as preeminent military power in the gulf area. Its armed forces, including an army of 190,000 men with reserves of 250,000 an air force of 28,000 and a navy of 4,000, are far larger than those of any other gulf state. The army and air force are well equipped principally with advanced Soviet and French arms.(38) Moreover, acquisition of substantial new elements of military strength is in progress, especially for the naval and air forces. Agreement has recently been reached with the French for purchase of a large number of fighters and fighter bombers together with tanks and naval vessels. Moreover, in late February 1980 reports indicated that a two billion dollar deal was being arranged with a group of Italian defense firms, the contract to include four frigates, six corvettes, and a complete naval base and facilities.(39)

Finally, speculation about the likelihood of Iraq developing an atomic weapons capability in the 1980s have intensified with a French decision to supply weapons-grade, enriched uranium to Iraq, after they failed to persuade the Iraqis to purchase uranium of a lower enrichment level.(40)

Enlarged ambitions, large and growing military forces, a pragmatically effective diplomatic approach, and a new self-confidence suggest that Iraq's role in the gulf will expand importantly. It must now be accorded very serious attention.

It is, of course, with Saudi Arabia, among the states of the gulf, that the United States has its most important relations. As the wealthiest of the gulf countries - indeed of all the Middle Eastern countries - it is regarded as an economic superpower and a major regional and international power in political terms. Its wealth is, however, a two-edged sword both internally and externally. When a degree of consensus and solidarity exists among moderate and radical Arab states, Saudi Arabia can play a significant balancing and mediating role in Arab affairs and exercise influence beyond the Arab world. But when splits and conflicts among the Arab states, as in the post-Camp David period, deprive Saudi Arabia of a principal Arab ally and force accommodation with erstwhile adversaries, its role is then restricted and its position vulnerable.

Threats to Saudi Arabia's security are generally similar to those faced by the smaller Arab states of the gulf; they are internal but prompted from the outside. This is true of both threats that assume a radical political guise, and in the wake of the Khomeini revolution, those that take the form of a conservative religious challenge. Like their smaller neighbors, the Saudis have endeavored to neutralize these threats principally through reliance on sources other than their own military forces. As with several of them, however, it has begun to look more seriously in that direction. Further, as has been noted in most of those states, the principal long-term security

threat for Saudi Arabia may derive from rapid economic development which creates and sustains massive dependence on
expatriate skills.

In large measure the Saudis have looked to a close political, economic and military relationship with the United States
since World War II, to counter major threats to the kingdom.
Ambiguities and uncertainties, however, have begun to cloud
the relationship with growing Saudi doubts as to American
constancy and purpose in opposing Soviet intentions in the
Middle East and elsewhere and with the increasing strains
inherent in the coexistence of the special American relationships with both Saudi Arabia and Israel.

Saudi Arabia faces no immediate external challenges to its
national security. To meet potential challenges it has been
making substantial efforts to create adequate defenses.
Modernization of the country's armed forces began in a serious
way in 1964, in the face of the radical Arab threat (particularly from Nasser's Egypt) to Saudi Arabia and other monarchical regimes.(41) Though sharing its general security concerns, Saudi Arabia feared the ambitions of the shah's Iran
and certainly views the successor Khomeini regime as hostile
and dangerous. It has regarded Ba'thist Iraq as a prime
threat - more immediately as a promoter of subversion, more
distantly as a direct military threat. Despite the current
signs of a Saudi-Iraq rapprochement, the danger from that
quarter, especially in light of Iraq's continuing major military
build-up, must still be regarded as continuing. Further, with
the Nasser era not far removed and the nature of Egypt's
leadership after Sadat unpredictable, renewed threat from that
direction is surely not discounted. Israel certainly is feared
in the event of a new round of Arab-Israeli fighting, especially since the Israeli leadership warned that Saudi possession of
the F-15 fighter bombers, sold as part of the Middle East arms
package that passed the U.S. Senate in May 1978, would make
Saudi Arabia a confrontation state in another Arab-Israeli
war.(42)

Events in the Horn of Africa and the PDRY undoubtedly
fuel Saudi fears of possible intervention of Soviet proxy forces
in the gulf area. While some sources of instability in the gulf
may be diminished with a substantial increase in the amount of
consultation between Saudi Arabia and its neighbors, major
threats to the country's national security from several sources
remain and are seen to call for reliance on the nation's own
military resources.

Dollar figures for Saudi purchases of military items tend
to exaggerate actual increases in the size of the Saudi military
establishment, since expenditures are largely for the basic
infrastructural needs of armed forces whose development into a
large, effectively modernized fighting force has only recently
begun.(43) Nevertheless, acquisition of new weaponry has

been impressive, dramatized by the F-15 sale in 1978. The small navy, whose development was begun only in the early 1970s, is now being substantially expanded.(44) Ground and air forces continue to be strengthened with major purchases of weapons and weapons systems. The Saudi National Guard, designed to counter internal threats, has been undergoing a modernization program with upgrading of its armaments.(45) It will take some time for sophisticated modern weaponry to be absorbed effectively and manpower shortages – the total personnel in the armed forces (not including the National Guard) number fewer than 50,000 - impose a severe constraint. Saudi military forces will not be equal to potential threats in the near future but may discourage attack by making it costly while preparing for future challenges. In the meantime, the country's principal defense against external threat remains diplomatic accommodation and the use of economic largesse and financial power.

The American military relationship with Saudi Arabia dates from World War II, beginning in rivalry with the British who were shortly supplanted. The United States has since continued as principal supplier of military weapons, infrastructure, and training, although the British role in providing certain weapons systems has been important and the French role in this regard is expanding.(46) As stated in a United States government document, the American military commitment in Saudi Arabia is designed to support the following U.S. policy objectives: access to oil, encouragement of a stable, moderate Saudi Arabia, and protection of the Saudi market for American imports.(47) To these should be added the economic rationale of promoting exports and American jobs and the strengthening of Saudi Arabia's capacity to play a regional role. All of these are vital interests. Even more basic interests are involved on the Saudi side, as the military relationship is intended to provide a dependable source of weaponry and expertise to develop the nation's defense establishment and a strategic umbrella, in the guise of American military strength to deter the Soviet threat and the various sources of radical threats that derive from it.

The military relationship, however, is only part of a larger special relationship, built over some four decades, that former President Carter acknowledged in stating that "Saudi Arabia is one of our closest allies, staunchest friends and economic partners."(48) The role of the United States in initiating and promoting Saudi Arabia's economic development has been unique. (This was overwhelmingly a role played by private industry, most dramatically and effectively by the Arabian American Oil Company). Greatly expanded and diversified American business involvement in the kingdom and the significant roles played by the U.S. Army Corps of Engineers and the U.S.-Saudi Joint Economic Commission in assisting with project development reflect the continuing importance of the economic dimension of the bilateral relationship. The military dimension, discussed above, and the political are closely related to the economic. The last has been close, generally reflecting shared perceptions and concerns internationally and in Saudi Arabia's regional setting. For some time, with the enormous acceleration of the pace of economic development, the once dominant American position in the economic relationship has begun to erode and the Saudis have begun, generally, to diversify their relationship abroad. Largely this has reflected the great access of Saudi wealth since 1973 and the natural tendency to broaden sources of imports under such circumstances. As an elder American statesman observed five years ago, this is undoubtedly desirable.(49) This process has, however, lately been accompanied by strain.

American products and services, once viewed as nearly synonymous with top quality, may now perhaps be questioned, as reflected in reported Saudi chagrin with American mismanagement of the program to modernize and upgrade the Saudi Arabian National Guard.(50) Other sources of technology have earned Saudi respect and assumed growing importance in their contribution to Saudi development. The weakness of the dollar and other American economic problems have both a direct bearing on Saudi economic interests and a psychological impact on perceptions of American strength. Acquisition of advanced technology is regarded as compensating for economic loss through inflation and a weakened dollar, and as an earnest of American seriousness of purpose in responding to Saudi needs.(51) Failure to provide new technology as desired is a source of strain in the relationship. The most serious problems in the economic relationship, however, are those that are also political, especially the issues of the level of oil production and the Arab boycott.

Strains in the military-strategic relationship derive from differing perceptions as to the appropriate responses to various threats and the relative priority to be assigned to those threats. The Saudis do not view the Soviet threat as an immediate, military contingency. A rapid deployment force and American bases in the immediate area may be more unsettling than reassuring, especially since only the United States has openly spoken of military invasion of the oil fields and Israel of breaking the Arab oil weapon. What is much more desired is a credible American deterrent to Soviet-supported activity in Angola, Somalia, and elsewhere, and more effective American support to declared friends and allies, such as the shah. The Saudis are uneasy with both too close an American embrace and what they see as insufficient resolve and constancy in providing a general strategic umbrella against Soviet and Soviet-backed threats. Hence American initiatives tend to provoke an ambiguous response.(52)

American military-strategic commitments may not be perceived as truly relevant. Especially in light of the shah's
fate, the Saudi royal family may wonder if the American commitment is to the territory - that is, the oil fields - or to the
family. (The latter is, after all, not really the sort of
commitment the U.S. government can make.) The American
security umbrella does little to ward off overt or other threats
from radical states in the area. Indeed, too close an association with the United States increases Saudi vulnerability. In
the Saudis' view, Israel and the Arab-Israeli conflict, promoting radicalism and instability in the Middle East, pose a
threat to their national security equal at least to that of
the Soviets, and the United States does not see this.(53)
Real evidence of American determination to advance a comprehensive Arab-Israeli peace settlement and of willingness to
provide a continuing and dependable supply of late-model
weaponry would be far more reassuring than American bases in
the Persian Gulf-Indian Ocean area or pledges to counter a
Soviet attack.

It is the Arab-Israeli conflict and the Saudi perception of
the American approach to its settlement which produce the
principal political strains in the countries' relationship. Saudis
perceive American support of Israel not as reinforcement of a
bulwark against Soviet penetration in the Middle East but as
an abettor to it.(54) After having informed the United States,
in advance, that they regarded the approach to settlement
taken at Camp David mistaken and dangerous, the Saudis were
pressured to support the Egyptian-Israeli treaty and criticized, even attacked, for not doing so. Their discomfiture
increased as the Begin government's intransigence on the issue
of Israeli settlements in occupied Arab territories reinforced
doubt as to the possibility of any meaningful agreement on
Palestinian autonomy. Failure to act more forcefully in
opposing Israeli actions which the United States has consistently characterized as being illegal and an obstacle to peace
causes Saudi Arabia to doubt American seriousness of purpose
and sincerity. Jimmy Carter's repudiation of the American
vote in the United Nations Security Council on March 1, 1980,
approving a resolution to condemn the Israeli settlements,
provided the most recent confirmation of this doubt. The
likely failure to achieve progress in the autonomy talks may
shift the balance within the Saudi leadership so as to strain
American-Israeli relations further.(55)

As with the other conservative Arab states of the gulf,
what is feared more than overt threats from the Soviets or
others is subversion promoted by external antagonists or by
an environment of hostile and unstable forces. Khomeini's Iran
is, therefore regarded with disquiet. Indeed, the small Shi'a
community in Saudi Arabia's Eastern Province has been restive.(56) While the Saudi government enjoys a legitimacy based

on close alliance with the nation's Sunni Muslim establishment, Khomeini's revolution is feared for its destabilizing impact in the area - that it may have provided an opening to the Soviets or other destabilizing forces.

The seizure of the Grand Mosque in Mecca in November 1979 did point to failure to discern a threat from the right, but it was an aberration, recurrence of which tightened security and more generosity toward disgruntled tribal elements should avert.(57) While this incident seems not to have caused a conservative turn away from rapid development and modernization of the economy, the pressures generated by that process and the debate thus stirred over the appropriate direction of national development constitute a basic source of concern about the country's stability and security. In this connection, massive continuing dependence on Arab and other expatriate labor accelerates change in social and political attitudes, provides possible openings for subversion, and in the case of the large numbers of semipermanent Yemeni workers, promotes discontent with discrimination against noncitizens. Moreoever, while foreigners have been segregated on infrastructural and turn-key projects, the future, continuing need for large numbers of non-Saudis in managerial and operational roles suggests the generation of still more rapid attitudinal change and the instability and uncertainty flowing from it.(58)

In this context the greatest threat is likely to be that of an Arab radical/nationalist-inspired coup. A more assertive form of Arab nationalism may be gaining support in Saudi Arabia and if the growth of the military forces, especially the air force, is excessively rapid, an attempt to overthrow the government might emanate from that quarter. This, however, is a future and by no means inevitable outcome. For the present the government is stable.

In 1972 Congressman Lee H. Hamilton, chairman of the Subcommittee on the Near East of the House of Foreign Affairs Committee (now the Subcommittee on Europe and the Middle East of the House Committee on Foreign Affairs), observed that "the Persian Gulf area is going to be increasingly, and perhaps vitally, important economically and politically to the United States." Further, he counselled that "the problems this area raises need to be addressed in the United States with much more vigor and intensity."(59) His prediction has been fully borne out and his adjuration is as valid now as it was then. The gulf and the area adjacent to it are arguably of greater concern to the United States at present than any other part of the world, yet it is not at all clear that current policy fully and effectively responds to threats to American interests or takes sufficiently into account the needs and concerns of the United States' friends in the area.

Given present American military capacities in or readily transferable to the area, former President Carter's 1980 state-of-the-union address rhetoric - "an attempt by any outside force to gain control of the Persian Gulf region will be regarded as an assault on the vital interests of the United States of America, and such an assault will be repelled by any means necessary, including military force" - lacks complete credibility.(60)   Moreover,   it   deflects   attention   from   the potentially serious political threat of the Soviets.   Not only might Soviet power enter the gulf through a political role in Iran but the possibility of a normalization of Saudi-Soviet relations should not be ruled out.   It is, in any event, erroneous in the view of a former American ambassador to Saudi Arabia to assume that the Saudis could never be pushed into the arms of the Soviets.(61)   Not only strains in the American relationship, but the prospect of using Soviet politi-cal leverage in the Arab-Israeli conflict could induce a degree of Soviet-Saudi rapprochement.   Moreover, the predicted So-viet domestic oil shortage of the mid-1980s might well lead not to military invasion but to commercial entry into the gulf.(62) This is not to suggest that the military threat is not real or that only the introduction of Soviet political influence and power need be seriously contemplated; it is simply to caution that the latter danger needs to be factored into policy calcula-tions more seriously than now appears to be the case.

At the very least, it is a dangerous mistake to assume that the Saudis and other conservative Arab states of the gulf hold to a view of the Soviet threat that is identical with America's, deep as their concern may be.   The tendency of the United States to take Saudi sharing of American percep-tions on this and other issues for granted and its seeming assumption that no American actions in the Middle East could turn the Saudis away from their close relationship with this country are causes for Saudi resentment.(63)   This tendency is part of a pattern of approach to smaller countries every-where that has caused us to view the Middle East "not as an inclusive system of a balance of forces or as a complex of problems linked to each other . . . but in a fragmentary or sectoral approach occasioned by circumstances and needs."(64) This has led to an inability to perceive fully the linkage between the Arab-Israeli conflict and political and security issues in the gulf.(65)

Perhaps most obviously that linkage is evident in the large numbers of Palestinians who play important roles in the educational, professional, commercial and, in some instances, even in the governmental affairs of the Arab states of the Gulf.   While most are politically circumspect because of their stateless vulnerability, they are, of course, subject to the frustrations of Palestinians generally.   Their restiveness, flowing from the continuing failure to move toward a resolution

of the conflict which provides for meaningful Palestinian self-
determination, could lead to disruptive expressions of dissent.
In the absence of a settlement the vulnerable, moderate regimes of Saudi Arabia and her neighbors will continue to be
threatened by dangerous political cross currents in the Arab
world.

Thus, it is not sufficiently appreciated that the kind of
security relationship the United States seeks with Saudi Arabia
and other conservative Arab states of the gulf can ultimately
be accomplished only in the context of a general peace settlement.   Dangerous strains in the American relationship with
these countries can, in the meantime, be meaningfully alleviated only by discernible progress toward that goal.

The effects of a lack of such progress are compounded by
various kinds of ill-considered actions in the conduct of
American diplomacy with these countries.   The response to
crisis in the area is all too often to send American officials
who lack an informed awareness of the countries in question or
the past American relationships with them, in order to urge
their support of American interests.   As the former commander
of the U.S. Naval Middle East Force has commented: "The
sending of Secretary Brown to Saudi Arabia to talk arms and
military language (at a time the United States needs help with
hostages in Iran and Russians in Afghanistan) or the sending
of a Secretary Miller to Kuwait to suggest use of Kuwaiti
money to bolster the U.S. dollar - such transparent visits to
further United States 'interest' are insulting to those who live
here."(66)   Moreover, while Saudis may have become accustom-
ed to hostile broadsides from members of Congress, it cannot
be presumed that they dismiss as easily such gratuitous insults
from the White House as the characterization of Crown Prince
Fahd as a weak leader and the false assertion that the Saudis
had informed Jimmy Carter that they did not favor a Palestinian state.(67)   The president's refusal to send congratulations
to Islamic heads of state on the occasion of the 1,400th
anniversary of Islam (in November 1979) was not only an ill-
advised discourtesy, but may well have suggested to the Saudis and their neighbors that the United States was permitting
Khomeini to drive it to further, self-inflicted injury.

These and other instances of petty, self-demeaning American behavior are a counterpoint to a continuing American
susceptibility to illusion, which has permitted the assumption
that the Saudis and other conservative Arab states would line
up behind the Camp David peace process.   In a more exaggerated form, such illusion embraces the idea of a strategic
alliance among Israel, Saudi Arabia, and other moderate Arab
states.(68)   When all this is superadded to the bewildering
discontinuity of recent American foreign policy, most dramatically manifested in the United Nations Security vote of March 1,
1980 and its subsequent disavowal, the effect is not reassur-

ing. The playing out of the Camp David process seems to suggest that policy is based on a kind of Micawberish faith that something will turn up.

There is a compelling need for awareness of realities in the gulf, the will to face up to them and the ability to make and carry out policy accordingly. It was well put almost eight years ago in a pioneering congressional study of the gulf that stated that "this new era calls for prudent, low-key policies which will enable these states to develop free from foreign intervention, great power politics or domination by any other state."(69)

In the wake of Camp David and its impact on the Arab world and of the Khomeini revolution in Iran, the conservative Arab states of the gulf are subjected to dangerous pressures. Saudi Arabia, which earlier played a central balancing role in the Arab world, is now vulnerable and obliged to accommodate radical Arab forces sufficiently to maintain a modicum of consensus within which to operate. Especially important in this context is the incipient Saudi-Iraqi rapprochement and the signs on both sides of a desire for looser alignment with superpower patrons, together with a growing disposition to provide, with the other states of the Arab littoral, their own regional security. The stability and security of the gulf will be preserved only if American policy takes full account of all the issues that significantly impinge upon these countries and their relations with the United States and only if it deals with them as equals.

NOTES

1. See Clayton Fritchey, "Oil Dominoes," in The Washington Post, February 11, 1980.

2. See "Democracy in Kuwait: Election of New Assembly Near," The Middle East, no. 53 (March 1979).

3. John E. Peterson, "Kuwait, Soviet Activities and Gulf Security," in The Impact of the Iranian Events upon Persian Gulf and United States Security, ed. Z. Michael Szaz, Studies on Middle East Problems (Washington, D.C.: American Foreign Policy Institute, 1979).

4. See "Kuwait Sets the Stage: Democracy Back on the Road," The Middle East, no. 57 (July 1979); and "Kuwait," Middle East Economic Digest 24, 7 (February 15, 1980): 33-34.

5. Rowland Evans and Robert Novak noted that the Kuwaiti government easily contained an anti-American demonstration of Iranian immigrants on December 1, 1979. See "Lamentations from the Gulf" The Washington Post, January 7, 1980.

6. See "Kuwait, Emirates, Iraq Raise Oil Prices by $2," The Washington Star, January 30, 1980; and "Kuwait Oil Minister Denies That OPEC Has Power Struggle," Wall Street Journal, February 13, 1980.

7. See Peterson, "Kuwait, Soviet Activities and Gulf Security," p. 75.

8. See ibid., p. 78; House of Representatives, Committee on International Relations, United States Arms Policies in the Persian Gulf and the Red Sea Areas, Committee Print, 95th Congress, 1st session (Washington, D.C.: U.S. Government Printing Office, 1977), pp. 87-90; The Military Balance, 1979-1980 (London: International Institute for Strategic Studies, 1979), p. 41; and Dan Smith, "Arms Sales-Recent Contracts," in Middle East Annual Review, 1979 (London: World of Information, 1978), p. 65. Data on all the military forces in the gulf are found in Alvin J. Cottrell and Frank Bray, "Military Forces in the Persian Gulf," The Washington Papers, 6 (Beverly Hills and London: Sage Publications, 1978). As the publication date indicates, this study was prepared before the fall of the shah.

9. Peterson, "Kuwait, Soviet Activities and Gulf Security," pp. 79-80.

10. "Kuwait Buying Soviet Missiles," The Washington Post, February 10, 1980.

11. Emile Nakhleh, Political Development in a Modernizing Society (Lexington, Mass.: Lexington Books, 1976), p. 96.

12. "Gulf Security Stressed: The Story of Bahrain's Unrest," The Middle East, no. 60 (October 1979), p. 18.

13. See Emile Nakhleh, "Bahrain and Persian Gulf Security," in Szaz, The Impact of the Iranian Events, pp. 117-118.

14. Nigel Dudley, "Bahrain 1979: A Middle East Economic Digest Special Report" (London: Middle East Economic Digest Ltd., July, 1979), pp. 21 and 23.

15. Emile Nakhleh, "Bahrain and Persian Gulf Security," pp. 118-124; and House of Representatives, Committee on International Relations, United States Arms Policies, pp. 104 and 105.

16. John Whelan, "Qatar 1979: A Middle East Economic Digest Special Report" (London: Middle East Economic Digest Ltd., November, 1979), p. 3.

17. See, for example, expressions of policy on superpower intervention in the gulf region, the Arab-Israeli conflict, and Egyptian-Israeli treaty and Islamic solidarity as reflected in Qatar News (issued by the embassy of Qatar, Washington, D.C.). 4 (July-August 1979); 5 (September-October 1979); and 2 (March-April 1979).

18. The Military Balance, 1979-80, p. 46; and Middle East Annual Review, 1979, p. 63.

19. James H. Noyes, The Clouded Lens: Persian Gulf Security and U.S. Policy (Stanford, Calif.: Hoover Institution Press, 1979), p. 40.

20. John Whelan, "United Arab Emigrates: A Middle East Economic Digest Special Report" (London: Middle East Economic Digest Ltd., December, 1979), p. 3.

21. For estimates of the indigenous-nonindigenous population figures for the UAE and Kuwait, respectively, see House of Representatives, Committee on International Relations, United States Arms Policies, pp. 63 and 86. For the same information on Qatar, see Ragaei el-Mallakh, Qatar: Development of an Oil Economy (London: Croom Helm, 1979), pp. 22-23.

22. On this, see James H. Noyes, The Clouded Lens, pp. 42-43.

23. Ragaei el-Mallakh, Qatar, p. 20. For a recent analysis of perceptions of the internal threat, see "Domestic Dangers to Gulf Principalities," Strategic Mid-East and Africa (London) 6, 1 (January 7, 1980).

24. H.D.S. Greenway, "Tiny Oman Guards the Strategic Strait of Hormuz," The Washington Post, January 2, 1980.

25. See House of Representatives, Committee on International Relations, United States Arms Policies, p. 54; and John E. Peterson, "Oman, the Persian Gulf and U.S. Security," in Szaz, The Impact of the Iranian Events, pp. 172-174.

26. See Peterson, "Kuwait, Soviet Activities and Gulf Security," pp. 177-178. For an insight into current Omani-Saudi relations, see "Foreign Minister Denies Offer of Facilities or Bases to America," in Asharq al-Awsat [The Middle East] (London), January 23, 1980. The story denied any Omani intention of making bases or facilities available to the United States or any other outside country. The minister was reported as saying that the government of Sultan Qaboos had adopted a resolution to that effect and observed that the states of the area could alone preserve its security. A few days later the United States and Oman had worked out a tentative agreement to give American air and naval forces increased access to Omani facilities. See George Gedda, "U.S. Granted Access to Oman Bases," The Washington Post, February 12, 1980.

27. Peterson, "Kuwait, Soviet Activities and Gulf Security," p. 176. On the recommendation of a 1973 U.S. Department of Defense study team against American involvement in Omani defense affairs and on the 1975 visit of Sultan Qaboos to Washington, which produced an American expression of interest

in occasional use of the former RAF facilities on Masirah island and the subsequent sale of TOW missiles to Oman, see House of Representatives, Committee on International Relations, United States Arms Policies, pp. 57-59.

28. George Gedda, "U.S. Granted Access."

29. The Military Balance, 1979-1980, p. 43.

30. "Iraqi Drive to Counter Omani Plan," The Middle East, no. 61 (November 1979), p. 16; H.D.S. Greenway, "Tiny Oman Guards"; and "Oman: Security Plan Rejected," Strategic Mid-East and Africa 5, 38 (October 3, 1979).

31. "Iraqi Drive to Counter Omani Plan," p. 16.

32. On the evolution of Iraqi policy toward the gulf, see Edmund Ghareeb, "Iraq and Gulf Security," in Szaz, The Impact of the Iranian Events, pp. 40-61. See also chapter 7, "Foreign Policy," in Majid Khadduri, Socialist Iraq: A Study in Iraqi Politics Since 1968 (Washington, D.C.: The Middle East Institute, 1978).

33. Jonathan Randal, "Arab Split on Invasion Clouds Islamabad Parley," The Washington Post, January 23, 1980; and Karen Elliot House, "Looking for Friendships in the Persian Gulf," The Wall Street Journal, February 8, 1980.

34. Claudia Wright, "Iraq - New Power in the Middle East," Foreign Affairs, vol. 58, no. 2 (winter 1979/80), p. 258.

35. Ibid., p. 273.

36. On recent domestic events, see ibid., pp. 264-268; and "Iraq Works on Domestic Image," The Middle East, no. 59 (September 1979).

37. Rowland Evans and Robert Novak discuss this on the basis of interviews with Iraqi officials in "Not-So-Neighborly Iraq," The Washington Post, December 24, 1979.

38. On military weapons and their sources, see The Military Balance, 1979-1980, p. 40; and Middle East Annual Review, 1979, p. 64.

39. On the former package see Wright, op. cit., p. 262; on the latter, Strategic Mid-East and Africa 6.

40. Milton R. Benjamin, "France Plans to Sell Iraq Weapons-Grade Uranium," The Washington Post, February 28, 1980.

41. Cottrell and Bray, "Military Forces," p. 16.

42. On these and other conflict scenarios, see Dale Tahtinen, National Security Challenges to Saudi Arabia (Washington, D.C.: American Enterprise Institute for Public Policy Research, 1978), pp. 3-8.

43. See, for example, George C. Wilson, "U.S. Military Sales to Saudis 5 Times Total for Israelis," The Washington Post, October 11, 1979. In The Military Balance, 1979-1980, p. 44, the projected Saudi defense expenditure for that year is given as $14.18 billion.

44. Cottrell and Bray, "Military Forces," p. 21; and Middle East International, no. 116 (January 18, 1980), p. 3.

45. On the National Guard see Cottrell and Bray, "Military Forces," p. 21. For types and sources of recently purchased military equipment, see Middle East Annual Review (1979), p. 67.

46. On the last point, see Mideast Markets (published by the London Financial Times), 7, 6 (March 10, 1980): 11.

47. The comptroller General of the United States, Report to the Congress: Perspectives on Military Sales to Saudi Arabia (Washington, D.C.: Government Accounting Office, October 26, 1977), p. 4.

48. Statement made at a news conference of February 17, 1978 in Cranston, Rhode Island, quoted by Malcolm C. Peck in ed., King Faisal and the Modernization of Saudi Arabia, ed. Willard A. Beling, (Boulder, Colo.: Westview Press, 1980), p. 230.

49. Senator Mike Mansfield, Saudi Arabia, A Report, Committee on Foreign Relations, United States Senate, 94th Congress, 1st session (Washington, D.C.: U.S. Government Printing Office, 1975), pp. 5-6.

50. Strategic Mid-East and Africa 6, 6 (February 11, 1980): 1.

51. See remarks of Ahmed Zaki Yamani, Saudi Arabian minister for petroleum and mineral resources in Alan L. Otten, "Saudi Arabia Warns of Oil Cutback Soon if Purchasers Don't Provide Technology," The Wall Street Journal, February 13, 1980.

52. See, for example, two quite different reports of Saudi reaction to American reassurances on defense of the gulf area following the Soviet invasion of Afghanistan, published in the same edition of The New York Times: Christopher S. Wren, "Saudis Shy Away from Westernizing," and Bernard Gwertzmann, "American Say Saudis Welcome U.S. Resolve to Defend Persian Gulf," February 5, 1980.

53. See "Saudis Tip the Balance: A New Direction," in The Middle East, no. 55 (May 1979), p. 28. Also see John K. Cooley, "Iran, the Palestinians and the Gulf," Foreign Affairs 57, 5 (Summer 1979): 1027.

54. James E. Akins, "Saudi Arabia, Soviet Activities, and Gulf Security," in Szaz, The Impact of Iranian Events, pp. 89-90.

55. Cooley, "Iran, the Palestinians and the Gulf," p. 1031.

56. See Evans and Novak, "An Anxious Oil Kingdom," The Washington Post, December 17, 1979; and "Four Killed in Shiite Riot in Saudi Arabia Province," The Wall Street Journal, February 6, 1980.

57. Frank Giles, "Saudi Royal Family Moves to Defuse Threats to Rule," The Washington Post, March 2, 1980; and "After Mecca Incident: Saudis Looking for Long-Term Solutions," The Middle East, no. 63 (January 1980), p. 10.

58. On these and related issues see House of Representatives, Committee on International Relations, United States Arms Policies, p. 18; Arnold Hottinger, "Does Saudi Arabia Face Revolution?" The New York Review of Books, June 28, 1979; and Joseph J. Malone, "Saudi Arabia: The Pace of Growth and Spreading Influence," Middle East Problem Paper No. 17 (Washington, D.C.: The Middle East Institute, 1978).

59. Preface to House of Representatives, Committee on Foreign Affairs, Subcommittee on the Near East, U.S. Interests in and Policy Toward the Persian Gulf, Committee Print, 92nd Congress, 2nd session (Washington, D.C.: U.S. Government Printing Office, 1972), pp. v and vi.

60. See "If Russia Did It Again," The Economist 275, 7124 (March 15, 1980): 13.

61. James E. Akins, "Saudi Arabia, Soviet Activities," p. 92. On Soviet and Saudi hints at diplomatic normalization, see Keven Klose, "Soviet Union Suggest Ties With Saudis"; and Thomas W. Lippman, "Saudi Signal Wish to Establish Ties With Soviet Union," The Washington Post, February 1 and March 4, 1979.

62. On the question of future Soviet petroleum production see The World Oil Market in the Years Ahead, prepared by the National Foreign Assessment Center, Central Intelligence Agency (Washington, D.C.: U.S. Government Printing Office, 1979), pp. 37-42.

63. Akins, "Saudi Arabia, Soviet Activities," p. 99.

64. Jacques Freymond, "La crise iranienne. Révolution national - Dimension internationale." Politique Etrangére, no. 2, 1979 (Paris), p. 162.

65. See R. K. Ramazani, Beyond the Arab-Israeli Settlement: New Directions for U.S. Policy in the Middle East (Cambridge, Mass.: Institute for Foreign Policy Analysis, Inc., 1977), p.

16. The destabilizing effects of the Arab-Israeli conflict on the states of the Persian Gulf were noted in a pioneering House committee report. See House of Representatives, Subcommittee on the Near East of the Committee on Foreign Affairs, The United States and the Persian Gulf, Committee Print, 92nd, Congress, 2nd session (Washington, D.C.: U.S. Government Printing Office, 1972), p. 10.

66. Marmaduke G. Bayne, "Why Arabs Look Down on the American Eagle," The Christian Science Monitor, Tuesday, March 11, 1980.

67. William B. Quandt, "The Middle East Crisis," Foreign Affairs 58, 3, America and the World, 1979 (January 1980): 554.

68. See Rita Hauser, "Israel, South Africa and the West," The Washington Quaterly 2, 3 (Summer 1979): 80-81. For comment on the illusory nature of such a scheme, see George Ball, "Crisis in Israeli-American Relations," Foreign Affairs 58, 2 (Winter 1979/80): 250.

69. House of Representatives, Committee on Foreign Affairs, Subcommittee on the Near East, The United States and the Persian Gulf, Committee Print, 92nd Congress, 2nd session, (Washington, D.C.: U.S. Government Printing Office, 1972), p. 10.

5 Iran: Political and Security Assessment

Charles G. MacDonald

The Iranian Revolution has cast a cloud of uncertainty over the entire Persian Gulf region as the United States and other Western states scramble to protect their strategic interests and oil-dependent economies. While the final impact of both the seizure of the American hostages and the Soviet invasion of Afghanistan is yet to be determined, the Islamic Republic of Iran remains caught in the throes of an internal power struggle, the outcome of which could affect the stability of other gulf governments. The political situation remains mercurial as Iran aspires to form a unified Islamic republic, free of foreign influences, but faces a continuing political struggle between opposing religious, nationalist, and ethnic forces. Multiple power centers have created an anarchic situation in which no government has had a single voice since the departure of the shah.

Ayatollah Khomeini, meanwhile, has remained the guiding spirit of the revolution and has been recognized as the ultimate guardian of the constitution (Vilayat-i Faqih). He has been successful in avoiding a direct confrontation with difficult political issues, while systematically isolating the "enemies of the revolution" that threaten his power. He has proved to be a master at balancing opposing forces against one another, and has given his full support to no individual or group.

While the Iranian Revolution has brought dramatic change, its achievements have been severely limited by political infighting. Each issue facing the government, from the various elections to the question of the American hostages, has become politicized. Sporadic fighting between ethnic minorities and the central government, and incidents between vying political and religious factions have come to weaken Iran's defenses, as the Soviet Union's presence looms on the northern horizon and Iraq eyes Iran's western provinces.

117

The purpose of this chapter is to assess Iran's political context and security situation with a view to understanding the current developments and the factors and forces that influence Iran's future. The political context is examined first in terms of the changing political scene, the struggle for power, and the search for legitimacy. Finally the security situation is assessed according to the status of the military, threats to Iran's security, and the question of regional stability.

POLITICAL CONTEXT

Iran has been transformed from a monarchy that former American President Jimmy Carter described in January 1978 as "an island of stability in one of the most troubled areas in the world,"(1) to an Islamic republic in search for an identity and suffering from a continuing revolutionary upheaval. The shah's power and legitimacy were swept away by the forces of the revolution. The consolidation of these disparate forces into a new Islamic republic has proven to be a slow and difficult process.

Changing Political Scene

Iran has experienced a series of governments since 1979. In the wake of increasing antigovernment violence, General Azhari resigned as prime minister on January 1, 1979. His military government was followed on January 4 by the civilian government of Shapur Bakhtiar. The Bakhtiar regime was established as a transitional government to maintain authority after the shah. A regency council was created on January 13, 1979 to assume the shah's duties. The shah departed three days later.

In Paris Ayatollah Khomeini, who was preparing for his return to Iran, announced the formation of the Islamic Revolutionary Council on January 13, 1979. After political maneuvering between the Bakhtiar government and Khomeini's supporters, the Ayatollah returned to Iran on February 1, 1979 to the cheers of millions. His charisma and widely recognized opposition to the shah made him the emergent authority in Iran, despite the continued presence of the Bakhtiar regime. Shortly after Khomeini's arrival, Bakhtiar called for a government of "national unity" with Khomeini. Khomeini was uncompromising and demanded Bakhtiar's resignation.

On February 5th Khomeini named Mehdi Bazargan to head a "provisional government" that came to exist simultaneously with the Bakhtiar government. When it appeared that civil

war would ensue, the military announced its neutrality.
Without military support, Prime Minister Bakhtiar resigned on
February 11, 1979. Bakhtiar's departure signaled a victory
for the Bazargan "provisional government" and for the revolution. Prime Minister Bazargan soon named others to his
government, including nationalist leader Karim Sanjabi as
foreign minister.

The Bazargan government, however, realized only a
semblance of authority as it vied with Khomeini aides,the
Islamic Revolutionary Council, and the revolutionary komitehs.
At the end of February Bazargan threatened to resign as the
komitehs, who were responsible for secret courts, summary
trials, and executions, continued to ignore the government.
Finally, Bazargan traveled to Qum on the eighth of March,
reportedly to resign. (Khomeini had left Tehran for Qum the
week earlier, indicating that he would guide the revolution
from there.) Khomeini refused to accept Bazargan's resignation, and indicated that the provisional government had his
full confidence. This followed an earlier criticism of the
government by Khomeini; he had called the government
"weak." In mid-March Khomeini reportedly took steps to curb
the komitehs; he required that future trials be held under the
direct supervision of the Islamic Revolutionary Council and the
provisional government.

At the end of March a two-day referendum formally approved the establishment of the Islamic Republic, thus ending
the 2,500-year-old monarchy. On April 1st Khomeini announced the establishment of the Islamic Republic of Iran and
proclaimed "the first day of the Government of God."

After the referendum the government of Prime Minister
Bazargan continued to be at odds with the komitehs and the
Islamic Revolutionary Council. The summary courts and
executions continued. Shortly after former Prime Minister
Hoveida was executed on April 7th, Foreign Minister Sanjabi
resigned. He denounced the continued excesses of the
komitehs and openly criticized the council as being "despotic."

The provisional government and the Revolutionary Council
continued to act independently, and often at odds, until the
middle of July. Prime Minister Bazargan then announced that
four members of the Revolutionary Council would assume
positions in the government, and that cabinet members would
participate in the Revolutionary Council. The two institutions
continued to act separately even though some memberships
(and competing factions) overlapped.

The next step in the revolution was to establish a new
constitution. A draft constitution, published in mid-June
1979, provided for an "all-powerful legislature and a strong
President,"(2) but only a minor clerical influence. A constituent assembly of about 300 was to have been elected to debate
and approve the constitution, but a smaller Assembly (Council)

of Experts, numbering 73, was decided upon by Khomeini. The smaller Assembly of Experts was reportedly justified by the unsettled conditions within the country. The Assembly of Experts was elected on August 3-4, 1979, but a number of political groups boycotted the elections.

The Assembly of Experts, in session from August 19   to November 15, 1979, refashioned the original draft of the constitution. It strengthed the power of the clerics and undercut the powers of the president and the Majlis. Most important in this regard was the recognition of virtually unlimited powers of "the Great Ayatollah Khomeini" as the faqih (leader). After approval by the Assembly of Experts, the constitution was formally approved by a referendum on December 2-3, 1979, but again not without opposition.

While the Assembly of Experts was considering the draft constitution, a group of militants calling themselves the "Students who Follow the Line of the Imam," seized the American embassy and took hostages November 4, 1979. The seizure of the American embassy, among other things, brought an end to the provisional government of Mehdi Bazargan, who finally succeeded in his resignation attempt. Khomeini then ordered the Revolutionary Council to assume responsibility for the government.

After initially keeping the same government, the Revolutionary Council announced a new government on November 15, 1979 that included Abolhassan Bani-Sadr as minister of finance and economic affairs and supervisor of the foreign ministry. The November 15th change of government coincided with the approval of the new constitution by the Assembly of Experts and the disclosure of the names of the members of the Revolutionary Council. Ayatollah Beheshti was identified as chairman of the council. Later in the month Bani-Sadr was removed from his role in the Foreign Ministry, and Sadegh Ghotbzadeh, the former head of National Iranian Radio and Television, was named foreign minister.

The presidential election, held in accordance with the new constitution, was the next significant development. After the withdrawal of Jalal al-Din Farsi, who was the Islamic Republican Party's candidate, Bani-Sadr was elected on January 25, 1980 with a reported 75.7 percent of the vote. Ayatollah Khomeini formally installed Bani-Sadr as President on February 4, 1980. Bani-Sadr did not, however, name a prime minister at that time. In an apparent political compromise, Bani-Sadr assumed the chairmanship of the Revolutionary Council, the post held by Ayatollah Beheshti. The council continued to be responsible for the government. The ministers were not changed.

The month after Bani-Sadr was installed as president, the first round of the Majlis (National Consultative Assembly) elections were held. The Islamic Republican Party claimed

victory with an estimated 49 seats to 18 seats for supporters
of Bani-Sadr. The second round, not held until May 9th
because of an investigation of voting irregularities in the
March 14th round, again resulted in a victory for the Islamic
Republican Party. Not all of the 270 seats in the Majlis were
filled, however, because ethnic unrest had prevented elections
in some areas, and some of those elected had their credentials
rejected.

As the newly constituted Majlis was preparing to approve
a new prime minister, prior to dealing with the hostage question, it appeared in June 1980 that the Islamic Republic of Iran
was about to establish its first constitutional government. New
uncertainty then arose as Ayatollah Khomeini publicly decried
the power struggle between president Bani-Sadr and Ayatollah
Beheshti's Islamic Republic Party that controlled the Majlis.
Khomeini stated that he was worried "about the incompatibility
that exists in the Islamic Government organs," and that "the
Islamic Republic could be defeated by those who are on our
side."(3) This criticism by Khomeini signaled that the political
future of neither President Bani-Sadr nor the newly elected
Majlis was certain.

Struggle of Power

To understand the nature of Iran's changing political scene, it
must be viewed as an ongoing struggle for power and legitimacy. This struggle can be seen as the political process in
which the various participants attempt to affect the structure,
identity, and goals of the Islamic Republic of Iran.

Iran's revolution has seen a number of disparate groups
vying for power. Although they have been commonly identified by such labels as the right (religious extremists), the
center (Mossadegh-style nationalists), the left (communists),
and the ethnic minorities, these labels were and are misleading. The politically active groups tend to be much more
complex and to defy categorization because of crosscutting
loyalities, competing factions within groups, and shifting
alliances. The shah faced a broad spectrum of opposition that
encompassed many unlikely allies. The shah's departure
brought the differences within the opposition to the fore.

Those commonly referred to as the "right" consisted of
the religious opposition. This religious opposition was by no
means monolithic. Foremost were the followers of Ayatollah
Khomeini. Following his exile to Iraq, Khomeini became the
symbol of resistance to the shah. His supporters called for
the establishment of an Islamic Republic in which Khomeini
would provide moral direction. In addition to Khomeini's
leadership, Dr. Ali Shariati, a sociologist, philosopher of
history, and teacher of Islam, had a large and varied follow-

ing.   His teachings were part of a popular Islamic reform
movement centered at Husayniyah Irshad from 1967 until 1973,
when it was closed by the government.   The original managing
board of Husayniyah Irshad included, among others, Ayatollah
Mutahhari.   (Mutahhari was later identified as the chairman of
the Revolutionary Council at the time of his death in May
1979.)

Ali Shariati died in London in 1977, but the impact of his
writings and his philosophical contributions to the Iranian
Revolution remain at the heart of Iran's continuing power
struggle.   Strongly influenced by the philosophy of Frantz
Fanon, Dr. Shariati, challenged the traditional roles of the
clergy and emphasized the importance of social commitment and
the revolutionary content of Islam.   Shariati echoed the Third
World writings of Fanon, focusing in particular on his criticism
of imperialism and his call for revolutionary change.

Shariati and Khomeini were each adamantly opposed to the
rule of the shah and shared many supporters.   Their policies
differed, however, on the subject of the role of the clergy in
government.   Khomeini, more traditional in his beliefs, maintained that the people should follow the guidance of religious
leaders.   Shariati, like Fanon, was strongly opposed to political roles for the clergy.   This has subsequently become a
central issue in the struggle between the religiously based
nationalists supporting President Bani-Sadr and the hard-line
clerics of the Islamic Republican Party under the leadership of
Ayatollah Beheshti.

In much the same way that numerous groups and individuals have claimed to be followers of the line of Khomeini, many
different groups also claim to be followers of the writings of
Shariati - notably the Mujahidin-i Khalq and the Furqan.   It is
the revolutionary philosophy of Shariati that has served as the
conjuncture for the secular and religious nationalists and has
confounded   any   simple   right/left   interpretation   of   Iran's
political spectrum.

The Mujahidin-i Khalq is often referred to as Iran's
largest leftist group, but is also a militant religious group with
socialist leanings.   It has opposed the rising strength of the
hard-line clerics of the Islamic Republican Party, and had
earlier aligned itself with Ayatollah Shariat-Madari in the
debate over the revision of the constitution.

The clandestine Furqan is a group that claimed responsibility for the assassination of a number of revolutionary
figures, including Ayatollah Mutahhari and General Gharani.
It has been called "counterrevolutionary" and "anti-Islamic."
Its supposed basis on the Koran, however, and its alleged
leader being Hojatoleslam Akbar Qudasi suggest that the Furqan has acted within the revolution, rather than against it.

Mossadegh-style nationalists represent what has been
called the center of Iran's political spectrum.   The National

Front of Karim Sanjabi and the Freedom Front of Mehdi Bazargan have been the most prominent, and each had their roots in
the Mossadegh era.   The Freedom Front worked more closely
with the Khomeini movement at first, despite the sometimes
uneasy alliance between secular nationalists and Islamic
leaders.   The National Front, active under Mossadegh and
again in the early 1960s, resurfaced in December 1977.   It
consisted of the Iran Party led by Kazem Hassibi and Shapur
Bakhtiar, the Iranian Nation's Party of Dariush Foruhar, and
the League of Iranian Socialists of the National Movement led
by Reza Shayan.(4)   The National Front initially appeared to
seek a constitutional monarchy with a strong Majlis, but after
Sanjabi's public support for Khomeini, came to advocate the
Ayatollah's uncompromising position.   Bakhtiar was expelled
from the National Front following his assumption of the care-
taker government just prior to the shah's departure.
     At first, members of the Freedom Front and the National
Front assumed prominent positions in the "provisional government"; later they became the target of rumor, accusation, and
arrest as the rivalry between the hard-line clerics and the
nationalist leaders reemerged.   The center appeared to be the
target of a well-orchestrated campaign of character assassination by the militants holding the American Embassy – a campaign that served the interests of the Islamic Republican
Party.   Among those accused were Abbas Amir-Entezam, a
former deputy prime minister under Bazargan and ambassador
to Scandinavia; Hassan Nazih, head of the National Iranian Oil
Company and president of the Iranian Bar Association; Nasser
Minachi, minister of information; and Admiral Alavi, head of
the Iranian Navy.   Others, including Admiral Madani and Mehdi Bazargan, were also the target of rumors.   In addition,
National Front Majlis candidate Abolfazl Qassemi's credentials
were rejected after his election, and controversy delayed the
run-off election in Isfahan where Karim Sanjabi was a candidate.   Qassemi was subsequently reported linked with the
alleged July 1980 coup attempt and arrested.
     The apparent disintegration of the center, and especially
of the National Front, has been the result of intragroup
feuding, as well as its rivalry with the Islamic Republican
Party.   In May 1980 eight members of the Central Council of
the National Front resigned over internal procedural questions
concerning party leadership.
     Within the center a number of moderate religious figures
can also be found.   Ayatollah Taliqani, prior to his untimely
death, was viewed by many as an intermediary between the
hard-line clerical right and the secular nationalists.   Ayatollah
Shariat-Madari, though regionally based, had assumed positions
that would place him in the center.   After the Majlis elections,
a number of clerics who were candidates of the Islamic Republican Party were also reported to be supporters of President
Bani-Sadr.(5)

The National Democratic Front, led by Hedayatollah Matin-Daftari, represented a left-of-center group that was quick to challenge what was seen as a move toward a clerical "dictatorship." The National Democratic Front, together with Ayatollah Shariat-Madari, opposed the decision to elect an Assembly of Experts instead of a Constituent Assembly. In August 1979 the National Democratic Front was attacked when it demonstrated for press freedom; hundreds were injured. The National Democratic Front became an early casualty in Iran's internal power struggle and is now banned.

The left has consisted primarily of the Tudeh Party, the Fedayin Khalq, the Fedayin Khalq guerrillas, and the previously mentioned Mujahidin-i Khalq. Despite Khomeini's early charge that those who were not Islamic were "enemies of the revolution," the leftist groups have claimed to be supporters of Khomeini and to follow his "line." The leftists, however, have strongly opposed Ayatollah Beheshti's Islamic Republican Party. The leftists became the subject of an attack from the right when on April 18th at Friday prayers the hard-line clerics called for all political groups on university campuses to close their offices. President Bani-Sadr announced the removal of the leftists on April 22, 1980 when he proclaimed the "great cultural revolution."(6) Then in June a rally of the Mujahidin-i Khalq was attacked by religious extremists known as Hezbollahi, and fired on by the Revolutionary Guard.(7) Leftist leaders charged that the Hezbollahi extremists were directed by Ayatollah Beheshti.(8)

While the left has suffered from the power struggle within the revolution, it has also experienced internal schisms. Some leftists have come to oppose the clerics, while others support the clerics because of their antiimperialist philosophy.

The ethnic minorities, representing a composite of the right, center, and left, have primarily sought autonomy from the central government. The Kurds and Azerbaijanis represent the most significant opposition, but are not unified among themselves in determining their goals. Fighting has continued off and on in Kurdistan, where Kurdish rebels have defied the efforts of the central government to restore its control. A potentially more dangerous conflict appeared to be developing in Tabriz in January 1980. A civil war launched by the 12 to 15 million Turkish-speaking Azerbaijanis could pose a "greater threat to Khomeini's efforts at unity than all the other ethnic groups combined."(9) The Azerbaijani religious leader, Ayatollah Shariat-Madari, played down the developments and effectively diffused the crisis at a time when Soviet troops were reported across the border. The Azerbaijani leadership apparently did not wish to trade their difficulties with the disorganized Iranian central government for potential Soviet rule.

Ethnic unrest has also included the Arabs of Khuzistan, the Turkomans, the Balouchis, and the Qashqais. While the various groups seek increased regional autonomy, there has been little coordination among the different ethnic groups. Moreover, competing factions within the ethnic groups have often been played off against each other by the central government.

As the revolution progressed, opposition to Khomeini was reported to have formed outside of Iran behind former Prime Minister Shapur Bakhtiar, General Gholam Oveisi, and General Bahram Aryana.(10) Supporters of Bakhtiar formed a group in the United States called the Iran Freedom Foundation which unsuccessfully sought permission to broadcast on Voice of America.(11) General Oveisi, however, reportedly established a radio transmitter in Iraq after receiving support from Iraqi President Saddam Hussein.(12)

As the various protagonists participate in the struggle for power in Iran, the number and makeup of the groups continue to change and the list of casualties continues to grow. While Ayatollah Khomeini has periodically shifted his support to keep an internal balance, he has also persisted in calling for Islam to be spread to all spheres of Iranian life. To accomplish this Islamic "purification," a "great cultural revolution" has been declared and an ever-growing number of institutions have been purged of "all that is not Islamic." This list includes, among others, the military, the mass media, the bureaucracies, and the universities. An apparent result of this Islamic "purification" is the gradual solidification of power by the hard-line clerics, the vanguard of Iran's Islamic revolution.

Search for Legitimacy

Legitimacy in revolutionary Iran has been tied to the two driving forces of the revolution, Islam and nationalism. These have been uniquely blended in the person of Ayatollah Khomeini. In fact, Khomeini has been the foremost source of legitimacy throughout the revolutionary turmoil. His charisma has given him a much greater popular following than the shah ever had. His banners and large colored posters are displayed throughout Iran, among the Shia in Iraq, and even among the Sunni. Khomeini's personal support has been sought and claimed by various groups from the central government to the militants who call themselves the "Students who Follow the Line of the Imam." Iran's historic personalism is manifest in Ayatollah Khomeini, who is now perceived by many as the Imam.

A second source of legitimacy in revolutionary Iran has been opposition to the shah, which initially served as a unifying factor. Groups and individuals with a history of anti-shah activity, suffering at the hands of Savak, and years of imprisonment became highly revered. Opposition to the shah has proved to be limited as a unifying factor, however, as cooperation among revolutionary groups began to unravel with the shah's departure.

By the fall of 1979 a new cohesive factor was needed as the revolution seemed to be losing its momentum and disintegrating. In November, prior to the seizure of the American embassy, Khomeini began to use anti-American rhetoric to fuel the revolution. He stated, "All our problems come from America. All the problems of the Muslims stem from America."(13) By playing upon the close ties between the shah and the United States, anti-American feelings were easily cultivated as a unifying factor. This reflected both the anti-Western and antiimperialist sentiment in the writings of Khomeini and Shariati. The seizure of the American embassy proved to be an instant focal point for new revolutionary enthusiasm. It also provided a ready-made scapegoat.

Legitimacy in Iran is now in transition. Khomeini's health is fragile. His ability to continue to play an active role is limited by his age and condition. Anti-American energies have subsided as the hostage question became locked in Iran's internal politics. Now that the Majlis has met to approve a prime minister, and the Islamic republic has established its first constitutional government, the new constitution is becoming the symbol of legitimacy.

The constitution, as revised by a clergy-dominated Assembly of Experts, has shifted power away from the president and to the clergy. It places absolute power in the hands of the "Great Ayatollah Khomeini," the faqih. Clerical power is also to be exercised through the Council of Guardians, Assembly of Experts, High Council of the Judiciary, and what has become a cleric-dominated Majlis.

At the top of the power structure is the faqih. The faqih has the authority to appoint the six religious jurists of the twelve-member Council of Guardians (the six lawyers remaining are to be named by the High Council of the Judiciary and approved by the Majlis); to appoint the highest judicial authorities; to command the armed forces; to appoint the chief of the general staff, the commander of the Revolutionary Guards, and the commander-in-chief of the three armed forces; to approve presidential candidates; to dismiss the president; to declare war; and to grant pardons (Principle 110). The constitution provides that the faqih (or if no single candidate is acceptable, a Leadership Council of three or five) be selected by an elected Assembly of Experts according to provisions established by the Council of Guardians (Principles 107, 108). A faqih or a member of the Leadership Council can be removed by the Assembly of Experts (Principle 111).

The Council of Guardians, consisting of the six religious jurists appointed by Ayatollah Khomeini and six lawyers named by the High Council of the Judiciary headed by Ayatollah Beheshti, has the authority to interpret constitutional law (Principle 98). A majority of the Council of Guardians can decide that a constitutional law contradicts Islamic decrees, but a majority of the six religious jurists can veto a Majlis law for not being in accord with Islam (Principle 96). In addition, the religious jurists are given the authority over the creation of the Assembly of Experts that is to select the new faqih (Principle 108) or remove the faqih (Principle 111). Once the Assembly of Experts is established, the law providing for the number and qualifications of the experts, the manner of their election, their terms, and the internal regulation of their sessions, cannot be changed except by the Assembly of Experts itself (Principle 108).

The Majlis (270-member National Consultative Assembly) is empowered to enact laws within the limits set by the constitution (Principle 71), but cannot pass laws that contradict Islam (Principle 72). The Majlis can also conduct investigations (Principle 76) and should approve international agreements (Principle 77). The Majlis approves the president's choice of prime minister (Principle 124). The ministers, appointed by the prime minister and approved by the president, must also receive a vote of confidence from the Majlis (Principle 133). The Majlis can also interpellate ministers and can dismiss ministers by not granting a vote of confidence (Principle 89).

The president, theoretically the "holder of the highest official power next to the office of the leader" (Principle 113), is primarily an administrator. His power was greatly reduced by the revision of the constitution. While he is responsible for the workings of the government, the Majlis must approve any agreements he reaches with other governments (Principle 125) and his nomination for prime minister (Principle 124). Should the president be unable to fulfill the term of his office, a Temporary Council of the Presidency is to assume his duties (Principle 130). The Temporary Council is to be composed of the head of the Supreme Court, the head of the Majlis, and the prime minister. The Temporary Council is, in fact, granted more power than the president; its government cannot be interpellated by the Majlis, nor receive a vote of nonconfidence (Principle 132).

The High Council of the Judiciary, in addition to naming the six lawyers on the Council of Guardians (Principle 91), "is responsible for bringing about justice" (Principle 156). It consists of the Head of the Supreme Court and the Attorney General, each appointed by Khomeini, and three judges who are elected by the judges of the country (Principle 158).

While the constitution does include internal checks and balances pertaining essentially to the everyday administration

of the government, the clerical element has the power to
stalemate all opponents. If the faqih (Ayatollah Khomeini or
his successor) choses to exercise absolute authority, the
constitution so provides.(14)

SECURITY SITUATION

Security and freedom of action have long been Iranian objectives. Iran, with a history of foreign influence and at times
domination, is sensitive to potential threats to its sovereignty
and territorial integrity. Under the shah Iran's security
interests were tied to both threats of external attack and
internal subversion. In addition, the shah identified Iran's
security with regional stability and extended Iran's "security
perimeter" to the Indian Ocean.(15)

   Since the revolution, the security goals of the Islamic
republic have been unclear. Revolutionary goals have emerged
that appear to contradict Iran's traditional defensive concerns.
Accordingly, Iran's security goals must be assessed with a
view to the complex internal situation and the desire by some
to export Iran's revolution.

Military in Revolutionary Iran

Iran's military mushroomed in the 1970s after the British
decision to leave the Persian Gulf in 1971 and after the oil
embargo and price rise of 1973-1974. Iran's defense expenditures soared from $1.023 billion in 1971 to $5.5 billion in 1974,
and to $9.942 billion in 1978.(16) These massive expenditures
under the shah provided the new Islamic republic with an
estimated $60 billion arsenal.(17)

   Despite the presence of this highly sophisticated arsenal,
the military nearly disintegrated in the first days after the
shah's departure. Even though the military assumed a neutral
position vis-a-vis the Bakhtiar regime, many of its ranking
officers either fled or became targets of the summary justice of
the komitehs. Many of the soldiers deserted.

   By March 1980 the military seemed to be regrouping.
Defense Minister Chamran in an interview placed the 500,000-
man military at about 75 percent strength.(18) This represented quite a contrast with the almost deserted barracks at
the beginning of the revolution. The military, however,
continued to suffer from a serious lack of maintenance and
spare parts. Chamran indicated that only about "a quarter of
the helicopters and fixed-wing aircraft were being kept air-
worthy."(19) Revolutionary Iran had earlier turned to the
United States for spare parts in October 1979, but this flow

was abruptly halted the next month when the American embassy was seized.

Apart from the initial purges and desertions and the continuing maintenance problems, the military has not fared well in Iran's internal power struggle. Admiral Alavi, the Harvard-educated head of the Navy, was accused of ties with the United States by the embassy militants and arrested by the Revolutionary Guards. Admiral Madani, a presidential candidate and important figure in the revolution, was rumored to be involved in an attempted coup in January 1980. Although he was considered by some as President Bani-Sadr's initial choice for prime minister, the press again speculated about his alleged involvement in an attempted coup in July 1980. Controversy surrounded General Amir-Bagheri, chief of the Air Force, following the surfacing of a photo showing him with the shah; he reportedly fled in an F-4 Phantom. The continuous turnover of military chiefs has not contributed to the strength of the military.

Following new rumors of a pending coup attempt and reports that some members of the military had refused to fight in Kurdistan, the military became the target of a new purge in July 1980. The purge, touched off by an alleged plan to bomb Khomeini's residence and return Bakhtiar to power, resulted in the closure of Iran's borders, hundreds of arrests, and a new wave of executions. Ayatollah Khomeini demanded that everyone involved be executed and called for a new "people's army" to be established, thus echoing similar calls by leftists in February 1979. It is unclear whether the July 1980 purge and call for a "people's army" represent a new development, or are part of the transformation of the military outlined by Chamran in March of 1980.

The plan Chamran described provided for the military establishment to be cut to a "reserve-based backbone of sophisticated weapons specialists and planners."(20) This was to be supplemented by the Revolutionary Guards (then numbering between 20,000 and 30,000) and a "home defense army of 20 million capable of fighting 'peoples' wars."(21) Such a 20-million-strong force was first mentioned with the arrival of the American naval task force in December 1979.

While the military has been implicated in the alleged coup attempt in July 1980 (the sixth in four months), the Revolutionary Guards have come to dominate the internal security limelight. The Revolutionary Guards, believed by some to be under the influence of the Islamic Republican Party, fired upon a Mujahidin rally in June 1980, leaving 300 injured. Such an incident raises questions concerning whose security interests are being served by the Revolutionary Guards. Bani-Sadr's appointment to head the Revolutionary Guard, Abu Sharif, resigned in June 1980 because of what he called "power seeking and group divisions."(22) His resignation was report-

edly due to "free-lancing activities" and the manipulation of
the Pasdaran (Revolutionary Guards) by clerical factions.(23)

Threats to the Islamic Republic

Threats to the security interests of the Islamic Republic are
variously perceived and have internal and external dimensions.
The most significant threat comes from the Soviet Union. Iran
stands between the Soviet Union and its historical desire for a
warm-water port. The Soviet invasion of Afghanistan in December 1979 and movement of troops near the Iranian border in
January 1980 brought the Soviets within reach of the Persian
Gulf and the Indian Ocean. Should the Soviets decide to move
into Iran via one of the historical invasion routes, or simply
down the road from Zahedan to the port of Chah Bahar, the
Iranians could offer little military resistance. To protect
itself, Iran appears to be relying upon the historical doctrine
of "equilibrium," movazeneh, that is "deep-rooted in Iranian
foreign policy thinking."(24) Iran, despite its anti-American
rhetoric and its holding of hostages, continues to depend upon
the United States to block any Soviet move. This was so
indicated by Defense Minister Chamran in March 1980.(25)
        The seizure of the American hostages created a potential
threat of American intervention. In turn, Iran looks to the
Soviet Union to deter any American attack. Iran also dis-
counts the likelihood of any overt American intervention
because of the continued reliance by the United States and the
West on Persian Gulf oil. Bordering on the strategic Strait of
Hormuz, theoretically Iran is in a position to close the strait to
all shipping. Foreign Minister Ghotbzadeh threatened such an
action when there was press speculation about the possibility
of the United States mining Iranian harbors.
        While the superpowers are balanced against each other,
Iran faces a more immediate threat from neighboring Iraq.
Iran's relations with Iraq, worsened since the departure of the
shah, have been characterized by repeated border incidents
and mutual accusation of fomenting unrest. In October 1979
Iraq called upon Iran to return control of the entire Shatt-al-
Arab River to Iraq, to withdraw from Abu Musa and the Tumb
Islands, and to grant autonomy to its Arab, Kurdish, and
Balouchi minorities. Iran refused all three requests. The
possibility of war between Iran and Iraq has surfaced periodically, but is limited by the location of their respective oil
fields and the potential for creating domestic unrest. Iran can
stir up the Iraqi Shiah population that strongly supports
Khomeini. Iraq can provoke the Arabs of Khuzistan where
much of Iran's oil is found. Each can cater to the Kurdish
aspirations in the other.

War became a reality, however, September 22, 1980, when Iraqi bombers struck deep into Iran. The Iraqis met with greater resistance than expected, and the war slowed to a relative stalemate with Iraq holding much of Khuzistan. Each side remained adamant in its claims but was unwilling to escalate the conflict through the first year. The Iran-Iraq War is significant in establishing a dangerous precedent for the Gulf; oil facilities and population centers were targeted.

Each of the perceived external threats has an internal dimension in Iran. Accusations of intelligence activities and subversion by the Soviet Union, the CIA, and Iraqi intelligence are commonplace in the Iranian media.

Apart from the struggle for internal control of the revolutionary government, the increasing alienation of the various national minorities is creating a constituency for antigovernment activities. So far, however, there has been no coordination among the various ethnic minorities that would suggest any threat of fragmentation. While some Soviet support for the minorities has been reported, the older ethnic leadership has not been receptive to the possibility of working with the Soviets.

One additional group, the Tudeh Party, was considered to be an internal security threat by the shah's regime, but appears to be supporting the Islamic republic. While there has been speculation that the Tudeh Party is waiting in the wings, the broad support for the Tudeh Party that has been suggested is yet to materialize.

Regional Stability?

The promotion of regional stability was central to the shah's perception of Iranian security. Revolutionary Iran denounced any "regional policeman" role, but initially voiced an interest in Persian Gulf stability. The "provisional government" of Bazargan often explained away calls for the export of revolution by the hard-line clerics by stating that they were not members of the government. In September 1979 Ayatollah Montazeri attacked the leadership of other gulf governments as "oppressing" Moslem citizens and governing through the "power of the bayonet."(26) He went on to proclaim that "Iran's Islamic revolution will be exported to all other Muslim countries."(27) Although Ibrahim Yazdi, foreign minister at the time, followed Montazeri's comments the next day with a public denial of any intention of Iran to export revolution, such calls by hard-line clerics are foreboding. Now that the hard-line clerics are assuming control of the government, and with Ayatollah Montazeri himself being named as a possible successor to Khomeini, Iran's move toward a destabilizing rather than a stabilizing role appears to be in the offing.

A ready-made issue for exporting the revolution and fueling the revolutionary energies, the Islamic energies, is Jerusalem. An Islamic attack on Zionism, built upon anti-Western and antiimperialist emotions, is likely to be used to broaden the Iranian Revolution, to undermine those Arab governments that are closely tied to the West, and create a new threat for Israel. This could bring the Arab-Israeli conflict to the Persian Gulf.

NOTES

1. Kayhan (Tehran; Weekly International Edition), January 7, 1978, p. 3.

2. For an English translation of the constitution and a discussion of developments surrounding the establishment of the constitution, see "Constitution of the Islamic Republic of Iran" and "Introductory Note" by Rouhollah K. Ramazani in Middle East Journal 34 (Spring 1980): 181-204.

3. New York Times, June 11, 1980, pp. A-1, A-9.

4. See Amir Taheri, "Parties Galore," Kayhan, October 1, 1978, p. 5.

5. Vahe Petrossian, "Voters Give Bani-Sadr a Mixed Bag at Elections," Middle East Economic Digest (March 21, 1980), p. 3.

6. William Branigan, "Bani-Sadr Heralds Cultural Revolution," Washington Post, April 23, 1980, p. A-1.

7. See Eric Rouleau, "Iranian Left and Right Slugging It Out in Chaotic Fighting," New York Times, June 14, 1980, p. 2.

8. Ibid.

9. Vahe Petrossian, "Dilemmas of the Iranian Revolution," World Today (London) 36 (January 1980): 23.

10. John K. Cooley, "Bakhtiar, Others Seek Help to Oust Khomeini Regime," Christian Science Monitor, April 30, 1980, p. 4.

11. Ibid.

12. Richard Burt, "Shah's Army Leader Says Iran is Weary of Khomeini," New York Times, June 12, 1980, p. A-12.

13. Iran Times, November 2, 1979, p. 14.

14. It should be noted that Ayatollah Montazeri, the head of the Assembly of Experts that revised the constitution to give increased power to the clerics, has been identified as the possible successor to Ayatollah Khomeini.

15. See _Kayhan_, November 9, 1974, p. 1.

16. For complete statistics on Iranian defense expenditures for this period, see Institute for Strategic Studies, The Military Balance, 1969-70 through 1978-79 (London: Chatto and Windus, 1970-79).

17. Jonathan C. Randal, "Iran is Expecting U.S. Military Aid If Soviets Attack," _Washington Post_, March 21, 1980, p. A-34.

18. Ibid.

19. Ibid.

20. Ibid., p. A-1.

21. Ibid., pp. A-1, A-34.

22. _New York Times_, June 18, 1980, p. A-12.

23. _Iran Times_, June 27, 1980, p. 14.

24. See Rouhollah K. Ramazani, "Iran's Changing Foreign Policy: A Preliminary Discussion," _Middle East Journal_ 24 (Autumn 1970): 433.

25. Randal, "Iran is Expecting U.S. Military Aid," p. A-1.

26. _Iran Times_, September 21, 1979, p. 14.

27. See _Iran Times_, September 21, 1979, p. 14; and _Arab News_ (Jeddah), September 18, 1979, p. 3.

6 Middle East Economies: An Overview

Hossein Askari

INTRODUCTION

To describe and analyze economic conditions and prospects of a single country in a few pages is by itself a challenge, but to undertake the same subject for all of the countries of Middle East and North Africa within similar space limitations is almost foolhardy. The sheer number of countries presents a problem. Moreover, it is difficult to do justice in comparisons because of the prevalence of a number of significant similarities and dissimilarities between the numerous countries in question. As a result, valid generalizations are difficult to establish. For reasons of space, however, it is expedient to terminate the list of excuses. Suffice it to warn the reader that this chapter is intended only to provide an overall glimpse into these economies.

BASIC ECONOMIC FACTS

The countries in this area exhibit an unusual dispersion of characteristics in physical size, population, GDP, GDP per capita, basic economic structure, and the like. Most economists, however, succumb to the temptation of accepting two broad country groupings that are perceived as homogeneous - oil exporters and non-oil exporters. Although such a broad classification has merit, there are, as will be seen, major anomalies within such groupings.

There is no universal definition of oil-exporting countries. For instance, the IMF classifies the members of OPEC plus Oman as oil exporters. But, one could justify shortening the list by omitting Oman, or lengthening it to include Bahrain, Egypt, and Syria. We will define oil-exporting countries as Oman and Bahrain, in addition to the OPEC countries. It is clearly "difficult" to omit OPEC countries from the list of oil exporters but the inclusion of Oman and Bahrain may be justified by certain important features.

Among the oil exporters, the variation in "basic" facts is significant (see Table 6.1). Algeria is physically the largest country at over 2.4 million square kilometers and Bahrain is the smallest at 674; four of the countries are over 1.5 million square kilometers, while four are under 100,000 square kilometers. In terms of population, Iran has a population in excess of 38 million as compared to a little over 200,000 in Qatar. GNP figures vary from a high of $80 billion in Iran to a low of $1.5 in Bahrain.(1) As to GNP per capita, the three countries having the highest per capita income in the world are in this group - UAE, Kuwait, and Qatar. The combined population of these three countries, however, is around only 2 million. In the same group, Algeria has a per capita income of only $1,260. In fact, the average weighted per capita GNP is only around $3,000, a figure substantially below the average for the EEC.

The non-oil exporters of the region show much less variance on all counts. In physical size, Egypt is the largest at about one million square kilometers and Lebanon is the smallest at about ten thousand square kilometers. In population, Egypt has the largest population at about 39 million and Yeman (PDR) is the smallest at 1.7 million. Similarly, in GNP per capita the range is again much smaller than that for the oil-exporting group: from a high of $1,200 in Lebanon to a low of $400 in Egypt.(2) As to GNP, Egypt has the largest economy at about $15 billion and Yemen (PDR) has the smallest at $740 million.

At first glance, one might conclude that the major difference between the oil exporters and the non-oil exporters is a tremendous gap in economic prosperity. Such a conclusion may be greatly exaggerated, at least in a dynamic sense. On the one hand, a country such as Saudi Arabia has very limited flow of output from a sustainable source. That is, if depletion of oil is not compensated by accumulation of productive wealth or foreign assets, then in the long run the future is not promising. On the other hand, countries such as Egypt or Syria have agricultural and industrial sources of sustained production. The alternatives for the oil-exporting countries are elaborated in the following section and then the important structural differences are discussed.

Table 6.1. Basic Facts (1978).*

Countries	Size (in sq. km)	Population (mid-year) (in thousands)	GNP/Capita (U.S. $)	GNP at market prices (millions US$)
A. Oil Exporters				
1. Algeria	2,400,000	17,701	1,260	22,290
2. Bahrain	674	368	4,100	1,510
3. Iran	1,648,000	35,849	2,273	80,000
4. Iraq	438,317	12,216	1,860	22,720
5. Kuwait	24,280	1,212	14,890	18,040
6. Libya	1,760,000	2,745	6,910	18,960
7. Oman	300,000	839	2,570	2,160
8. Qatar	10,365	223	12,740	2,840
9. Saudi Arabia	2,240,000	7,870	8,040	63,310
10. UAE	77,000	804	14,230	11,440
B. Non-Oil Exporters				
11. Egypt	1,002,000	38,686	400	15,520
12. Jordan	90,240	2,985	1,050	2,270
13. Lebanon	10,400	3,011	1,200	3,613
14. Morocco	446,000	18,914	670	12,610
15. Syria	185,170	8,088	930	7,490
16. Tunisia	164,200	6,050	950	5,760
17. Yemen, Arab Rep.	195,000	5,098	580	2,960
18. Yemen, PDR	337,800	1,749	420	740

*Figures for population, GNP/capita, and GNP are preliminary estimates.

Source: 1979 Work Bank Atlas, Washington, D.C. For Iran the GNP figures were derived from national sources. For Lebanon the GNP figures are estimates for 1977 from national sources.

ALTERNATIVES FOR THE OIL-EXPORTING COUNTRIES

To different degrees, all the oil-exporting countries face one important question - the optimal transformation of their limited and nonrenewable oil wealth. In some of these countries, oil and associated gas are the only significant natural resources. Agricultural potential is limited by rugged terrain, harsh climate, the absence of adequate water resources, rudimentary infrastructure, and limited supply of indigenous professional and skilled labor.

Oil is the major natural wealth of these countries. These countries are confronted with the uncertain outcome of transforming their oil wealth into productive assets with which they may sustain their economy. If oil is not perceived in such a light, the long-run consequences for these countries will be disastrous. In the short and medium term, depletion of oil wealth will, in terms of traditional accounting methods, result in oil revenues and thus in high levels of GNP in some countries. If, however, the depletion of oil does not result in the development of a productive non-oil sector, then current GNP will be derived from a depletion of oil wealth; a process which is unsustainable in the long run. In other words, exports, GNP, and external position of major oil exporters are not comparable to those of economies where output is a flow derived from a sustainable productive base with exports and external position being a byproduct. In the case of oil exporters, exports and external surplus are not a flow but are instead derived from an exchange, or transformation, of a nonrenewable asset. Thus, potential GNP is maintained in these countries if oil is not extracted, or if extracted oil is transformed into other capital, with the condition that the present discounted value of the transformed capital (net of depreciation) is equal to the discounted value of the oil had it not been transformed.

The oil sector has other important characteristics. First, unlike much of industry in other countries, the oil sector is not integrated into the rest of the economy through various backward and forward linkages. A change in the level of oil production has a limited impact on domestic inputs of materials, capital, equipment, and labor. While this may be seen as generally undesirable from a development perspective, it does have the benefit of limiting reallocation of resources between the oil and non-oil sectors as output fluctuates. Second, the oil industry provides employment opportunities that are limited in number and restricted to a narrow range of skills and professions that may not match overall aspirations and domestic supplies. Third, the government, by owning oil resources, receives the revenues from oil exports. While this theoretically affords the government unusual control over expenditure rates and resource allocation between sectors, it does not provide a mechanism for distributing income. Furthermore, as oil revenues are received by the government without a great deal of physical labor, current generations feel a direct claim to their "fair share" without hard work, with little understanding of the implication for future generations if oil depletion were to finance current consumption. Government ownership of oil reserves presents additional difficulties. The government is given the task of determining major investment projects, and thus the specifics of economic diversification, without the benefit of receiving indications through the market mechanisms as indicated in a more gradual process of industrialization through the private sector. For growth to proceed realistically, however, the government must simultaneously provide the private sector with appropriate incentives.

The process of asset transformation or oil depletion implies two viable long-run alternatives for these countries - to build a non-oil productive base, and to acquire foreign assets. The available opportunities in these areas in turn affect the rate of oil depletion.

Domestic economic development potential in the oil-exporting countries is diverse to say the least. In Algeria, Iran, and Iraq, agriculture has been in the past and has the potential of becoming an even more important source of output. While in Kuwait, Libya, Qatar, Saudi Arabia, and the UAE, there is little potential for a large agricultural sector. In Algeria, Iran, and Iraq, the availability of non-oil resources and professional and skilled labor has promoted industrialization and the expansion of the service sectors of the economy. While in Kuwait, Libya, Qatar, Saudi Arabia, and the UAE reliance on imported materials and labor has made expansion of industry and services both costly and difficult.

The rapid absorption of oil revenues by dramatically increasing domestic incomes can result in noticeable and immediate difficulties. A quantum increase in incomes can occur over a short span of time, while the development of infrastructure and a domestic productive base require a longer gestation period. Thus, as incomes increase, expenditures on all goods increase - tradeables (importables) and nontradeables (housing, health, and the like). Initially, inflation is all-pervasive as infrastructural bottlenecks cannot accommodate the large increase in imports. In the case of nontradeables, inflation is more noticeable as imports can by definition do little to augment domestic supply and domestic supply is highly inelastic. After the expansion of base infrastructure, the input of tradeable goods can be accommodated. But in the case of nontradeables, much more time is required for the productive structure to adjust to the higher and changing composition of demand. The most noticeable areas of excess demand tend to be housing and social services. The governments have very little leeway in arresting these effects. Taxes and similar measures are not sufficiently developed to discourage the consumption of nontradeable goods and services selectively. Thus, a general reduction in government expenditures and demand is called for. This is, however, socially and politically difficult to implement. Moreover, such a policy would also result in higher external surpluses which is on the one hand a cause of international recriminations, and on the other hand results in the accumulation of depreciating external assets. In essence, the oil-exporting countries find themselves in a vicious circle which, unlike the traditional form of the vicious circle in the development literature, is not caused by too little current revenues but by too much current revenues from a nonsustainable source coupled with unattractive domestic investments.

As to the second alternative in the process of asset transformation (oil extraction), the acquisition of foreign assets, the issues are well known. From a purely theoretical standpoint, an oil-exporting country should extract its oil at a rate such that the social rate of return on the marginal investment (domestic or abroad) is equal to the expected rate of increase in the net price of oil (net of extraction cost). In reality, however, rate of oil extraction may not exactly satisfy such a condition. Some oil exporters may be willing to extract oil at a rate in excess of the optimal, for a short period of time, in view of certain externalities; for example, in order to meet some global requirement due to unexpected supply short-falls in other countries or to bring order to the international oil market. Over the longer term, however, surplus (on balance of payments) oil exporters cannot be expected to produce at current levels unless appropriate investment opportunities are forthcoming, either domestically or internationally. Domestic social rates of return are unlikely to change significantly as the speed with which oil revenues can be invested domestically are subject to both economic and social constraints; in other words, domestic rates of return cannot be readily manipulated. Rates of return on foreign assets (issued by major oil-importing countries), however, are, subject to special policy considerations by the countries for whose benefits the higher oil production is intended.

It is in such an economic setting that international cooperation is clearly called for. The price of oil has risen over two decades toward a price reflecting its scarcity value as opposed to an approximation of its extractive cost. It could rise even more dramatically if alternative sources are not developed (i.e., current price being below its scarcity value) or if demand is not restrained (i.e., conservation and efficiency of oil consumption). Actions of the oil-importing countries will therefore, in large part determine the expectations of oil exporters as to future price of oil and thus affect their current production decisions given existing investment opportunities. It is in this latter regard - that is, investment opportunities abroad - that international cooperation is specifically called for. Mr. de Larosière, the managing director of the IMF, has said that if the major oil-exporting countries are to continue transforming their underground oil wealth into financial holdings at current levels of production or higher, such countries must be able to invest their current account surpluses in financial instruments that will make it worthwhile for them to keep on pumping oil. (3) If such accommodation is made by the international community, then international investment opportunities would allow the oil exporters to take pricing and production decisions without the constraint of short- and medium-term considerations of their domestic economic development opportunities.

External investment opportunities have been quite dismal in recent years. Some of the oil exporters, with substantial net foreign assets, have had very little choice but to hold dollar-denominated assets, earning a real-dollar rate close to zero, and with a depreciating dollar resulting in a substantial negative real yield in terms of internationally traded goods. Two broad approaches would be helpful to ameliorate this problem. First, one helpful solution would be the floating of bonds (off market) bilaterally by the strong currency countries - Germany, Japan, Switzerland, and possibly other industrial countries. Germany and Japan have initiated such a policy on a small scale, but it is questionable whether the yield is still sufficiently attractive. Such initiatives, however, at least offer a beginning for process of orderly reserve diversification. Second, a broad international effort to create an asset with appropriate characteristics would be a desirable course of action. Such a proposal could be adopted by the industrial countries or by the entire international community through the IMF. If such proposals were forthcoming, then oil-production decisions would be more immune to domestic investment opportunities.

If these or similar proposals are not adopted, the choice for capital surplus oil exporters is very restricted. If oil extraction is maintained at current levels, they can: (1) acquire depreciating foreign assets; (2) increase their import of goods for current consumption; and (3) increase expenditures on domestic (nontraded) investment and goods with resulting high rates of inflation as supply is highly price-inelastic and labor is fully employed. For the reasons explained above, these three outcomes are undesirable for oil-exporting countries - the first two for their long-term implications and the third both for its short- and long-term effects. Thus, in the absence of attractive foreign assets, oil exports of the capital surplus countries are likely to drop in the medium and long term, resulting in higher oil prices and potential international economic disruptions.

ECONOMIC STRUCTURE

Oil has been by far the single most important factor determining structural differences in the countries of the Middle East and North Africa. In Table 6.2, percentage shares of agriculture, manufacturing, other industry (mining, construction, electricity, and water), and services in GNP are shown. For all of the oil exporters, the share of agriculture has fallen sharply over time to less than 10 percent in 1977; in large part owing to rising oil prices and in part owing to the neglect of the agriculture sector. On the other hand, for the non-oil exporters, the share of agriculture has been relatively stable and in nearly all cases it was substantially higher than 10 percent (even in excess of 30 percent) in 1977. In manufacturing, Algeria, Iran, and Iraq display shares that are similar to that of the non-oil group but in other oil-exporting countries, the share of manufacturing was significantly lower than 10 percent in 1977. In these latter oil-exporting countries, the share of other industry in GDP ranged from 70 to 91 percent. This sector includes the oil and construction sectors, with the output value of the former increasing with oil prices and the latter benefiting from infrastructural expansion. The size of this ratio is much higher than that of the more diversified oil exporting of Algeria, Iran, and Iraq - approximately 40 percent in these countries. But for oil exporters, as expected, the relative importance of this sector (value of oil activity and construction) has increased with higher oil prices. For the non-oil-exporting countries, the share of this sector was much lower, ranging from 5.5 percent in Egypt to 23.2 percent in Yemen (PDR). The relatively smaller size of this sector is in large part a reflection of little or no domestic oil production.(4)

In Table 6.3., the structure of the export sector clearly shows the importance of oil to the economies of the oil-exporting countries, with the exception of Bahrain. Even in the "diversified" economies of Algeria, Iran, and Iraq, fuels, minerals, and metals respectively comprised 97.0, 96.5, and 99.2 percent of total merchandise exports. These countries are net importers of agricultural goods. Their industrialization has occurred in protected markets. There is ample local demand to absorb production of such goods, resulting in little incentive to seek foreign markets. Moreover, these countries are not yet competitive in international markets for manufactured goods. For the non-oil-exporting countries, their export structure is much more diversified. The share of all

Table 6.2.   Economic Structure
(Percentage of GDP at Current Factor Costs)
(1960, 1970, 1977).

Country	Agriculture			Manufacturing			Other Industry			Services		
Oil Exporters	1960	1970	1977	1960	1970	1977	1960	1970	1977	1960	1970	1977
Algeria	20.5	12.8	7.5	9.9	15.2	11.0	23.5	28.6	45.5	46.1	43.4	36.1
Bahrain			2.1									36.7
Iran	29.1	19.4	9.3	11.0	13.8	12.0	21.9	28.8	42.0	38.0	38.1	36.7
Iraq	17.3	17.3	--	9.6	9.7	--	41.8	35.4	--	31.2	37.6	--
Kuwait	--	0.4	0.2	--	3.5	5.5	--	67.2	71.2	--	29.0	23.1
Libya	13.7	2.4	1.7	8.5	2.1	2.8	--	66.5	70.2	--	29.0	25.3
Oman	--	15.5	2.8	--	0.2	1.0	--	77.1	72.1	--	7.2	24.2
Quatar												
Saudi Arabia	--	5.7	0.9	--	9.6	3.8	--	53.8	77.5	--	30.9	17.8
United Arab Emirates			0.9			1.7			91.0			6.4
Non-Oil Exporters												
Egypt	29.9	29.4	30.2	20.1	15.2	11.0	4.2	6.2	5.5	45.8	42.4	40.9
Jordan			9.9			20.3			7.6			62.2
Lebanon			9.0			16.6			13.8			60.6
Morocco	23.4	20.5	16.3	15.5	15.6	16.5	10.9	11.4	16.7	50.1	52.5	50.5
Syria	--	21.5	19.6	--	15.8	10.3	--	7.4	18.1	--	55.4	52.0
Tunisia	--	19.3	18.4	--	9.2	10.6	--	15.7	20.1	--	55.8	50.9
Yemen Arab Republic			44.5			5.8						
Yemen, PDR			21.8			8.2			23.2			46.8

Source: World Tables 1980.   IBRD, Washington, D.C.   1980.
For Bahrain, UAE, Jordan, Lebanon (1974), Yemen Arab Republic, and Yemen, PDR the figures are derived from national
sources.

Table 6.3.
Foreign Trade Structure - Export Composition
(Percent of Total Merchandise Exports in 1977).

	Food and Beverages	Nonfood Agriculture	Fuels, Minerals, and Metals	Machinery and Equipment	Other Manufactures
A. Oil Exporters					
1. Algeria	2.3	0.1	97.0	0.1	0.6
2. Bahrain	6.9	0.5	27.7	28.1	36.9
3. Iran	0.6	1.2	96.5	0.3	1.4
4. Iraq	0.6	0.2	99.2		0.1
5. Kuwait	0.6	0.1	88.4	2.8	8.0
6. Libya					
7. Oman	0.3		99.7		
8. Qatar			98.7	0.4	0.9
9. Saudi Arabia			99.7	0.2	0.1
10. UAE	0.7		96.5	0.9	1.9
B. Non-Oil Exporters					
11. Egypt	18.6	29.9	26.4	0.2	24.9
12. Jordan	35.0	0.7	23.6	13.3	27.4
13. Lebanon					
14. Morocco	30.6	2.3	46.1	0.5	20.5
15. Syria	6.2	17.7	65.8	1.9	8.5
16. Tunisia	15.2	2.0	49.4	1.3	32.2
17. Yemen, Ar. Rep.	33.7	56.1		1.0	9.2
18. Yemen, PDR					

Source: World Tables 1980, IBRD, Washington, D.C., 1980.

export sectors is in general significant, with the exception of exports of machinery and equipment; this is to be expected as the growth of this sector occurs at a later stage, after the exhaustion of goods that are easily import substitutable.

The importance of oil exports is also manifested through external balance (Table 6.4). All of the non-oil-exporting countries have incurred a current account deficit in every year from 1975 to 1978. This is to be expected for developing countries where borrowing should result in real resource transfers for development purposes. On the other hand, the oil-exporting countries have by and large experienced substantial surpluses on the current account arising from oil exports in excess of their domestic financial requirements. The surplus of the oil exporters, however, declined dramatically from its peak in 1974 to a near balanced position in 1978, before increasing again into a large surplus position. This decline in surplus was due to an unexpectedly rapid expansion of imports following oil-revenue increases. But as mentioned earlier, the surplus of oil exporters cannot be seen in the same light as that of industrial countries. The oil sector is not linked to the rest of the economy; it is instead more akin to an enclave. The managing director of the IMF described the reason underlying such surpluses in an interview: "Saudi Arabia was running a 'very important surplus' in its BOP for one essential reason: the rest of the world wanted Saudi Arabia to produce oil at much higher levels than it needed for its own BOP. So in a way the oil surplus of Saudi Arabia is an internationally requested surplus. There would be one very simple way for Saudi Arabia to eliminate this surplus and that would be to cut down on its production."(5) In the same interview, regarding the surpluses of the past (i.e., in industrial countries), Mr. de Larosière said: "They were not internationally requested and they often had their source in divergencies in economic activity levels throughout the world and differences in the way to handle economic policies."

By increasing the pace of domestic economic activity, expanding oil revenues have markedly affected the structure of the labor force in some oil-exporting countries. Interestingly enough, this structural change has in turn affected the labor market in nearly every country of the Middle East and North Africa by affecting the flow of expatriate labor.

In the smaller oil-exporting countries of the Middle East, expatriate labor was large even before the substantial increase of oil revenues; the ratio of expatriate labor to total workers was 74.1 percent in Kuwait (1971), 56.7 percent in UAE (1968), and 83.2 percent in Qatar (1971). The case of Kuwait (see Table 6.5) represents perhaps the most dramatic importance of expatriate labor prior to 1973. Nearly three-fifths of the phenomenal 260 percent increase in the population of Kuwait between 1957 and 1970 resulted from the influx of Arabs,

Table 6.4.   Current Account Balance
(Goods, Services and Private Transfers,
in $ Millions).

Country	1974	1975	1976	1977	1978
A. Oil Exporters					
Algeria	584	-1,650	-871	-2,307	-3,526
Bahrain					
Iran	12,299	6,332	4,734	5,091	
Iraq	2,855	2,971			
Kuwait		6,684	7,172	5,645	6,967
Libya	1,900	96	2,581	3,058	1,297
Oman		-13	-3	-12	-31
Qatar	1,667	1,130	1,020	426	692
Saudi Arabia	24,022	17,059	17,127	16,679	2,900
U. A. E.		3,900	4,600	3,700	3,200
B. Non Oil Exporters					
Egypt	-981	-1,772	-826	-1,219	-1,244
Jordan	-255	-366	-287	-493	-617
Lebanon					
Morocco	221	-528	-1,346	-1,843	-1,367
Syria	-244	-561	-1,174	-1,300	-1,242
Tunisia	9	-221	-437	-640	-525
Yemen Arab Republic	-59	-22	-193	-181	-48
Yemen, P.D.R.	-93	-87	-97	-136	-55

Source: National sources.

Iranians, Indians, Europeans, and others attracted by Kuwaiti opportunities. On every level the country depends heavily on non-Kuwaiti labor. For example, in 1970 only one doctor in 15, one nurse in 32, one engineer in 15, one accountant in 37, and one teacher in five was a Kuwaiti citizen, while 72 percent of the jurists; 79 percent of the managers; 65 percent of the post office workers; 96 percent of the cobblers; 95 percent of the bricklayers, carpenters, and construction workers; 97 percent of the tailors and dressmakers; and 90 percent of the stenographers and typists were expatriates. In only a handul of occupations is Kuwait self-sufficient in labor, and these are generally jobs reserved for citizens as government executives and administrators, firemen, and policemen.

Table 6.5. Expatriates in the Labor Force, Kuwait, 1970.

Category	Number of Workers	Percent Expatriate
Professional, technical, and related	25,622	85.4
Administrative and managerial	1,780	65.7
Clerical and related	28,204	59.3
Sales	21,093	69.0
Service	57,737	59.8
Agriculture and fishing	3,943	77.4
Production and machinery	96,966	86.2
Total	237,755	74.1

Source: Government of Kuwait, Census of Kuwait, 1970.

After the oil price increase, expatriate labor increased in the smaller countries but showed a particularly large jump in Iran, Libya, and Saudi Arabia (see Table 6.6); this labor has been absorbed in all sectors with the largest concentration being in construction, services, and commerce and finance (Table 6.7). Since 1975, there have been further substantial movements in the flow of expatriate labor. The flow of expatriate labor to Iran subsided, and in fact expatriate labor in Iran has become almost non-existent. In the other countries

(Table 6.6), however, the flow of expatriate labor has continued. For Saudi Arabia, preliminary information suggests that in 1980, expatriate labor was around one million, representing around 43 percent of the total labor force.

With the increase of oil revenues in the 1970s, most oil exporters in the Middle East were unable to absorb such revenues immediately. Such an observation is most readily seen in the current account surplus of these countries in 1974 and 1975. Such bottlenecks were in large part and in varying degrees due to shortage of infrastructure (port capacity, transportation, power, and communication) and labor (managerial, professional, skilled, and in some cases unskilled). The inflow of manpower has made a significant contribution to the rapid development of these countries. Without such labor, infrastructure could not have been completed so quickly, development plans and their implementation would have lagged, health care would not have become so advanced, and educational programs would not have become so expansive.

The benefits of such labor inflows to the importing country are clear but there have also been costs. The inflow of such labor in many countries has led to social difficulties. The imported labor has been housed in restricted areas; they have not received the normal benefits available to citizens – educational, health, social security, land ownership, and the like. In other instances, such as the Bell Helicopter operations in Iran, the immigrant workers (Americans) received greater benefits and did not adapt to the local society and its customs. As a result, in both instances, such realities have led to social tensions. Furthermore, in countries where foreign labor is a large proportion of total labor force and total population, Kuwait, Qatar, and UAE, the political implications for unrest are clear. Finally, much of the labor is still committed to the country of origin where in many cases the family resides. Thus, when sufficient funds have been accumulated, the worker will go back home, taking with him his acquired skill and experience. In turn, the labor-importing countries may have to retrain new labor from abroad.

For the labor-exporting countries, the outflow of labor has normally occurred with the existence of high levels of unemployment coupled with a high expected wage differential (i.e., wage differential adjusted for the probability of finding a job and for the fixed cost of relocation). In addition, the migrating labor normally leaves his family behind and thus sends funds home for their support and also intends to return home when he has accumulated sufficient funds.

The first benefit to the labor-exporting country has been a reduction of unemployment; unemployment compensation, pressures on domestic resources, and social tensions are thus reduced. Second, most of these labor-exporting countries have severe foreign-exchange constraints; the inflow of work-

Table 6.6. Immigrant Labor in the Middle East and
North Africa by Source and Destination, 1975 (In Thousands).

Source	Bahrain	Iran	Iraq	Kuwait	Libya	Oman	Qatar	Saudi Arabia	United Arab Emirates
					Destination				
Egypt	1.2	--	2.3	37.6	175.0	5.3	2.7	...	(12.7)
Europe and N. America	4.4[1]	(35.0)[2]	0.7	2.0	28.0[3]	3.6	9.2	...	(9.1)[4]
India	9.0	(4.4)	0.3	21.5	2.0	24.8	19.8	...	(73.0)
Jordan[5]	0.8	--	3.1	47.7	7.0	2.6	1.7	...	(6.4)
Morocco	--	--	--	--	1.8	--	--	...	--
Pakistan	6.7	(2.4)	0.9	11.0	5.0	20.2	14.5	...	(94.0)
Syrian Arab Republic	0.1	--	0.2	16.5	15.0	1.5	0.4	...	(3.4)
Tunisia	--	--	--	--	29.0	--	--	...	--
Turkey	--	(1.2)	--	--	8.0	--	--	...	--
Yemen Arab Republic and PDR of Yemen	1.3	--	--	11.4	--	1.0	2.6	...	(3.5)
Other Asia	1.0	(5.0)	--	1.1	--	--	0.5	...	(0.4)
Other	5.0[6]	(134.0)[7]	0.9	62.7[8]	24.2	8.2	10.5	...	(43.3)[9]
Total	29.4	(182.0)	8.4	211.4	295.0	67.2	61.8	770.0	(245.8)
Percent of total employment	38	2	1	71	33	64	77	39	89

Figures in parentheses are rough estimates.

--Data nil or insignificant.

...Not available.

[1] Includes the Untied Kingdom 3.497; the United States 843; and others 43.

[2] Includes about 25,000 Americans.

[3] Includes Bulgaria 2,000; France 2,000; Poland 6,000; Romania 3,000; the United Kingdom 4,000; the United States 2,000; and Yugoslavia 9,000.

[4] Includes France 1.572; the United Kingdom 3,167; and the United States 1,318.

[5] Jordanians and Palestinians.

[6] Includes Africa 58; Iran 1,980; Iraq 126; Kuwait 65; Lebanon 128; Oman 1,385; Saudi Arabia 226; the United Arab Emirates 411; and other 656.

[7] Includes about 120,000 Afghan workers and others from the Gulf states.

[8] Includes Iran 28,953; Iraq 17,999; Lebanon 7,232; Saudi Arabia 2,644; Sudan 873; and others 4,954.

[9] Includes Bangladesh 2,450; Iran 25,444; Iraq 620; Lebanon 4,068; Somalia 1,620; Sudan 1,776; and others 7,035.

Source: A. Ecevit and K.C. Zachariah, "International Labor Migration," Finance and Development (December 1978), p. 35.

Table 6.7.   Sectoral Structure of Immigrant Labor
in Selected Labor Importing Countries, 1975
(In Percent).

	Kuwait	Libya	Saudi Arabia
Agriculture	1.87	10.36	14.58
Mining	3.16	2.87	1.47
Manufacturing	14.97	7.74	4.55
Utilities	2.94	1.36	.95
Construction	22.92	49.45	32.26
Commerce and finance	14.81	4.22	19.21
Transport and communication	5.63	1.60	9.41
Services	33.70	20.40	17.57
Others	--	2.00	--
Total	100.00	100.00	100.00

Sources: Kuwait - 1975 census; Libya - The Plan of Economic
and Social Transportation 1976-1980; Saudi Arabia - Development Plan, 1975-1980.

ers; remittances have become a major source of foreign exchange. The inflow of such remittances are shown in Table
6.8. In many instances such inflows clearly sustain the development of labor-exporting countries. An indicator of this is
the size of remittances expressed as a percent of exports in
1976: Egypt (28 percent), Morocco (43 percent), Turkey (50
percent), Jordan (198 percent), and Yemen Arab Republic
(5.897 percent).(6)
    The costs of such labor outflows are twofold. First, in
some cases, labor shortages have begun to appear in certain
labor-exporting countries, especially in the skilled areas as
their own development has picked up. This has led to imports
of labor from third countries.(7) Such problems are likely to
be most severe when intersectoral labor mobility is low in the
labor-exporting country. A second problem may be caused if
the migrating labor does not return, especially if skilled.
    For the labor-importing countries, the inflow of labor
must be seen as a temporary phenomenon. In the skilled

Table 6.8. Inflow of Remittances
(In Millions of U.S. Dollars).

	1973	1974	1975	1976	1977	1978
Egypt	87	189	366	755	894	1,750
Jordan[1]	75.3	166.7	396.3	424.4	457.2	
Lebanon[2]	120E	150E	200E	250E	400E	450E
Pakistan	146.8	189.5	258.0	412.0	869.6	1,302.8
Syria						662.4[3]
Yemen Arab Rep.[1]		151.4E	324.0E	649.8E	930.5E	
Yemen, PDR	32.9	41.1	55.9	115.2	179.2	

[1] Net.

[2] Remittances are believed to be understanded; two-thirds of remittances are estimated to origin from ME oil-producing countries, the remainder from Europe and Latin America.

[3] Official estimate.

Source: National authorities and balance-of-payments statistics.

categories, countries should simultaneously train their own indigenous labor force to replace imported professional and skilled labor. For the imported labor, countries should provide adequate facilities so that social and political tensions are relieved. But if imported labor remains in the country for prolonged periods, political needs and requirements may become most severe.

For the labor-exporting country to benefit fully from such movements of labor, it should adopt appropriate policies. First, it should encourage repatriation of earnings. It is, therefore, essential to avoid an overvalued exchange rate. If, however, the exchange rate is overvalued, countries should adopt a special rate for remittances. As a part of such a package, countries should maintain adequate levels of domestic interest rates (or a special rate for remittances) and should attach no exchange controls to such deposits for a fixed period of time. Second, after such an inflow of remittances has been realized, countries should adopt policies to channel these funds into productive investment as opposed to consumption. Third, references to the notion that governments want added compensation or to tax the movements of such labor is likely to be self-defeating. Such labor movements are by and large temporary and the reverse flow, when it occurs, is likely to be a more experienced labor force. Labor, unlike wine, does not improve by aging through idleness. Fourth, to ensure that the outflow of labor is not permanent, countries should adopt specific financial incentives for repatriation. Fifth, to avoid domestic shortages, governments should adopt comprehensive labor training programs to elevate the skills of the entire labor force.

ECONOMIC PERFORMANCE

Expanding oil revenues in the oil-exporting countries can therefore, be expected to have increased population growth (largely from labor inflow), growth in GDP, inflation (from higher demand and bottlenecks), and increased national savings and investment rates. These expectations are confirmed to varying degrees in each country (Table 6.9). Population rates of growth of 16.7 percent per annum are observed in UAE, 10.3 percent in Qatar, 7.1 percent in Bahrain, and 6.2 percent in Kuwait; the figures for Iran and Saudi Arabia, however, appear low at 3 percent. Real economic growth rates are high by any standard. Inflation rates have shown a very large increase. And savings and investment rates have been exceptionally high: for Saudi Arabia an investment rate of 52.6 percent and a savings rate of 67.6 percent. These latter figures should be expected, given that these countries are transforming one asset to another.

The performance of the non-oil exporters, though less dramatic, has been laudable when compared to other non-oil-exporting, developing countries. There was substantial increase in real GDP growth from 1965-1970 to 1970-1977, in the range of 6.4 to 9.6 percent per annum in the latter period. Unfortunately this has been accompanied by higher rates of inflation, but again the range (6.9 to 16.0 percent) compares well to other non-oil-exporting, developing countries. A large part of the explanation for the above-average performance of these countries has to be related to large workers' remittances, expansion of exports to oil-exporting countries, and increased levels of aid from the oil-exporting countries. The markets in the oil-exporting countries have been the most buoyant in the world and this, coupled with labor shortages in these economies has greatly enhanced the external balance-of-payments position of the non-oil exporters of the region.

Table 6.9. Selected Economic Development Indicators (Average Annual Growth Rate).

	Population 65-70	Population 70-77	GDP 65-70	GDP 70-77	GDP/Capita 65-70	GDP/Capita 70-77	CPI 60-70	CPI 70-77	GDP Deflator 60-70	GDP Deflator 70-77	Gross Domestic Investment 1970-77	Av. National Savings Ratio 1972-77
A. Oil Exporters												
1. Algeria	3.7	3.2	8.1	5.4	4.2	2.2	1.5	6.1	2.3	13.7	11.7	39.1
2. Bahrain	2.9	7.1	..	10.7	..	3.2	..	12.4	-0.5	23.7	22.0	39.4
3. Iran	2.8	3.0	12.6	7.4	9.5	4.3	1.6	7.3	1.7	17.5		
4. Iraq	3.2	3.4	4.1	8.1	0.9	4.7	2.1	8.9	0.9	22.1		
5. Kuwait	9.6	6.2	5.7	-0.1	-5.3	-6.0	..	..	5.2	24.0	11.1	69.4
6. Libya	4.2	4.1	..	6.8	..	..	7.6	5.4				
7. Oman	2.7	3.2	39.7	..	36.0	3.5	..	13.8	2.4	34.6	38.7	33.4
8. Qatar	6.9	10.3	..	..	..	..	..	..				
9. Saudi Arabia	2.8	3.0	9.1	12.7	6.1	9.4	1.8	19.1	1.0	30.4	52.6	67.6
10. UAE	13.7	16.7	..	12.5	..	-2.1	..	..				
B. Non-Oil Exporters												
11. Egypt	2.1	2.1	3.2	6.4	1.1	4.2	3.8	7.6	2.7	6.9	25.4	13.2
12. Jordan	3.2	3.3	..	7.0	..	3.6	..	12.3	..	12.0		
13. Lebanon	2.8	2.5	..	..	..	..	..	..				
14. Morocco	2.9	2.7	5.7	6.4	2.8	3.6	2.2	8.3	2.0	7.3	17.9	17.1
15. Syria	3.3	3.3	5.6	9.6	2.3	6.2	2.0	12.4	1.9	13.5	15.6	16.3
16. Tunisia	2.1	2.0	4.9	8.5	2.8	6.4	3.1	5.4	3.7	7.4	12.5	20.3
17. Yemen, Ar. Rep.	1.5	1.9	..	8.4	..	6.4	..	25.3	..	16.0		22.1
18. Yemen, PDR	1.9	1.9	..	6.8	..	4.8	..	..				

Source: World Tables 1980 (Washington, D.C.: IBRD, 1980).

152

Given the existence of supply bottlenecks (ports, roads, electricity, labor, housing, and other social services) and high rates of inflation, the oil-exporting countries by and large shifted their policies during 1975-1977 to restrain domestic demand and reduce inflation to acceptable levels. These policies appeared to have been successful. The rate of growth in real, non-oil GDP declined from about 12 percent in 1975 to about 7 percent in 1978 and average inflation (CPI) rates declined significantly from around 20 percent in 1975 to less than 10 percent in 1978. Although short-run supply bottle-necks are less likely, the slower increase in expenditures and expansion of money supply is still prevalent after the 1979/80 oil price increases.

The economic performance of Saudi Arabia aptly illustrates the recent development of an oil-exporting country. Over the last five fiscal years the percentage growth rate of real non-oil GDP has been high by any standards but has shown a decline from its peak in 1975/76 - 13.0 (1974/75); 19.8 (1975/76); 16.9 (1976/77); 13.8 (1977/78); 12.7 (1978/79): Initially, this growth was in large part stimulated by a more rapid expansion of the public sector but beginning in 1976/77, the role of the private sector showed a marked increase. Over the same period, inflation, as measured by the percentage change in non-oil GDP deflator, reached its peak in 1974/75 but then declined owing to both the amelioration of supply bottlenecks and the restraint in monetary and fiscal policy - 61.3 (1974/75); 40.5 (1975/76); 22.4 (1976/77); 14.6 (1977/78); 7.2 (1978/79). These results were achieved during the course of the Second Development Plan. The major thrust of the plan was to expand infrastructure and petrochemicals. Under the Third Development Plan, launched in 1980, the authorities will endeavor to diversify the productive base of the economy to achieve sustained productive output in the non-oil sector; specifically to support light industry, agriculture, education and vocational training, and social services. It is only after the completion of basic infrastructural needs that a policy of economic diversification has become feasible. But even now, bottlenecks in certain skilled labor categories may hamper such efforts.

ASSESSMENT

The economies of the Middle East show many striking similar-ities and dissimilarities, but the most important fundamental difference contributing to observed differences between the countries of the Middle East is the existence and nonexistence of oil. Oil has dramatically affected developments in these economies. Given, however, that oil is finite in quantity and is in several cases the only known physical resource, to be successful over the long run, these countries must transform their oil asset into productive non-oil domestic assets and attractive (real yield) foreign assets. To assess the likelihood of such success in historical perspective, it may be useful to compare circumstances surrounding economic development in the Middle East oil-exporting countries to that of the gold rush era,(8) as the magnitude and swiftness of changes recalls few historical parallels. Among these are the 19th century gold rushes, particularly in California in the late 1840s and early 1850s and in the Yukon and Alaska in the 1890s.

In both gold and oil booms, the consequent inflation has been clearly of a demand-pull nature, coupled with severe supply bottlenecks. On the demand side, purchasing power multiplied severalfold within a few months. Not only did the local per capita money supply increase significantly, but the numbers of consumers also climbed dramatically. The characteristic "rush" of population associated with gold in the 19th century has its counterpart in the Middle East in the mid-1970s.

The gold rushes occurred in areas that were quite isolated from the major suppliers of basic goods - in western North America, months away by ship around Cape Horn from Atlantic coast suppliers.(9) Local production was limited (for example, some agriculture in California), and inventories of basic goods at the onset of the gold rushes reflected the low population levels before the discoveries. In the Middle East case, physical isolation has not been the specific cause of supply bottlenecks. Rather, the transportation infrastructure, often inadequate even before 1973, was simply not able to handle the rapid expansion of imports.(10) While local population in the Middle East was much more numerous than in California or the Yukon, local production nonetheless was limited by the specific skill requirements for increased output. These countries were not and are not developed industrial economies; local production does not satisfy domestic demand for items such as automobiles and some of them have little domestic capacity even for basic simple consumer goods.

The marked degree of inflation that occurred in gold and oil boom regions was essentially a geographically limited phenomenon. Once supply bottlenecks were eased, the most exaggerated price increases slowed down and were then reversed over time. Since most goods imported into these regions were purchased at world prices and represented minor shares of world production, the increase in local demand had little effect on international price trends.

The transformation of an economically backward country with an exhaustible resource is dependent upon the quality of investments. In the case of gold, California was put on the road to becoming a major overall economic producing region of the United States - first of other natural resources and agricultural goods, then of manufactures. In the Yukon and Alaska, the gold rushes were short-lived phenomena, with little permanent economic effect.

As we have seen above, there are many similarities between the economic phenomenon surrounding the gold rush era and the current economic position of many OPEC countries. The basic reason for such a parallel is the discovery or increase in value of an exportable natural resource and fundamental similarities of economic structures of OPEC countries and those countries which experienced a gold rush.

In all cases, there has been a rapid expansion of the money supply. But in the face of this increase in purchasing power the economy has been unable in the short and intermediate time frame to expand domestic production of goods and services. In addition, owing to distance or to physical constraints of infrastructure (ports, roads, warehousing, etc.) and to some extent because of the time required for procurement and transportation of imports, imports have not increased rapidly enough to satisfy demand. As a result of this excess demand, domestic inflation has been very rapid. And in the Middle East, disastrous government economic policy such as uncontrolled and haphazard expansion of imports and domestic production has often resulted in a great deal of economic waste, such as food rotting aboard ships. More importantly, expansion has occurred in industries in which the country does not have comparative advantage, while others with such advantages, as in agriculture, have been neglected.

Such prevailing economic forces have in most instances resulted in several similar economic patterns. Foreign labor or labor outside of the region have moved in to supplement domestic labor supply. In OPEC countries, as with the gold rush economies, this labor movement has been pronounced and has consisted of both skilled and unskilled labor. With the initiation of these rapid forces for change, these countries have accelerated toward becoming market economies, and with such a change in economic structure a more sophisticated financial and banking system has developed. But all the while prices increased, the increases being most pronounced in nontradeable goods where imports would not supplement domestic availabilities. With higher prices, domestic supplies responded positively. In the short run, however, this expansion was not enough to satisfy demand, even when supplemented with imports.

The interesting question from the Middle Eastern and OPEC perspective is whether, in view of recent availability of financial resources, a sustained drive to development, as in California, is likely or whether the boom may be a temporary phenomenon, as in Alaska and the Yukon.

Certainly, much OPEC capital is reinvested regionally, as gold capital was retained in California. But many early indications are not promising that these investments will pay off in the Middle East. There are signs that, as in the Yukon, private capital holders are looking elsewhere for future activity.

There is, however, a major difference between the gold rush cases and the Middle Eastern countries - the oil boom seems likely to last somewhat longer, giving local governments the opportunity of gaining experience from the excesses of the mid-1970s. This opportunity does not extend equally to all the Middle Eastern countries. Though most people are aware that not all of the Middle East is equally endowed with oil, there is a tendency to forget how uneven the distribution is. Almost 60 percent of the area's residents are citizens of countries with little or no current production. Among the major oil exporters, three (Algeria, Iran, and Iraq) have another 35 percent of the Middle East's people, but pump only about one-third of the oil; the rest comes mostly from Saudi Arabia, Kuwait, and the UAE.

While some of the world's poorest countries are in the Middle East (for example, the two Yemens), all the oil producers are well off by Third-World standards. Still, as the recent GNP per capita figures show, the variation is considerable. Algeria, with more than 17 million people, is OPEC's poorest Middle Eastern member, with per capita GNP about equal to that of Peru or Chile, while Kuwait and the United Arab Emirates (with populations of about one million and 600,000 respectively) lead the list.

Even among the oil states then, the disparity is fairly wide - Qatar, Kuwait, and the UAE have about 11 to 12 times Algeria's per capita GNP. This gap becomes even wider if we remember that in most of the smaller gulf states, half or more of the population are noncitizens, with no real claim on national wealth. Thus, the common myth that all Middle Easterners, or even all those from OPEC states, are oil rich is obviously misleading. Across the OPEC Middle East as a whole, average GNP per capita was only about $3,000 in 1978.

These GNP per capita figures, which indicate current income, are less helpful when the long-run prospects of the Middle East are being considered. For this purpose, a measure of the region's wealth of proven oil reserves would be more interesting. Here as well, tremendous changes took place during the early 1970s. On a per capita basis, this oil wealth (1975 prices) is considerable by any standard (Table 6.10). And if current oil prices are used, this wealth would be more than double the 1975 value.

Table 6.10. Middle Eastern Income and
Oil Wealth (1975).

Country	GNP/Capita	Value of Proven Oil/Capita
Algeria	$ 870	$ 5,720
Iran	1,660	22,595
Iraq	1,250	36,800
Kuwait	15,190	848,000
Libya	5,530	124,340
Oman	2,320	89,475
Qatar	10,970	347,375
Saudi Arabia	4,010	301,325
United Arab Emirates	13,600	572,390

Source: World Bank Atlas, The World Bank, 1977. The
International Petroleum Encyclopedia (Tulsa: 1976).

The transformation of this oil wealth will face many pit-
falls. But given the magnitude of such wealth, the richer oil
states have considerable leeway to get their investments in
order. They may, however, have increasingly to look abroad
for promising investment opportunities. But, other producers
(notably Iran and Algeria) enjoy less leeway and must take
greater care to avoid waste, lest the Yukon example become
appropriate when oil production begins to decline, perhaps as
soon as the mid-1980s.

The effects and consequences of the gold rush and the oil
boom on the political and social arenas have been also great.
As an example, the gold rush in California resulted in institutional developments such as government. These evolutions out
of the mining camps and towns provided the new society with
its framework for order. This frame was thought crude at
first, developed rapidly and promoted an environment that
over the next hundred years made California the nation's most
populous and wealthiest state.

In the Middle Eastern experience, two different cases
should be briefly mentioned - Kuwait and Iran. The Kuwaiti
approach has been to give priority for social programs for
citizens of the country. Industrialization has taken a backseat
but instead surplus revenues have been invested abroad to

provide for a "social" fund for all future generations of Kuwaitis.

The Iranian experience is, on the other hand, much less simplistic. Iran's per capita oil revenue is much less than that of Kuwait; this fact, coupled with Iran's potential for economic development, encouraged the government to embark on a rapid program of industrialization. But even more important than industrialization was the commitment to military expenditures, other prestige projects, and foreign investments. This path resulted in neglect of agriculture, of education, of health, and other social expenditures and in fact, because of large military expenditures and foreign commitments, even industry received little attention. Specifically, even the form of the commitment to industry was ill conceived and no result of long-run advantage was given to the economy. These glaring facts, coupled with dismal income distribution, contributed in large part to the political and social disruptions of 1978-1979. That is the neglect of society at large and the phenomenal wealth of a few ripped apart the social fabric.

In short, although the gold rush and the oil boom have many similarities, the end result may be different in certain areas. The gold rushes in Alaska and the Yukon were short-lived with little permanent impact. To California the discovery of gold was in large part a blessing but to Iran the oil boom could, up until now, be more appropriately referred to as the "oil curse." For other oil-exporting countries the results have been a mixed bag. But the future is uncertain and success depends on how oil wealth is transformed into productive domestic assets and foreign holdings of both financial and real assets.

For the non-oil-exporting countries of the region, future prospects depend on five major factors. First, like any other country, the authorities should adopt appropriate adjustment policies; restraint on demand coupled with medium- and long-term policies to stimulate supply, while conserving energy and promoting more efficient (reducing the ratio of energy consumption to GNP) use of energy in industry. Second, to the extent that countries increase the output of indigenous energy sources, as in Egypt and Syria, the availability of foreign exchange for development financing will be enhanced. In addition to these general factors, the future performance of these non-oil-exporting countries will depend on some special regional issues. What will be the future level of workers' remittances from the oil-exporting countries? How will import markets develop in oil-exporting countries? And what will be the future level of economic assistance from the oil-exporting countries? For the recent past, these factors have been critical determinants, to varying degrees, in the development of the economies of non-oil-exporting countries. The future in these areas, however, though it is promising, is uncertain.

NOTES

1. Currently, owing to political and economic upheaval, Iran's GNP may be substantially lower than this figure.

2. The Lebanese figures are subject to a wide margin of error.

3. Address by J. de Larosière before the International Monetary Conference, New Orleans, June 3, 1980.

4. For this reason, it may be expected that the relative share of this sector may have increased since 1977 for Syria and especially Egypt.

5. As quoted in the London Financial Times, June 9, 1980, p. 17.

6. A. Ecevit and K.C. Zachariah, "International Labor Migration," Finance and Development (December 1978), p. 36.

7. In this regard, the case of Jordan in 1976 and 1977 is mentioned in Ecevit and Zachariah, "International Labor Migration," p. 37.

8. This relies heavily on an unpublished paper; for further details, see H. Askari, J.T. Cummings, and H. Reed, "Middle East: Gold Rush or Economic Development," (Austin: University of Texas, 1978).

9. The gold sites in the Yukon and Alaska were also a hard journey inland from entry ports.

10. For example, ship demurrage charges in 1974 approached and then exceeded actual transport costs as freighters backed up in established ports like Jeddah, Khorramshahr, and Dubai for unloading waits as long as 200 days. The often poorly graded highways of Turkey began to crumble under convoys of overloaded trucks bound for Iran and Saudi Arabia, while delays at undermanned customs stations all the way from Europe to the Middle East added weeks to truck journeys that might have taken ten days in 1972.

FURTHER READING

Askari, H. and J.T. Cummings. "The Middle East and the United States: A Problem of Brain Drain," International Journal of Middle Eastern Studies 8 (1977).

Askari, H., J.T. Cummings, and H. Reed. "Middle East: Gold Rush or Economic Developoment," Austin: University of Texas, 1978.

de Larosière, J.   Address before the International Monetary
    Conference.   New Orleans: June 3, 1980.

Ecevit, A. and K.C. Zachariah.   "International Labor Migra-
    tion," Finance and Development (December 1978).

Financial Times (London).   June 9, 1980, p. 17.

Gerakis, A. and S. Thavanity.   "Wave of Middle East Migration
    Raises Questions of Policy in Many Countries," IMF Sur-
    vey (September 4, 1978).

Government of Kuwait.   Census of Kuwait, 1970, 1975.

The International Petroleum Encyclopedia.   Tulsa: 1976.

World Bank Atlas.   Washington, D.C.: IBRD, 1979.

World Tables 1980.   Washington, D.C.: IBRD, 1980.

7 U.S.-Middle East Trade

Peter B. Hale
Cherie A. Loustaunau

The history of commercial relations between America and the
Middle East dates from early in the 18th century. The British
North American colonies used sea-borne trade to establish their
economic viability early in their history. The developing merchants of New England moved quickly beyond their initial role
as a source of supply to Great Britain of American raw materials and products, and developed a thriving three-corner trading pattern with Britain, the West Indies, and North America.
The success of this trade and the relative ease of transportation by ship compared with the difficulty of the land transport
needed to develop the American hinterland soon led these
merchants farther afield.

Although the colonists were prohibited from direct commercial relationships with North Africa and the Levant by the
British Acts of Trade, American manufactures were carried to
the Barbary Coast on British vessels or on American ships in
British convoys before 1750. American wheat, flour, cloth,
and other commodities were sold in North Africa in return for
wine, salt, and Moroccan leather.(1)

After the Declaration of Independence of the United
States was signed and issued in 1776, the Americans lost their
trading privileges with other British colonies and American
shipping lost the protection of British men of war. When
American merchants sought to renew commercial contacts after
independence had been won, they found that trade was no
longer possible with their former partners in the West Indies,
because they were still part of the British Empire. So the
Americans turned more attention to the East, only to find the
Barbary pirates across the sea lanes to the trading centers of
the Mediterranean and North Africa. Commercial contacts with
the region expanded, but they were increasingly costly. By
1800, almost $2 million or one-fifth of the country's annual

revenues was paid to the North Africa states to permit access to the Mediterranean for American ships and to ransom prisoners.(2)   Efforts got underway early to reach a less expensive accommodation.

In 1787, America's first treaty with a non-European power was ratified: a treaty of peace and friendship between the United States of America and the sultan of Morocco, Sidi Mohammed Ibn-Abdullah. The treaty assured protection to American ships in Moroccan waters, in addition to establishing a special trading relationship. Though superseded by a new treaty in 1837, the basic provisions of the 1787 treaty have never been changed, making it the longest unbroken treaty relationship in American history. Treaties with Algiers, Tripoli, and Tunis were longer in coming and it was not until 1816 that a military expedition against Algiers finally freed American shipping from Barbary piracy.

Despite the treaties with the Barbary states, little trade developed with the North African countries. The elimination of the menace to American shipping did, however, allow trade to develop with the countries of the eastern Mediterranean. This trade grew slowly, fluctuating widely from year to year. "Turkey, Levant and Egypt" appeared as a separate listing in the Treasury Department's import and export statistics for the first time only in 1803,(3) and U.S. trade with the Middle East was not a consistently significant portion of total U.S. trade until after World War II (see Table 7.1.)

There were both political and commercial reasons for the relatively limited amount of goods exchanged between the United States and the Middle East before the middle of the 20th century. Most Americans, including those in Washington, wanted to keep ties of any sort with other countries to a minimum. They were drawn reluctantly into the affairs of Europe, but only missionaries, and a few hardy entrepreneurs ventured into other parts of the world. Prior to the discovery of oil in the region in the 1920s, a minimum American political involvement followed the traders and missionaries into the Middle East.

Commercially, prior to the middle of the 19th century, the United States and the countries of the Middle East had little to trade with each other. Both regions largely exported raw materials and imported manufactured goods. In fact, though industrialization changed the nature of U.S. exports, U.S. non-oil imports from the region are today fairly similar to those of the colonial period.

The American merchants, however, maintained into the mid-1800s the pattern of multilateral trade that they had developed before independence. Goods imported from South America and elsewhere were shipped from the United States to the eastern Mediterranean in exchange for goods that were sold in still another part of the world. As late as 1840, U.S.

Table 7.1.   U.S. Trade with the Middle East, 1825-1945
($ Thousands).

	Domestic Exports	Reexports	Total Exports	Percent of Total U.S. Exports	Imports	Percent of Total U.S. Imports
1825	37.9	368.3	406.2	0.4	864.4	1.0
1830	413.3	337.5	750.8	0.6	417.4	0.7
1835	63.2	216.8	280.0	0.2	387.6	0.3
1840	276.6	156.9	433.5	0.2	563.5	0.6
1845	165.1	49.5	214.6	0.2	781.5	0.7
1850	257.7	53.3	311.0	0.2	801.0	0.5
1855	958.0	163.8	1,121.8	0.4	790.9	0.3
1860	880.4	60.9	941.3	0.3	970.2	0.3
1865	428.7	185.5	614.2	0.4	326.9	0.1
1870	2,565.3	13.0	2,578.3	0.7	678.7	0.2
1875	4,244.9	*	4,244.9	0.8	579.9	0.1
1880	1,913.1	*	1,913.1	0.2	1,171.5	0.2
1885	428.7	185.5	614.2	0.1	2,036.8	0.4
1890	176.4	*	176.4	**	4,622.8	0.6
1895	309.3	0.4	309.7	**	6,809.2	0.9
1900	3,152.1	1.0	3,153.1	0.2	17,748.9	2.1
1905	2,806.0	3.9	2,809.9	0.2	22,050.0	2.0
1910	2,835.2	7.8	2,843.0	0.2	23,164.7	1.5
1915	6,851.9	*	6,851.9	0.2	31,532.8	1.9
1920	92,724.9	1,230.8	93,955.0	1.1	145,860.2	2.8
1925	119,145.8	93.4	119,239.2	2.4	79,283.7	1.9
1930	33,197.2	286.1	33,473.3	0.4	42,636.0	1.4
1935	34,593.8	227.7	34,821.5	1.5	28,996.2	1.4
1940	53,449.0	368.2	53,817.2	1.3	44,896.0	1.7
1945	240,924.4	3,718.0	244,642.3	2.5	118,904.1	2.9

*Less than $50

**Less than 0.05 percent

Source: Treasury Department, 1825-1903; Department of Commerce, 1904-1946.

reexports of foreign goods to the Middle East were equal to exports of American products and, in 1821, U.S. domestic goods were less than 10 percent of total American exports to the region. The port of Smyrna (Izmir) in Turkey was the center for this trade. Americans shipped wheat, cotton, rum, coffee, refined sugar, and tobacco to Turkey in exchange for animal hides, raw wool, wine, olives, figs, raisins, and opium. By 1828, New England merchants were purchasing almost the entire Turkish opium crop for resale in China.(4)

Hoping to capitalize more on the commercial potential in Turkey and the other countries on the Black Sea, the U.S. government in Washington finally agreed in 1830 to negotiate a treaty that had been sought by the Turkish government for years. The treaty assured most-favored-nation status to American goods and gave American merchant vessels access to the Black Sea. The commercial consequences of the treaty, however, never lived up to the expectations that motivated its negotiation. The prevailing winds and currents through the straits made passage into the Black Sea difficult, and waiting out nature's vagaries was too costly a proposition for many of America's sailing captains. In addition, the exorbitant duties on the import of raw wool placed by the "tariff of abominations" of 1828 had already begun complicating the problem of return cargoes.(5) Nevertheless, Americans maintained a small but steady trade in Turkey and the Levant.

Although statistically insignificant, there are interesting trading stories involving other Middle Eastern countries. The efforts of a certain Edmund Roberts of Portsmouth, New Hampshire, who was related by marriage to the secretary of the navy, resulted in the signing in 1833 of the Treaty of Amity and Commerce with the sultan of Muscat. Roberts had lost a considerable amount in commercial ventures in Zanzibar because British merchants, protected by a most-favored-nation treaty, prevented him from establishing a foothold in the lucrative East African trade. Roberts sought to recoup his losses by changing the ground rules. He negotiated a treaty with the sultan of Muscat, who was also the ruler of Zanzibar, that gave the United States most-favored-nation status. Though Roberts did not live to benefit from the treaty, it did facilitate a small amount of trade from which others profited.(6)

The sultan's treaty ratification papers arrived in the United States on May 2, 1840. His personal emissary, Ahmed bin Na'aman, and the ship in which Ahmed sailed, al-Sultanah, were the first Arab emissary and the first Arab vessel to visit American shores. The al-Sultanah's cargo included 1,300 bags of dates, 21 bales of Persian wool carpets, and 100 bales of Mocha coffee from Muscat and 108 ivory tusks, 81 cases of gum copal, 135 bags of cloves, and 1,000 dry salted hides from Zanzibar. The ship returned, after a stay of several months and a complete refitting, with a cargo for the sultan's account and for general purchase that included gray sheeting, red, white, and blue beads, muskets, gunpowder, glass and china plates, sperm candles, gold thread, paper, sugar, vases, perfume, music boxes, mirrors, chandeliers, and candies. As a result of the treaty, Muscat also was able to purchase several brass 24-pounders from the United States in 1842.(7)

Though American ships had visited Alexandria off and on since 1800, trade with Egypt was fairly small in the early part of the century, but there were a number of unusual commercial contacts. For instance, it was rumored that the pasha, Mohamed Ali, had bought two warships in the United States in the 1820s and from that time had kept an agent in this country shopping for naval stores.(8) In 1837, the U.S. vice-consul also purchased a quantity of U.S. cotton-ginning equipment and other machinery for the pasha.(9) Sometime after the Civil War, Pullman palace cars were purchased for the pasha's special train, and there was the emigrant from the state of Maine who prospered for a time "by cooling the champagne of the Pasha with the product of ice houses which he had established on the Danube."(10)

In 1848, U.S. economic and commercial ties with Egypt had become important enough to establish a consulate general at Alexandria and Egypt appeared as a separate listing in the U.S. trade statistics just before the Civil War. The primary imports from Egypt were cotton and cotton rag, much of which was used to make paper money in the United States. American exports to Egypt were primarily timber and wooden furniture.

There was little or no direct trade with Persia until late in the 19th century, though a commerce in American rum was carried on by foreign flag vessels. The possibilities of profitable trade with Persia were noted as early as 1832 by the U.S. consul at Smyrna, but American contact with the country was almost exclusively the province of the missionaries.(11) It was only out of concern for their effort that Congress finally appropriated the money for a legation in Tehran in 1883, 27 years after a treaty of friendship and commerce was signed.(12)

After the Mexican-American War and the conquest of California, there was a large increase in shipping from the U.S. East Coast to California which drew vessels out of the trade with the Mediterranean. The American shipbuilding industry, however, soon caught up with the new demand, and despite the California gold rush and despite - or maybe because of - the revolutions in Europe, American commerce with the countries of the eastern Mediterranean began to expand more rapidly. American ships were calling at Beirut and Jaffa to take on olive oil and wool. By 1855, the city of Constantinople "was seeing the weekly arrival of an American ship bringing cotton textiles, rum, sugar, and flour for the armies fighting the Crimean War and a problem of distressed seamen for the diplomats."(13)   The ships returned with wool, fruit, gums, resins, licorice paste, and, of course, opium.

Following the American Civil War, U.S. interests shifted to other parts of the world, tariffs rose, and American shipping went into a decline.   After a large drop in trade during the war, however, exports to the Middle East climbed steadily through the remainder of the century.   The large-scale export of petroleum and arms and ammunition even reversed the U.S. balance of trade with the Ottoman Empire from one in which the United States purchased three to four times the value of the goods it sold to a healthy surplus.

In the United States, new forms of energy had been revolutionizing manufacturing and transportation.   As production of the new industrial goods increased, their export increased and the export of raw materials and rum declined in relative importance.   U.S. merchants continued to purchase about half of Turkey's opium crop and quite a large amount of raw wool, but imports of fruits decreased and imports of licorice root, birdseed, and rags for the manufacture of paper increased.   U.S. exports changed radically and became dominated by petroleum, armaments, and machinery and transportation equipment.(14)

As strange as it may seem today, the United States had an effective world monopoly on petroleum from 1860 until the late 1880s.   By 1868, illuminating oil was America's chief export to Syria and Egypt and was equaled in value only by rum among consumer goods shipped to Constantinople.   The American consul at Constantinople reported in 1879 that "even the sacred lamps over the Prophet's tomb at Mecca [sic] are fed with oil from Pennsylvania."(15)

In addition to the change in the composition of trade, American goods were increasingly carried on foreign bottoms. American shipping never recovered from its catastrophic decline at the beginning of the Civil War and by the turn of the 19th century, the tonnage of U.S. shipping in foreign trade was less than it had been at the turn of the 18th century.(16) American attempts to inaugurate direct shipping service before World War I were thwarted by the British "shipping ring" and other competitors, or operated under foreign flags.(17)

After 1890, Egypt began to emerge as America's primary trading partner in the region.   Long staple cotton was Egypt's largest export, but sugar, onions, gum arabic, and animal hides also found their way into the American marketplace. U.S. exports consisted of petroleum, especially kerosene, iron manufactures, lumber, agricultural implements, and a rather large volume of wheat and flour.

Around the turn of the century, American commercial prospects and interests in the Middle East increased considerably.   This was reflected in the trade statistics by an increased volume and the separate listing of Aden, Persia, and

Morocco, in addition to Turkey and Egypt. The fashions made popular by U.S. industrialists generated even larger imports of hides and skins from Morocco and Aden, and coffee and ivory from Aden and wool carpets from Persia. Dates, selected by hand from the product of an estimated four million trees, were arriving in considerable quantities from Muscat and nearly all the figs and sultana raisins imported into the United States came from the region around Smyrna.(18)

In the early 1900s trade with and through Turkey also increased in importance. By 1912, the American Tobacco Company was spending $10 million a year in the purchase and preparation of tobacco in Turkey that was mixed in the United States with American leaf for "Turkish blend" cigarettes, and the firm of McAndrews and Forbes had a virtual monopoly on the U.S.-Turkey trade in licorice root, shipping 40,000-50,000 tons per year to the United States.(19)

The American commercial presence in Constantinople included a varied group of firms. The Singer Sewing Machine Company conducted a million-dollar business annually in Asiatic Turkey selling U.S. products through nearly 200 agencies and stores. The largest American export business was conducted by the Standard Oil Company of New York (Socony), through its subsidiary the Vacuum Oil Company, which had branches in Egypt as well as Turkey. Socony's brisk business continued in Anatolia and the Levant even after Russian and Rumanian oil began to cut into its market in Egypt.(20) At the other end of the scale, the Starr Piano Company of Richmond, Indiana established a sales office in Constantinople around the turn of the century, often trading American pianos for oriental carpets - each product enjoying a vogue in the others country of manufacture.

The expanded commercial involvement in the region also was reflected in the establishment of an American Chamber of Commerce at Constantinople in 1911. The chamber quickly set up branches in Smyrna, Beirut, Cairo, and other major commercial centers. Within a year, it could claim 500 members.(21)

With the exception of trade with Turkey and the import of carpets from the entire region, U.S. trade prospered during World War I. Turkey's close relationship with Germany during the war brought American-Turkish trade to its lowest level in many years. The exchange of goods was nearly eliminated, except for U.S. imports of Turkish dates. The war reinforced Egypt's predominant position as America's main trading partner in the region. A sharp increase in the demand for Egyptian cotton brought imports into the United States from $18 million in 1913 to $32 million in 1917. The growth in U.S. exports to Egypt was largely attributable to sales of mules which rose to $7 million in 1917.

Outside of Turkey, the United States began to export automobiles to the region and maintained sales of petroleum products, oilfield equipment and other machinery, and textiles. The United States temporarily stopped importing carpets after 1915, but continued to import gums, opium, goat and sheep skins, and coffee.

Following World War I, there was some expectation that the United States was about to embark on a period of tremendous growth in its commercial relationships with the countries of the Middle East. Indeed, as they had been doing since the late 18th century, American consular and diplomatic reports stressed the great potential for American businessmen in the region and criticized their lack of foresight and entrepreneurial ability in failing to take full advantage of these markets. The protectorates, however, established by the Great Powers under the League of Nations mandate system effectively divided the region from Iran to Morocco, with the exception of Saudi Arabia and North Yemen, into spheres of British and French influence. So the promise of greatly expanded trade failed to materialize. (22)

This does not mean that trade did not grow. It did; but, as before, it grew slowly. The traditional imports and exports continued to show up in the statistics. Turkey began exporting carpets again, along with fruits, wool, opium, and licorice root. Carpets also reappeared from Iran, which became America's third-largest trading partner in the region, and cotton continued to be Egypt's largest export. The United States, however, began to purchase some new items from the Middle East. Chrome ore was added to Turkey's exports, and manganese and copper ores to those of Egypt. Americans were now purchasing pistachio nuts from Iran and sausage casings from Iran, Turkey, and the countries of North Africa. The North African countries were also exporting olive oil and cork products to the United States and Palestine was shipping wines and potash from the Dead Sea.

Americans exported to the region larger quantities of food and food products and machinery and transportation equipment than they had prior to the war. Transportation equipment included automobiles, trucks, buses, and even some airplanes. Machinery exports were primarily agricultural implements and mining, and later, oilfield equipment. Food items included sugar, wheat, apples, pears, and vegetables.

The United States also continued to export petroleum products. Increasing production of crude oil in the area, however, and fear that domestic oil supplies were about to run out, finally brought significant U.S. government interest and involvement in the Middle East on the side of American commercial interests. Gradually, in the late 1920s and 1930s, American companies won sizable concessions in the exploitation of the oil resources in the area through the application of diplomatic pressure on their behalf.

During World War II, U.S. imports from the Middle East declined somewhat with the exception of the purchase of a huge quantity of raw tobacco from Turkey and purchases from the nascent diamond industry in Palestine. Following the war, the development of refrigerated transportation allowed increases in sales of fresh fruits and vegetables to the United States and the countries of the region began to export more semiprocessed and processed goods, particularly textiles. The most significant development in the U.S. import picture, however, was the gradual growth of the Middle East as a major source of petroleum.

World War II permanently affected both the character and size of U.S. exports to the Middle East and altered the composition of those exports. For the first time, U.S. goods began to enter the countries of the region under government-to-government bilateral agreements rather than strictly as a result of the efforts of the U.S. private sector. Though the nature of the agreements have changed periodically, and they vary from country to country, they have supported and still support a significant proportion of U.S. exports to the Middle East.

During the war, most American exports to the Middle East entered under lend-lease financing. Egypt received by far the largest share of this aid - $870 million of a total of $891 million - but it was also provided to Algeria, Iraq, Turkey, Morocco, Iran, Syria, Palestine, and the Arabian Peninsula States. Though a wide variety of agricultural and industrial goods continued to appear on the ledgers, purchases of munitions and weaponry drove the export statistics up sharply. Bahrain's purchase of a large quantity of oilfield equipment was the only instance of a significant increase in non-lend-lease exports.

Although the United States had periodically sold military goods and technical assistance to Egypt and Turkey, the changed nature of the U.S. involvement in the Middle East made these items a fixed part of American exports to the region following World War II. The construction of a military airfield in Dhahran, Saudi Arabia, in 1945, by the U.S. Army Corps of Engineers, began a relationship that now has the corps overseeing billions of dollars in military construction in Saudi Arabia. Iran, Israel, Turkey, Egypt, Jordan, Libya, and Morocco have also purchased, or received through military aid programs, varying amounts of weaponry and other military equipment and services.

After World War II, the increasing U.S. strategic interests in the region also made economic development aid programs a permanent part of the U.S.-Middle East trade picture. The U.S. Agency for International Development (USAID) and its predecessor agencies have funneled over $8.2 billion in aid to the countries of the Middle East, primarily to

Egypt, Iran, Israel, Jordan, Lebanon, Libya, Morocco, Syria, Tunisia, Turkey and the Yemen Arab Republic (see Table 7.2). U.S. economic aid to these countries from the end of World War II through 1981 accounted for 26.4 percent of total U.S. foreign economic assistance. This assistance has been utilized both for industrial and infrastructure project financing and for general support for import needs. Of the total figure for the Near East, Egypt ($2.8 billion), Israel ($1.8 billion), and Turkey ($1.5 billion) have accounted for almost 80 percent.

In addition, the United States has provided assistance in the form of agricultural commodities under Public Law 480 to 12 countries. The dollar value of this assistance from mid-1954 (when the program started) through September 1979 reached $4.9 billion or 17 percent of total worldwide food assistance (see Table 7.3). The major Near East beneficiaries of the PL-480 program have been Egypt ($1.9 billion), Turkey ($681 million), and Tunisia ($446 million).

U.S. exports to the Near East increased steadily, but generally not dramatically, from World War II until the Arab oil embargo in 1973-1974 (see Table 7.4). Machinery and transport equipment for use in agriculture, construction, and the development of petroleum and mineral deposits became the most important component of this trade. In addition, U.S. agricultural products, especially food-grains and edible oils, became a more significant element of U.S. exports with the addition of PL-480-financed shipments to the usual commercial sales.

Turkey was the United States' largest trading partner in the region for the first decade and a half after World War II, followed by Israel and Iran. During the 1960s, Israel took the lead and Turkey dropped to third place. From World War II until 1970, Egypt and Saudi Arabia were the only Arab countries to which U.S. exports rose over $100 million annually. The continuing influence of the British in the sheikdoms of the lower Arabian Peninsula and of the French in North Africa prevented a significant increase in U.S. trade with those countries. Growth in U.S. trade with Syria and Iraq was blocked in the late 1970s by the shift of their political allegiances, and therefore their purchases, to the Soviet Union and Eastern Europe. By 1970, U.S. exports to all of the Middle East were still only 4.7 percent of total U.S. exports.

The Arab oil embargo of 1973-1974 and the resultant, sharp OPEC price increases changed this situation radically. In 1973, U.S. exports to the Near East had reached 5.4 percent of U.S. exports worldwide (see Table 7.5). This figure, however, jumped to 6.8 percent in 1974, 10 percent in 1975, and reached a high of 10.6 percent in 1978, before the revolution in Iran. Total U.S. trade with the region showed a positive balance of almost $2 billion in 1973; by 1979, it was almost $12 billion in deficit.

Table 7.2. U.S. Aid Commitments to the Middle East (Ending 12/31/79, $ Thousands).

	AID's Predecessor Agencies	Development Loans	Supporting Assistance	PL-480 Economic Development	PL-480 Cooley Loans	PL-480 Miscellaneous Non-food	M.E. Special Requirements Fund	Miscellaneous Development Assistance	Country Total
Egypt	16,754	41,138	2,273,768	457,891	1,032				2,790,583
Iran	177,594	27,393	19,554	25,709	3,332	4,612*			258,194
Israel	96,410	138,599	1,275,000	243,951	28,416	2,498**			1,784,874
Jordan	2,467	19,724	157,650	3,681			10,000	7,400	200,922
Lebanon	4,892								4,892
Libya	7,014								7,014
Morocco	190,246	54,641	73,137	44,160	3,095			21,000	386,279
Syria	2,787	427	322,700	17,727			78,000		421,641
Tunisia	44,823	151,614		69,896	1,893			20,850	289,076
Turkey	361,562	809,797	120,518	168,425	58,992				1,519,294
Yemen (Sana)								1,349	1,349
*Total Middle East	904,549	1,243,333	4,242,327	1,031,440	96,760	7,110	88,000	50,599	7,664,118
% of World Total									26.4

*Common defense

**Triangular trade

Source: Office of Financial Management, Agency for International Development, "Status of Loan Agreements as of December 31, 1979."

Table 7.3. PL-480 Commodity Assistance to the
Middle East Through FY 1979
($ Thousands).

	TITLE I*	TITLE II**	TOTAL
Egypt	1,666,599	247,381	1,913,980
Iran	115,344	48,356	163,700
Israel	643,253	17,694	660,947
Jordan	65,642	92,441	158,083
Jordan (West Bank)	-	16,124	16,124
Lebanon	26,409	36,350	62,759
Libya	-	32,900	32,900
Morocco	195,489	353,861	549,350
Syria	111,622	35,691	147,313
Tunisia	199,197	246,944	446,141
Turkey	550,104	130,417	680,521
Yemen (Aden)	-	457	457
Yemen (Sana)	-	21,466	21,466
Total Middle East	3,573,659	1,280,082	4,853,741
% of World Total	17.4	15.2	16.8

---

*Government-to-government concessional sales.

**Food for peace.

Source: U.S. Department of Agriculture.

    This radical change has been caused by two factors.
Growing U.S. needs for imported energy resources, coupled
with sharply higher prices for crude oil, have driven U.S.
import figures upward. At the same time, the massive revenues generated by oil exports have allowed the Near East pro-
ducer countries to embark on massive social and economic
development programs and to assist with the development of
their less wealthy neighbors. Improved political relations with
many of the Arab countries, reflected in the ties formed by
government-to-government joint economic commissions and private business councils, support of U.S. exports (especially to

Table 7.4. U.S. Trade with the Middle East, 1946–1970 ($ Millions).

	EXPORTS, INCLUDING REEXPORTS					GENERAL IMPORTS				
	1946-50 average	1951-55 average	1956-60 average	1965	1970	1946-50 average	1951-55 average	1956-60 average	1965	1970
TOTAL MIDDLE EAST	445.1	598.0	803.0	1242.0	2020.0	155.3	285.8	411.3	723.8	502.0
% of U.S. TOTAL	3.8	3.9	4.2	4.5	4.7	2.3	2.6	3.0	3.4	1.3
Algeria	37.7	19.3	26.7	20.5	61.1	3.3	4.9	1.5	4.8	9.5
Bahrain	10.4	10.2	7.4	10.0	11.8	1.2	1.1	3.3	2.4	7.7
Egypt	43.5	70.5	90.7	157.6	80.4	29.2	39.1	19.6	17.1	22.9
Iran	49.7	38.0	100.3	162.1	326.1	24.3	27.4	43.7	87.3	66.8
Iraq	11.2	29.0	35.3	40.0	22.2	9.6	18.9	32.2	18.9	3.0
Israel	51.5 }	93.2 }	108.6 }	184.6	569.5	9.4 }	13.4 }	22.4 }	61.5	149.6
Palestine			*	9.3	-			*	*	-
Jordan			10.8	19.5	63.4			0.1	0.3	0.1
Kuwait	14.7	13.3	40.1	65.8	61.6	18.7	61.6	131.1	48.7	25.4
Lebanon	35.8 }	30.7 }	41.6 }	74.4	63.1	9.6 }	4.0 }	4.0 }	6.4	12.8
Syria			20.8	13.0	11.1		11.9	8.3	3.8	2.1
Libya	0.3	2.4	24.4	63.6	104.2	0.3	*	0.2	30.5	39.1
Morocco	39.5	48.1	89.1	55.3	88.9	4.4	11.4	20.4	6.4	9.6
Saudi Arabia	57.8	70.5	59.6	128.5	140.4	12.9	52.7	62.1	106.3	19.7
Tunisia	11.0	6.9	10.9	43.6	49.2	1.2	1.5	2.2	4.7	3.0
Turkey	80.5	79.6	128.4	160.3	314.6	58.5	69.1	71.6	81.8	69.8
Yemen (Aden)	1.0	4.8	1.6	5.6	2.7	0.1	0.1	0.4	201.9	0.1
Arabian Peninsula State, n.e.s.	0.5	1.5	6.5	28.5	49.2	1.8	7.8	7.8	41.0	60.8

*Less than $0.1 million.

Source: Foreign Commerce and Navigation of the United States, 1946–1963, Bureau of the Census, U.S. Department of Commerce; U.S. Imports and Exports, 1965 and 1970, Bureau of the Census, U.S. Department of Commerce.

Table 7.5. U.S. Trade with the Middle East, 1973-1979 ($ Millions).

EXPORTS, INCLUDING REEXPORTS

	1973	1974	1975	1976	1977	1978	1979
Total of area	3,824.8	6,736.0	10,738.0	11,641.2	12,765.2	15,188.9	14,134.0
% of U.S. total	5.4	6.8	10.0	10.1	10.6	10.6	7.7
Arab Countries	1,744.3	3,334.0	5,337.2	7,005.0	8,164.4	9,222.3	10,903.9
Algeria	160.5	315.1	631.8	487.0	526.5	374.0	404.1
Bahrain	41.4	79.7	90.2	279.5	203.3	157.1	159.5
Egypt	225.4	455.2	682.7	810.0	982.4	1,134.1	1,433.3
Iraq	55.9	284.7	309.7	381.8	210.9	316.6	441.6
Jordan	79.4	105.2	195.4	234.0	301.8	235.0	333.7
Kuwait	119.5	208.5	366.1	471.5	547.8	744.8	764.7
Lebanon	161.6	286.9	402.3	48.5	123.8	142.2	227.4
Libya	103.7	139.4	231.5	276.6	313.7	425.0	468.1
Morocco	112.9	184.0	199.5	297.0	371.6	406.4	271.3
Oman	9.1	36.5	74.7	57.1	56.9	65.1	87.9
Qatar	18.8	33.6	50.3	78.7	113.1	76.7	138.3
Saudi Arabia	441.9	835.2	1,501.8	2,774.1	3,575.3	4,370.1	4,875.0
Syria	20.7	39.6	127.8	272.2	133.6	142.5	229.3
Tunisia	60.2	86.9	90.8	82.4	111.3	83.0	175.1
United Arab Emirates	121.1	229.7	371.5	424.8	515.1	493.2	666.8
Yemen (Aden)	2.6	12.3	2.8	4.4	30.9	25.9	13.7
Yemen (Sana)	9.6	1.5	8.3	25.4	46.4	30.6	214.1
Non-Arab Countries	2,080.5	3,402.0	5,400.8	4,636.2	4,600.8	5,966.6	3,230.1
Iran	771.5	1,733.6	3,241.7	2,776.0	2,730.8	3,684.4	1,019.4
Israel	961.6	1,205.7	1,551.2	1,409.2	1,446.5	1,925.1	1,856.6
Turkey	347.4	462.7	607.9	451.0	423.5	357.1	354.1

(continued)

Table 7.5. (Continued)

GENERAL IMPORTS

	1973	1974	1975	1976	1977	1978	1979
Total of area	2,005.8	6,009.2	8,011.6	15,206.6	20,018.8	19,417.4	25,901.1
% of U.S. total	2.9	6.0	8.3	12.6	13.6	11.3	12.6
Arab Countries	1,262.2	3,453.6	6,154.5	12,916.0	16,514.3	15,646.0	22,167.3
Algeria	215.1	1,090.6	1,358.6	2,343.7	3,064.5	3,481.6	4,940.2
Bahrain	16.6	60.7	100.4	33.1	74.4	28.8	10.6
Egypt	25.9	69.8	27.5	111.0	170.0	105.0	381.0
Iraq	15.8	0.9	19.4	123.2	381.5	243.4	618.4
Jordan	0.3	0.2	0.3	1.5	3.2	0.6	4.1
Kuwait	64.9	13.4	111.4	41.1	214.5	49.6	86.8
Lebanon	32.7	29.9	33.3	4.9	42.5	14.8	14.6
Libya	215.8	1.4	1,044.5	2,406.2	3,796.1	3,779.3	5,256.0
Morocco	13.7	19.7	10.2	18.4	21.0	43.5	39.3
Oman	24.0	20.8	52.7	251.1	424.3	354.0	316.7
Qatar	13.3	79.6	56.5	132.7	292.2	318.0	279.1
Saudi Arabia	514.5	1,671.2	2,623.3	5,846.8	6,358.5	5,306.5	7,983.4
Syria	5.8	2.1	7.0	10.3	16.2	36.8	165.2
Tunisia	32.6	21.4	26.0	59.2	11.2	21.1	95.4
United Arab Emirates	67.2	366.3	682.3	1,531.2	1,640.8	1,867.9	1,971.0
Yemen (Aden)	3.8	5.0	0.5	0.8	2.8	4.7	4.0
Yemen (Sana)	0.2	0.6	0.2	0.3	0.6	0.4	1.5
Non-Arab Countries	743.6	2,555.6	1,857.1	2,290.6	3,504.5	3,771.4	3,733.8
Iran	342.5	2,132.0	1,398.2	1,631.2	2,788.8	2,877.4	2,783.7
Israel	268.6	282.4	314.1	437.1	570.3	719.4	749.1
Turkey	132.5	141.2	144.3	222.3	145.4	174.6	201.0

Source: U.S. Department of Commerce, Bureau of the Census, Washington, D.C.

Algeria) by the U.S. Export-Import Bank, and huge quantities
of USAID money to Egypt and Israel, and to a lesser extent
Jordan, Tunisia, and Morocco, have allowed the American
business community to play a major role in the design and
construction of the huge industrial and infrastructure projects
that have been a part of these development programs.

American suppliers of aircraft, cereals, motor vehicles,
power-generating machinery, telecommunications apparatus,
chemicals, consumer goods, agricultural and construction machinery, and mining and materials-handling machinery have
been able to enter these markets on the heels of the large
American engineering and construction firms that have taken
the prime contracts for most of these projects. Though these
companies face increasing competition from their Western European and Japanese counterparts and some disincentives to
operating overseas, such as U.S. tax and antiboycott legislation, their presence in the region is enormous and continues to
grow. In Saudi Arabia alone, more than 1,000 American companies have an agent or distributor and close to 500 companies
maintain an office in the country. There are approximately
175 U.S. firms working in Egypt. Several Middle Eastern
capitals also are the site of the regional headquarters for U.S.
firms. There are over 200 of these offices in Athens, about
60 in Bahrain, 50 in Tunis, and 30 in Amman.

The major change in the U.S. trade picture with the
Middle East after 1973 is best illustrated by a look at Saudi
Arabia. U.S.-Saudi relations essentially began with the oil
concession won by Standard Oil for California, which discover-
ed oil at Dhahran in 1933 and found commercially exploitable
quantities of oil in 1938. The United States has been the
preeminent supplier to Saudi Arabia since World War II and has
held about one-fifth of the share of the Saudi market since the
late 1960s.

Trade with Saudi Arabia, however, grew slowly. In
1947, the United States sold $67 million worth of goods to the
kingdom and purchased $3 million. By 1970, these figures had
only reached $140 million and $20 million, respectively. In the
mid-1970s, however, the levels increased by huge amounts.
By 1979, U.S. sales to Saudi Arabia had reached $4.9 billion
and purchases almost $8 billion. At these levels, Saudi Arabia
has become the United States' sixth-leading trading partner,
just ahead of France.

Total U.S.-Middle East trade was about $40 billion in 1979
and it continues to grow at rates exceeding 10 percent a year
- a far cry from the miniscule beginnings in pre-Revolutionary
War times and the slow growth prior to the last decade. Even
trade with the so-called "confrontation states" - Syria, Iraq,
and Libya - rose sharply in the past year. Assuming steady,
if slow, progress in the Middle East peace negotiations, U.S.
political and strategic interests in the region and the avail-

ability of money to pay for quality U.S. goods, services, and technology will maintain a high level of U.S. trade with the region for the foreseeable future.

NOTES

1. J. D. Anthony, "Arab-American Relations: From Evangelism to Interdependence," MEED Special Report: Arab American Commerce (November 1977), p. 9.

2. S. E. Morrison, Oxford History of the American People (New York: Oxford University Press, 1965), p. 363.

3. James A. Field, Jr., America and the Mediterranean World: 1776-1889 (Princeton: Princeton University Press, 1969), p. 113.

4. Ibid., p. 114.

5. Ibid., p. 186-187.

6. Herman F. Eilts, "Ahmed Bin Na'aman's Mission to the United States in 1840," The Essex Institute, Salem, Historical Collections 98, 4 (October 1962).

7. Ibid., p. 224.

8. Field, America and the Mediterranean World, p. 192.

9. Ibid., p. 194.

10. Ibid., p. 310.

11. Ibid., p. 188.

12. Ibid., p. 260.

13. Ibid., p. 247.

14. Ibid., pp. 309-310.

15. Ibid., p. 311.

16. Ibid., p. 312.

17. John A. DeNovo, American Interests and Policies in the Middle East, 1900-1939 (Minneapolis: The University of Minnesota Press, 1963), p. 42.

18. Ibid., pp. 40 and 41.

19. Ibid., p. 39.

20. Ibid., p. 40.

21. Ibid., p. 41.

22. Anthony, "Arab-American Relations," p. 10.

8 The Multinationals and Arab Economic Development: A New Paradigm

Riad A. Ajami

We say that our fathers rode on camels, and that our sons will travel by Concorde, but their sons will travel by camel again.
- A Qatari Businessman

What should we do when the oil runs out, go back to our camels.
- Dr. Mana Said Al-Otaiba, OPEC Secretary-General and Minister of Oil for the United Arab Emirates

Either Saudi development plans work, or it's back to the desert in un-airconditioned tents.
- A Saudi Government Official

We have finite hydrocarbon resources which we want to exchange for development. . . . Economic development is a long-term process and it needs time to convert developing countries into developed ones.
- Ali Jaidah, Former Secretary-General of OPEC; presently Director of Qatar General Petroleum Corporation

The above passages are a mere sample of the echoes, sentiments, and preferences of Arab elites and technocrats. These quotes were chosen because they illustrate the felt need and commitment to economic growth and technological transformation within the Arab states. These states wish to close the gap with the industrialized world and transform their economies, in anticipation of the day when the oil runs out. Oil is a finite and exhaustible asset and Arabs hope to exchange it for permanent assets. Arab economies without oil resources in the last part of the 21st century, yet without a viable economic alternative, is a future state of affairs that most Arab decision makers fear. They realize that now is their only chance to transform their economies and they are acutely aware that the process of economic transformation is at best difficult, long, and fraught with bottlenecks and difficulties.

The concern of Arab decision makers with industrialization gives added significance to the role of the multinationals. Arab elites are aware that multinationals corporate know-how and expertise, if properly harnessed, could spell the difference between success and failure.

This chapter looks at the process of interaction between the Arab states and the multinationals. It also assesses the role of the multinationals in Arab economic development. The evolution of this process is traced over time. The obstacles that characterized the earlier interactions will be highlighted and the potentially unfolding ones that might be generated will be pointed out.

THE MULTINATIONAL FIRM AND ECONOMIC DEVELOPMENT: THE ADVOCATES AND THE CRITICS

The activities of the multinational firm have naturally become a focus for those interested in development and industrialization. The commitment to development and economic transformation is the most powerful motivation within developing societies. Such a commitment is embodied in the United Nations General Assembly Declaration on the Establishment of a New International Economic order embraced by Arab countries and other third world states:

> All efforts should be made . . . to encourage the industrialization of the developing countries . . . and with a view to bringing about a new international economic structure which should increase the share of the developing countries in world industrial production. (1)

Such a concern in host countries with growth and development followed the disappointment with the unrealized expectations of the First Development Decade. Inadequacy of aid as an instrument of development shifted the focus to trade and investments - domains in which multinational corporations play an extremely important role. (2) This shift has given the concern with the relationship of the multinational firm to the process of development heightened and added significance.

Multinational firms-host society interaction is a subject upon which there is very little consensus. There are as many advocates as there are critics of direct foreign investment within developing countries. What follows is an attempt to look briefly at the arguments of both the advocates and the critics as to the impact of the multinationals upon host developing countries.

The Advocates

On the whole, the advocates of multinational corporate investment are confident of the contributions of such investments to the process of economic development. The advocates place their faith in the economic efficiency and the ability of multinationals to transfer capital, technology, and managerial and organizational skills. Some argue that developing countries often lack the ability to mobilize their resources: human, capital, and physical, and sees the multinational firm as the most efficient and effective "energizer" of these resources.(3)

Moreover, the advocates stress the benefits of corporate investments as a mechanism for linking host developing countries with the center of world finance and industry. According to Vernon:

> When a foreign enterprise sets up a subsidiary in a less developed country, the principal consequence is to link a business entity inside the country with a multinational mechanism.(4)

This link may often increase the export capacity of host countries and result in economies of scale. It provides jobs and could also increase the supply of capital locally, while providing easier access to foreign capital. Furthermore, the advocates argue that the immense payoff in labor skill formation, through the establishment of backward and forward linkages with local producers and consumers, is considerable.

There is a broad consensus among economists that the inflow of finance, technology, organizational skills, and knowledge are a prerequisite for industrialization and the concomitant economic growth and development.(5) Johnson suggests that if through no other mechanism other than selfish, profit-motivated pursuits, the potential of direct investment as an agent of economic development is likely to be immense.(6) He sees two areas of significant development: first, through the development and training of labor; and second, through the "input-output" activities of "backward-forward" linkages with indigenous producers and users. Caves also indicates that productivity gains are likely to accrue to domestic firms that are linked with multinational firms and indirectly through "demonstration effects" to other firms.(7)

The point here is that subsidiaries of multinationals provide examples of improved managerial practices and production processes that domestic firms may decide to emulate.

The ability of multinationals to mobilize domestic resources will also have a significant positive impact upon the level of indigenous economic formation. The infusion of foreign capital compensates initially for the lack of domestic savings and - over the long run - should generate high domestic savings.(8)

Advocates further argue that direct investment accelerates the process of import substitution and export promotion more efficiently than local entrepreneurs because these subsidiaries need not go through new learning curves as is the case for their domestic counterparts. The result is a rise in domestic economic efficiency and/or a lowering of the real costs of local production. On balance the available research indicates that in terms of mere economic efficiency, the multinational firm seems to be ahead of its local counterpart especially for export-oriented products.(9) Because of intraenterprise trade - movements of products and semifinished components within corporate affiliates - which accounts for about one-eighth the value of world trade, the export-generating capacity to other affiliates and also to third markets is likely to increase.(10) The proponents of direct investment further indicate that the balance-of-payment effect on host developing country is positive, especially in regard to the capital account. The benefits, however, are more evident in extractive investments but less than conclusive for manufacturing investments.

Finally, the advocates also argue that the direct contribution of multinational firms to increasing and upgrading local employment is considerable, especially in the manufacturing and service sectors, and the indirect effects through linkages with suppliers and distributors is equally substantial. Their contribution toward technical and professional skill formation is equally significant, and the benefit to local firms as a result of managerial mobility is immense.

Against the claims of the advocates of the multinationals are pitted the arguments of a wide spectrum of critical and generally pessimistic opinion as to the compatability between the multinationals and the process of economic development. Though sharper divisions can be made within each group, and there are also ways in which the perspectives converge; the critics all suggest, however, that there are many harmful aspects of multinational corporate investments: excessive profits, balance-of-payment drain upon the host economy, lack of transfer of applicable skills, and market-structure distortion.

Generally speaking, the critics divide into three broad groups. The three orientations are the nationalist school, the dependencia school, and the Marxists. The opposition of the nationalist school and others in the less developed parts of the world is in many ways similar to the opposition of nationalists in the home countries.(11) Whatever country it asserts itself in, the nationalist preference is for national autonomy, for limited participation in the world economy. On the whole the nationalists are hostile to the multinationals because they wish to exert maximum control over economic activities and they see the mobility of the multinationals as a threat to that control. The dependencia school opposes the activities of the multinationals because they are said to make the economic performance and conditions in the so-called periphery societies dependent on the growth, values, and lifestyles of the major economies of the world.(12) Finally, the Marxists are naturally critical of the multinationals.(13) In a way their opposition is inevitable and there is not much that multinational corporations could do to meet or to accommodate the Marxists. The reason lies in the fact that the Marxists' opposition to the multinationals is a derivative of their general opposition to capitalism as an economic system and as a mode of production. To Marxists from Lenin down to Magdoff and Sweezy, capitalism has been responsible for untold evils and sufferings; by this logic multinational firms, representing the most advanced sector of capitalism, its most internationalistic dimension, could hardly escape Marxist criticism.

The Critics

Among the critics of the multinational corporate system, the nationalists believe that the interdependent world economy has provided a favorable environment for the operation of multinational firms. They argue that the ability of the corporate system to reap the benefits of direct investments and to skew the costs to the disadvantage of the national economy is immense. Along with the more radical they cite charges that the profits of multinational firms are exorbitantly high and only a small proportion is reinvested within host countries.

They also argue that direct investment is concentrated in advanced technology industries, where the profits are higher, and ignores other sectors. The cost of capital is higher than what the government would be charged on capital markets. The transfer of technology is minimal, if any, and is usually tightly held by the parent through concentration of research and development at corporate headquarters. Its costs are exorbitantly high and it is often nonadvanced and inappropriate. The training and employment of local labor is minimal and so is the opportunity for nationals to reach managerial positions. Moreover, the activities of multinationals are hard to integrate into the domestic economy because they are under the control of the parent firm and thus represent an enclave. The sheer size and power of multinationals overwhelm local competitors; often they impose export-restrictive clauses that limit the ability of host societies to benefit fully from this linkage.

The more radical critics, the dependencia school and the Marxist school further challenge the partner-in-development motif of the business school and advance a more pessimistic and exploitive view of multinational firms. They see direct investment as an outgrowth of "corporate capitalism" and the process of "global exploitation" of the periphery by the center society.

Hymer sees this system as an exploitative system that produces affluent development for some - the center society - and dependent underdevelopment for others - the periphery society. On the issue of profits, the critics argue that multinational firms extract exploitive rents and also higher rates of return on their investments in developing countries. This done, they contend, through monopolistic returns on technology transfer and transfer-pricing manipulation with higher charges for "tied" imports and conversely lower prices for exports. Hymer and Resnick further contend that the technology-exporting countries receive proportionately higher income that host countries.(14)

Barnet and Muller, on the issue of profits suggest that:

> 122 of the top U.S.-based multinational corporations had a higher rate of profits from abroad than from domestic operations. . . . (Extraordinarily high profit on relatively low overseas investment is not uncommon. In 1972, for example, United Brands reported a 72.1 percent return on net assets, Parker Pen 51.2 percent, Exxon 52.5 percent).(15)

The critics further point out that oil investments - like most extractive investments - are a lucrative source of foreign profits in developing countries, with the majority coming from the Middle East.

Employment

As to the employment and training of nationals, the critics argue that the process of substitution of capital for labor in the manufacturing sector by multinational firms precipitates the high unemployment problems of developing countries. Vaistos further argues that significantly large sectors within developing countries such as extractive industries contribute very little to domestic employment.(16) Finally, the critics contend that multinational firms do not provide enough training of nationals for eventual participation in position within the upper echelons of management.

Rhetoric aside, on balance the net employment impact of multinationals is clearly positive. Jobs made available by multinationals in host developing countries might not be numerous, but without these jobs unemployment in these countries would have been even worse. It is understandable for at least two reasons that extractive industries do not contribute substantially to employment. Primarily, these industries are highly capital intensive, and no enterprise - domestic or foreign - could escape them.

On the other hand, manufacturing investments - especially those intended for the local market - do contribute directly and indirectly to employment; through linkages the employment potential of these investments is appreciable. Furthermore, indirect employment results through subcontracting and the creation of other supporting services such as accounting.(17) Again it is understandable that the employment potential of export-related manufacturing investments may be less than that of import-substitution investments. High capital intensity to ensure quality uniformity among various units of the multinational firm on the one hand and the lack of skilled labor and supervisors in host developing countries on the other hand usually preclude this. Without these investments, however, it must be said that the unemployment situation in developing countries would definitely be worse.

Competition

The ability to influence the domestic business climate, the critics argue, is likely to come about because of fewness and bigness. Multinational enterprises, they further contend, impede local entrepreneurs and contribute to their displacement, thus effectively stifling the development and growth of countervailing national firms.

In the same vein, the U.N. Report of Eminent Persons on the Impact of Multinational Corporations on Development and on International Relations - a group in which had a fair number of developing countries represented - stated that the size of multinational firms: "Make it possible for a few large firms to control substantial shares of local and sometime world markets."(18)

According to Dunning, if scale economy allows, multinational firms entry could then increase competition rather than reduce it.(19) Vernon equally points out that the emergence of multinational firms could have mixed results for international competition and monopoly power:

In some respects, as enterprises have thrust their way into foreign markets, competition has been fostered; on the other hand, as enterprises have linked up in international alliance and partnerships, the opposite effect has also occurred.(20)

This is true of national and multinational firms alike.

Technology Transfer

The literature on technology transfer by multinational firms to developing countries points out that the areas of concern revolve around the inappropriateness - in relation to factor endowment - of technology, its restricted "availability" and cost, and the contention that the policies and practices of multinational firms create a perpetual state of technological dependence upon the multinational corporate system.

Since multinational firms are the major source and sellers of commercial technology, the critics argue that the cost of technology transfer is prohibitive, owing to the monopolistic rents and returns demanded by the multinationals, and the unevenness in power between them and recipient developing countries, thus relegating the inferior position in the bargaining process to developing countries.(21) They also argue that the preference of multinationals for a total "package" of direct investment limits the options of developing countries and opens them to manipulation through transfer-pricing devices, fostering the retention of control within the multinational corporate system and perpetuating technological dependence.

The notion of inappropriateness of production technology stems from what Helleiner has labeled "technological fixity" or factor substitution inelasticity in the production process, which leads to a relatively higher level of capital intensity than is warranted given the factor endowment of less-developed countries. This comes about because the technology was initially designed to reflect existing factor availability and factor prices in advanced industrial societies; in most cases the technology is transferred without any variations and changes to fit other societies faced with different factor endowments, prices, and problems.

The critics also advance other criticisms that indirectly negate the so-called technology inappropriateness argument. One such criticism revolves around the notion that the transferred technology is standardized and nonadvanced, thus relegating recipient developing countries to a position of technological inferiority within the international production system. The proponents of this argument cite the product life-cycle theory, associated with the work of Vernon and Wells, to suggest that only standardized and mature products that are in the later stages of their life cycles are likely to be transferred abroad long after their novelty and quasimonopolistic advantages have been eliminated.(22) Thus, Vaistos argues, the product life-cycle model strengthens the monopolistic advantages of multinational firms vis-a-vis developing countries while weakening the latter by keeping them in a sequential state of perpetual dependency awaiting new mature products and new cycles.

Another spin-off argument from technological dependence deals with the concentration of R&D in metropolitan societies. It is argued that this concentration relegates host developing countries to a position of technological dependence and inferiority and will ultimately stifle their innovational capabilities. According to Sutter, total expenditures of U.S.-based multinationals on R&D in developing countries amounted to no more than $70 million during 1970, which is only 0.5 percent of the total amount spent worldwide by these multinationals on R&D.(23)

In summing up the conflicting views on technology transfer, if one looks at the technology generation as a dynamic process that is being always updated over time, the rationale is that the cost of the future technology is unknown and the cost of updating technology always has to be borne by the existing one. Add to this risks of failure, and the fact that only a small fraction of the total initial input of R&D results in new useful technologies, then a seemingly high price is not in fact so high. A Swedish executive points out that:

> Successful new products and processes have to carry the cost of the total research and development effort. The buyer of licenses and the like gets the final and tested technology with nothing of the risk to bring it forth. If he disregards this fact, he might think of the price as too high.(24)

The disagreement over a "fair" marginal cost of technology is a function of two differing views held by buyers and sellers. Vaistos argues that since information is a "public good" and nonexhaustible and the marginal cost to the firm supplying it to a developing country is zero unless a good deal of alterations and adaptations of that technology is required, then clearly the charged price is exorbitant. The donors of technology, however, argue that the total cost of developing technology from scratch, considering the associated risks with a new technology, and the economic value of the time foregone until such a technology materializes, given the inadequacy of the indigenous technological infrastructure in most developing countries, then the charged price is reasonable.

Finally, as to the inappropriateness of technology argument, and the centralization of R&D, both can be rationalized on economic grounds. The smallness of markets in developing countries makes it economically infeasible for a multinational firm to redesign products or to support local R&D on a large scale. With an enlightened economic policy, however, these tasks can best be handled locally, and thus give host countries the chance to redesign products and carry out supporting local R&D which will enhance the development of an indigenous scientific infrastructure.

Part of the intellectual confusion surrounding the activities of the multinationals and their contribution to development is suggestively resolved by Wells when he notes that the criticism of multinationals is not based on a claim that their activities are economically bad for host developing countries; rather it is "based on the belief that the benefits could be much greater than they are." (25) And if Wells is correct, the criticism conceals a vote of confidence of sorts in the potential efficiency of the multinationals: confidence that is pushed harder, they could mobilize their impressive talent to accomplish the developmental tasks more successfully.

These are the general areas of conflict and convergence between the multinationals and nation-states. They establish and illuminate the broad context within which multinational firms and host developing countries find themselves. The next part moves from the general to the particular: it turns to the Arab world to see how these issues manifest themselves and sort themselves out in an increasingly crucial part of the world economy.

PRE-1973: THE MAJOR ISSUES BETWEEN THE MULTINATIONALS AND HOST ARAB SOCIETY

The Arab countries have their share of traditionalists who oppose all modernization, quasi-Marxists who see all multinationals as capitalist instruments, and economic nationalists who urge their countries to go it alone and shut out all but the minimum essential dealings with multinational firms. But the national commitment in most Arab countries is a more moderate one that favors connectedness with the multinationals and substantial technology imports.

Interactions between multinational firms and host Arab countries tended to be at times stormy. The earlier negotiations over oil prices, the desire for participation in the ownership and running of oil industry at the refining and distribution stages, location of refineries within Arab countries, and employment of nationals were contested issues. Nonmarket issues such as the perceived identities of interests between the oil firms and their home governments also visited added problems to a potentially problematic interaction process. The multinationals were essentially viewed as alien enterprises coming from an antagonistic Western world.

These are the general issues of potential conflict. A brief look at these and other concerns of Arab society is now in order.

The Seven Sisters: A Challenge to Sovereignty

The "Seven Majors" prior to 1973 controlled the production, refining, and marketing of Arab oil, and in addition provided the major link between the Arab oil economies and the Western markets where the majority of Arab oil was consumed. The power of the multinationals came not only from their capacity to provide that link but from their dominance in the global oil market at all stages of production, refining, and distribution. As members of an oligopolistic industry, the "Majors" controlled, up until the early 1970s, over 70 percent of global crude production and over 50 percent of refining and distribution. The "Majors" market power and joint Middle Eastern ownership in Aramco, the Iraq petroleum company, and Kuwait Oil Company, effectively gave them a good deal of bargaining power vis-a-vis the host governments. The multinationals, moreover, were essentially sophisticated Western enterprises midst traditional and dependent economies. This represented a potential source of conflict between the multinational and the host Arab society. Moreover, the system of subsidiaries was subject to the criticism that managerial control and decision making lay at corporate headquarters located in home countries, while the impact of these corporate decisions was local and specific, and in a way had a major impact upon the viability of the local economies. This was unacceptable to the nationalist. The concession period was thus perceived as exploitive and restrictive.

The Mossadegh nationalization of foreign oil interest in Iran during 1951 and the role played by the U.S. government in restoring the shah to power created the impression of very powerful oil firms and closely identified the multinationals in the public mind with the policies of their home governments. Immense political power and leverage was attributed to the oil companies, thus making it difficult to separate their economic activities and operations from their "perceived" political role as agents of American and European policies.

The Major Economic Issues: Revenues and Profits,
Participation and Oil Enclave

Revenues and Profits

In the context of Arab economies, the importance of oil revenues to the government is obvious. In all the Arab oil-producing countries, oil revenue provides over 85 percent of the government's revenues.

Since oil revenues account for an extremely high proportion of the national income in all of the Arab oil-exporting countries, and since these countries have grown more dependent than ever on oil for their foreign exchange earnings and livelihood, it is easy to understand why the optimization of these revenues has occupied first priority.

The governments' share of revenues was based on the so-called "posted price" of crude. The Arab oil-producing countries viewed the posted prices as being below what they should be, and since they could not participate in the setting of posted prices, naturally the issue of oil revenues became a major source of conflict between the oil producers and the multinationals. The governments felt that their share of revenues was low and that the multinational's share was high.

Participation and Oil Enclave

The felt need for national participation by the governments in running the oil sector was great among the oil producers, especially since oil was the dominant sector within their economies. Participation in downstream operations (i.e., refining and marketing) was an issue of equal concern.

The talk about participation in "downstream operations" on the part of the producers provoked negative responses from the majors. If one considers the degree of their vertical integration as well as the diversity of their markets and sources of crude oil, it is no surprise that the majors would make no concessions to this demand. The majors draw their supplies from all over the world to supply the global market. The majors argued that it would be difficult to accept a situation in which any of their refining and marketing operations would be politically tied to any particular source; this would also imply a drastic reorganization of the entire structure of the industry.

Like all export-oriented extractive investments, the oil sector tended to be an enclave in the national economy, and as such the industry was not integrated with the rest of the economy. There are several reasons that explain this isolation. The shift from a final-product to a crude-export market and with it the shift in location of the refinery industry during the mid-1950s and early 1960s was viewed by the exporting countries as a lost chance to industrialize and to build subsidiary industries such as petrochemicals.

Process industries are highly capital intensive - a technological imperative, rather than an organizational policy of multinational firms. As such, the oil sector provides relatively few employment opportunities for the national labor force. But apart from this unmanageable fact there has been a widespread and deep-seated belief in the oil-exporting countries that the companies have tried to make sure that they are absolutely indispensable by avoiding having more than a token number of nationals in key positions. Early agreements with the companies, however, had provided for the appointment of one or two

directors nominated by the government to the companies' board
of directors. This, however, had a twofold drawback: first,
it did not contribute at all toward the employment of nationals
at middle- and upper-management levels; second, as OPEC
complained, these local boards of directors were not empowered to make many of the decisions in which the governments
sought participation.

Public Opinion: A Nonmarket Factor

Finally, a major source of tension between the multinationals
and host Arab society was the inability of the companies to
project a favorable public image. The companies did not
appreciate the importance of public relations within the Arab
world: one need not, however, blame the companies for the
difficulty they had with the public in the region; they often
suffered from their association with their home governments.

In the aftermath of the June war of 1967, the companies
suffered from the intervention of their home governments on
the part of Israel and equally in 1973 when a number of U.S.
multinational properties were nationalized because of U.S.
government support and airlifting of supplies to Israel.

These were the issues prior to 1973. The oil events of
1973-1974, by the turn of events, asserted the power of the
oil producers over oil pricing and revenues, participation and
thus rendered obsolete the notion of very powerful oil companies and weak Arab governments. Let us now look into the
post-1974 order.

POST-1974 ORDER: THE NEW ISSUES

The nationalization of oil investments by Arab governments and
the wresting of control over oil pricing from the multinationals
are events that mark the beginning of a new economicopolitical
era that thrust the Arab oil producers from the periphery of
the international economic order to its center. Some of the
previous issues of conflict between host Arab countries and
the multinationals were somewhat resolved. But the multinationals today are playing a vital part in the process of Arab
economic transformation. Arab society remains a hospitable
environment for foreign firms. Total ownership by the multinationals is no longer acceptable. Arrangements ranging from
minority ownership to service contracts to processing agreements are widely utilized. The expertise of the multinationals
and their marketing and refining outlets makes them indispens-
ible to the Arab producers, who are yet to develop their own
distribution outlets. Arab elites understand the benefits of
multinational corporate linkages, whether in the oil sector or

elsewhere, and they wish to maximize them. They believe that
the operations of the multinationals do have a positive impact
on Arab economic development. A survey of Arab elites' attitudes toward a multinational firm has confirmed this view.
The results of my survey have recently been published in
Arab Response to the Multinationals.(26) The survey findings
did not substantiate the view widely held by most economic
analysts and observers on this side of the Atlantic, that there
is an irreconcilable conflict of interest between multinational
corporations and host Arab societies.

This relationship between the multinationals and host Arab
societies, resilient as it may appear, will bring forth a number
of issues of conflict between these two actors during the
coming decade. These issues are:

- Resistance of the multinationals to the establishment of
  petrochemicals by the Arab countries.
- Overpricing by the multinationals of goods and services
  destined for Arab markets.
- Bribery and illicit payments.

Petrochemical Industries: The Center Stone to Industrialization

The Arab countries - oil and non-oil based economies - are
committed to industrialization. Such a commitment is echoed by
Arab technocrats and leaders. Algeria's drive to industrialize
is spelled out in the National Charter: "Basic industries, such
as metallurgical, mechanical, electrical and electronic,
petrochemical and chemical and ship-building play a decisive
strategic role since they insure the independence of national
industry and, more directly, of the country."(27)

The Arab oil producers are determined to develop petrochemical industries and go beyond being mere suppliers of
crude oil They see their participation in the petrochemical
market as a legitimate right. Their oil endowments, they
reason give them a potential comparative advantage in petrochemicals, which they envision as the cornerstone of their
drive toward industrialization. The Europeans, however, have
voiced their objections to the idea of an Arab petrochemical
industry. The established Western petrochemical firms are
concerned that the entry of the Arab producers will increase
capacity far in excess of demand, thus jeopardizing the viability of the existing firms within the industry. Arab countries'
commitments to increase their share in petrochemicals stems
from their belief that it is only natural for oil-rich countries to
develop petrochemical industries, and that the market will
expand sufficiently to allow the coexistence of their plants with
those in countries that are currently producing petrochemicals.

Handicapped by the lack of oil, the Europeans fear that they
will eventually disappear from the market. The Arab oil
producers see the attempts of some to withhold technology and
know-how so as to keep them out of the industry as an unfair
arrangement. Should they be kept out by multinational firms
by withholding technology, the existing linkages between the
multinationals and host Arab countries will be subject to
stress.

Profits

Critics of the multinationals in the Arab world and elsewhere
argue that the cost of technology and corporate linkages are
excessive. The concern about overpricing was put forth by
Faisal Bashir, a Saudi deputy minister for planning. Bashir
states: "the big international companies in the United States,
Western Europe, and Japan seem to have three sets of prices:
a regular price, a higher one for the oil-producing countries,
and a still higher one for Saudi Arabia."(28)
    The Saudi government, as a result, initiated a campaign
against high bids by multinational firms. The culmination of
that campaign resulted in the cancellation of a multibillion-
dollar contract to a Western consortium led by Phillips, to
install and supply telephone service in Saudi Arabia. The
Qatari government recently retendered a number of projects
after cancelling the previously awarded contract. The reasons
behind the two cancellations were Saudi and Qatari perceptions
that the bid prices and charges were excessive and unreasonable. Spokesmen for the two governments argued that the
bids were inflated and that what they calculated to be about a
40 percent rate of return was too high and unfair. The multinationals, without conceding that the rate of return was 40
percent, pointed out that the cost of doing business in the
region was too high. Projects, according to the companies,
are often subject to a great deal of delay and bottlenecks.
The costs of repair, maintenance, keeping expatriates, and
training local staff tend to grow geometrically with time.

Bribery

Bribery, according to Nye and Keohane, is a transnational
issue that involves the movement of tangible items "across
state boundaries when at least one actor is not an agent of a
government."(29) Arab countries see bribery as a visited
economic and social cost of multinational corporate linkages.
Bribery thus represents an infringement on resource allocation
as well as a distortion within the process of economic development. It is seen as an unnecessary cost with a potential

threat to sovereignty and efficient utilization of scarce economic resources. From that perspective, illicit payments by multinational firms in a number of Arab countries are a source of concern for host Arab societies. This concern has led Egyptian President Sadat to issue a warning to foreign firms that offer illicit commissions. In a speech to a gathering of Egyptian engineers, he stated: "There is no place among us for exploitation and opportunism. . . . Premier Mustafa Khalil . . . has agreed to adjudicate and give a decision if the need arises in these cases. We have established that companies that give bribes will be put on a blacklist. We shall sever all associations with them and the bribe takers will receive the severest penalties."(30)

Recently, a number of Egyptian officials have been tried for allegedly receiving improper payments from two American firms, Boeing and Westinghouse. In Syria, an anticorruption drive is also under way. Though its aim is to curb corruption by local businessmen, President Assad issued a decree on October 1, 1979, banning governmental agencies and private firms from dealing with middlemen or brokers, whether local or foreign.

Bribery is an inefficient way of conducting business. It taints the image of the multinationals and lends credence to allegations that multinationals corporate linkages represent corrupt forms of international commerce. As such its curb will remove a source of irritation in relations between multinationals firms and host Arab societies.

Nonmarket Factors

It is becoming more difficult for multinational firms to insulate themselves from their external environment; nonmarket considerations often do change the rules of the game and alter the fine-tuned ability to maintain rapport with their most important constituencies. The relationship between multinational firms and the host countries is not independent or self-contained. The policies of home countries can challenge accepted practices and call into question the workability of existing arrangements between firms and host countries. Likewise, the policies of host countries which the multinationals must try to manage effectively can come in conflict with the rules, established practices, and norms of the home country.

The nonmarket factors that will impinge upon the multinationals within Arab society relate to the image of the Arabs in Western popular culture, and the Arab economic boycott of the state of Israel.

Though the images of Arabs in Western popular culture is not a byproduct of multinationals' corporate activities, the impact of such distorted imagery on multinational firms-host

Arab society relations is considerable. This state of affairs
will somewhat mitigate the desire for harmonious economic
relationships. Arabs, according to an Arab official quoting
Harvard linguist Noam Chomsky, are regularly portrayed as
racists throughout the American press.(31) At a recent conference on the image of Arabs in the West held in London and
attended by former British Prime Minister Edward Heath, the
same official stated that Western media often characterize Arabs
as backwards and fanatic.(32) Mohammed Wahby, a correspon-
dent for the authoritative Middle East Economic Digest, traces
this development over time. Of this he writes:

> Following the start of the Arab-Israeli conflict, the
> Americans increasingly began to view the Arabs as
> "backward, fanatic, scheming, unscrupulous, over
> sexed, fatalistic and lazy." In the aftermath of the
> Arab defeat in the 1967 war and the rise of the
> Palestinian resistance movement, the Arabs were
> shown as either "cowardly and corrupt" or "irra-
> tional and blood-thirsty."

> The 1973 war and the rise oil prices in 1973/1974
> added a further dimension: that of the fat, vulgarly
> rich and blackmailing shaikhs.(33)

The oil events of the 1970s have, according to Arabs,
exacerbated an already distorted image of their countries.
They have often been portrayed as blackmailers who, through
higher oil prices, are out to destroy the existing global
economic order. Arabs point out that they are being used a
"scapegoats" for the "energy crisis" as well as other economic
ills of the Western economies. In the hopes of a better
understanding, the Arabs have sought to present their case.
Statements by the Saudi oil minister, Sheikh Zakhi Yamani,
about the interest of the Arabs in pursuing policies that will
minimize the impact of escalating oil prices upon the industrial
economic order are an example of such orientation. In the
same manner, Shadli Qlibi, the Arab League secretary-general,
recently told a joint gathering of the U.S. Chamber of Commerce and the American-Arab Association for Commerce and
Industry in New York that "Arab countries are not trying to
blackmail oil-consuming countries, but are seeking to syn-
chronise our economic and financial policies to the legitimate
quest for stability in economic relations."(34)
       From the perspective of the oil producer, oil is an
exhaustible and, in certain uses, the only asset of certain
Arab countries. In selling it, these countries are trading
their only asset and future livelihood. The exchange of this
wasting asset in the hope of creating a permanent one will
have to be viewed as a legitimate exchange.

Another source of friction impinging upon international economic linkages to Western industrial concern is the Arab boycott of the state of Israel. Coordinated by the League of Arab States and run by a special agency, this issue brings difficult political questions into the market. The Arab governments point out that they have the right to boycott firms that trade with Israel. They argue that if the U.S. boycott of the Soviet Union, among others, is legitimate, then theirs is legitimate too. Arabs defend their policies by stating that they are in a state of war with Israel and that embargoes and boycotts are legitimate during international conflict. While this has been controversial enough, the thorny issue of the boycott raises an additional conflict with business practice and legal commitments in the United States that prevent discrimination on the basis of race, creed, religion, or national origin.

The political objectives of the host countries thus clashed with the business norms and the legal culture of the home country. The expectations of the home country were that its firms would abide by its rules and its values. Compliance with host country demands would create an adverse atmosphere at home, and raise the question of business ethics as well as the compliance of multinational firms with home country law and regulations.

CONCLUSION

The future viability of the multinationals in a turbulent and changing Arab society is inescapably bound to the evolving capabilities and priorities of Arab economies, as well as the capacity of these firms to adjust to the shifting economic needs and demands of that host environment.

Past multinational corporate policies may have visited intended as well as unintended economic and social costs and dislocations upon host Arab countries. Arab decision makers, however, must confront the future on its promise, and the past need not present a mutually advantageous process between the two actors from developing further.

Arab elites are cognizant of the fact that their present economic leverage and improving fortunes in the world economy would not have been possible without the multinationals.

Arab decision makers commitments to industrialization reconcile them to viewing that linkage favorably. They realize that there are costs associated with such a linkage, but they see these costs as manageable and they view their transactions with these firms from a utilitarian perspective. Jonathan Rabin writes of this:

They're not going to give tuppence for your love of
Arabia, or your fourth-year Arabic from the School
of Oriental and African Studies; the only thing they
want from you is your technical knowledge, your
advice in investment or construction. The rest is
simply flummery.(35)

By way of final summation, the image of Arabs in Western
popular culture and the Arab boycott of Israel are examples of
nonmarket factors that will affect host Arab society-multina-
tional firms' interactions. The multinationals alone cannot
resolve these issues; their resolutions are likely to be left to
the global community.
Bribery is an issue that must be dealt with collectively.
Similarly, the other issues are: appropriate technology transfer, upgrading the training of human resources, fair pricing
and profits, development of petrochemical industries, and the
provision of external market linkage. If these concerns are
resolved to the satisfaction of host Arab countries, the
tenure of the multinationals will be secure.
In conclusion, careful survey of the economic activities of
the multinationals lends support to the reasoned arguments of
its advocates: the multinationals can and do provide access to
technology, capital, and markets. The conditions and terms
under which that access can be secured can be successfully
negotiated by host Arab countries. The process of bargaining
and negotiations is not a zero-sum game in which the host
Arab country is bound to lose to the corporation; nor is there
necessarily a conflict of interest. And the same can be said of
the contribution of the multinationals to training. Enlightened
governmental policies arrived at with the collaboration of the
multinationals can continue to make a contribution to this
overwhelmingly important problem.
Thus, the climate for multinational corporate linkages, in
spite of the apparent turbulence and noise emanating from the
region, is favorable. The Arab countries are committed to
industrialization and technological transformation. Cognizant of
the important role the multinationals can play, Arab decision
makers will accept these firms.

NOTES

1. U.N. General Assembly Resolutions 3201(S-V1) and 3202
(S- V1), "Declaration and Action Programme on the Establish-
ment of a New International Economic Order," May 1, 1974,
reprinted in Beyond Dependency: The Developing World Speaks
Out, ed. Guy F. Erb and Valeriana Kallab (New York Overseas
Development Council, 1975), pp. 185-202.

2. Lester B. Pearson, The Crisis of Development (New York: Praeger, 1970).

3. Peter F. Drucker, "Multinationals and Developing Countries: Myths and Realities," Foreign Affairs 53, 1 (October 1974): 121-134; C. Brown, ed. World Business: Promise and Problems (New York: Macmillan, 1970).

4. Raymond Vernon, The Economic and Political Consequences of Multinational Enterprises: An Anthology (Boston: Division of Research, Graduate School of Business Administration, Harvard University, 1972), p. 25.

5. W. W. Rostow, Stages of Economic Growth: A Non-Communist Manifesto (Cambridge University Press, Cambridge, England 1960); Harry G. Johnson, Technology and Economic Interdependence (New York: St. Martin's Press, 1975).

6. Johnson, Technology and Economic Interdependence.

7. Richard E. Caves, "International Corporations: The Industrial Economics of Foreign Investment," Economics (February 1971), pp. 1-27.

8. Peter Ady, Editor, Private Foreign Investment and the Developing World (New York: Praeger, 1971), p. 25.

9. Grant L. Reuber, Private Investment in Development (Oxford: Clarendon Press, 1973); Raymond Vernon, Sovereignty at Bay : The Multinational Spread of U.S. Enterprise (New York: Basic Books, 1971).

10. J. H. Dunning, ed. The Multinational Enterprise (New York: Praeger, 1971).

11. "The Multinational Corporation in a World of Militant Developing Countries," in George W. Ball, Editor, Global Companies: The Political Economy of World Business, ed. George W. Ball (Englewood Cliffs, NJ: Prentice-Hall, 1976), pp. 70-84.

12. Osvaldo Sunkel, "Big Business and 'Dependencia'": A Latin American View, Foreign Affairs 50, 3 (April 1972): 517-531; Steven Humer, "The Multinational Corporation and the Law of Uneven Development," Mimeo, 1970.

13. P. M. Sweezy and H. Magdoff, "Notes on the Multinational Corporation," Monthly Review 5 and 6 (October and November, 1969).

14. Stephen Hymer and Stephen Resnick, "International Trade and Uneven Development," in Trades Balance of Payments and Growth: Papers in International Economics in Honor of Charles P. Kindleberger, ed. Jagdish N. Bhagwat et al. (Amsterdam: North Holland, 1971) pp. 473-494.

15.   Richard J. Barnet and Ronald E. Muller, Global Reach: The Power of the Multinational Corporation (New York: Simon and Schuster, 1974), pp. 16-17.

16.   Constantine V. Vaistos, Employment and Foreign Direct Investments in Developing Countries: Some Notes and Figures, Junta del Acuerdo de Cartegeme, Mimeographed document J/AJ/ 35/Rev. 1, Lima, 1973, quoted in Multinational Corporations in World Development, St/ECA/190 (New York: United Nations) 1973 p. 53.

17.   S. Wantabe, "International Subcontracting, Employment and Skill Promotion," International Labor Review 105 5 (May 1972).

18.   Report of Eminent Persons on the Impact of Multinational Corporations on Development and on International Relations, E/5500/Rev. 1, 54/ESA/6 (New York: United Nations, 1974), p. 30.

19.   John Dunning, "Multinational Enterprise, Market Structure, Economic Power and Industrial Policy," Journal of World Trade Law 8 6 (December 1974):506.

20.   R. Vernon, "Multinational Enterprises: Performance and Accountability," in Multinational Corporations, Trade and the Dollar, ed. J. Backman and E. Black (New York: New York University Press, 1974), p. 79.

21.   Rolf Sutter, "Multinational Corporations: Technology Transfer into LDC's," Intereconomics, no. 12 (1974), pp. 380-384; G. D. Helleiner, "The Role of Technology," World Development 3, 4 (April 1975) Paul Streeten, "Bargaining With Multinationals," World Development 4 3 (March 1976); Vaistos, Employment and Foreign Direct Investments.

22.   R. Vernon, "International Investment and International Trade in the Product Cycle," Quarterly Journal of Economics 80 (May 1966); L. T. Wells, The Product Life Cycle and International Trade (Boston: Harvard University, 1972).

23.   R. Sutter, "Multinational Corporations."

24.   J. R. Basche, Jr., and M. G. Duerr, International Transfer of Technology: A Worldwide Survey of Chief Executive (The Conference Board, 1975), New York City, p. 4.

25.   Louis T. Wells, Jr., "More or Less Poverty? The Economic Effects of the Multinational Corporation at Home and in Developing Countries," in The Case of the Multinational Corporation, ed. Carl H. Madden (New York: Praeger, 1977), p. 1.

26.   Riad A. Ajami, Arab Response to the Multinationals (New York: Praeger, 1979).

27. "Algeria reassesses priorities after snags at Rouiba," Middle East Economic Digest (November 16, 1979), p. 8.

28. Robert D. Crane, Planning the Future of Saudi Arabia (New York: Praeger, 1978), p. vii.

29. Joseph Nye, Jr. and Robert Keohane, "Transactional Relations and World Politics: An Introduction," International Organization 25, 3 (1971):329-349, 332.

30. "Foreign Firms Warned on Commission," Middle East Economic Digest (October 19, 1979), p. 29.

31. Mohammed Wahby, "The Arabs and Their Image in the West," Middle East Economic Digest (October 5, 1979), p. 15.

32. Ibid.

33. Ibid.

34. "Qlibi Claims Arabs are 'Scapegoats,'" Middle East Economic Digest (October 19, 1979), p. 19.

35. Edmund Fuller, "A Vision of Paradise, A Portrait of Arabia," Wall Street Journal, January 22, 1980, p. 18.

9 Assessing Corporate Vulnerability

Brooks McClure

With the onset of the 1980s, the international business community can look back upon a decade of turbulent history and contemplate an uncertain legacy for the balance of the century. Trade imbalances and dislocation, currency fluctuation, inflation, rising operating costs and growing concerns about pollution, overpopulation, hunger, and revolutionary disruption in the Third World have all matured as problems over the past ten years, and none with a glimmer of hope for easy solution.

And then, in the midst of it all, is the perplexing phenomenon of political terrorism - this type of low-level conflict flowered in the 1970s and seeks to become an instrument of world revolution in the 1980s. It has little chance of achieving this goal based on its record so far, but it may be capable of causing costly damage and disarray in both the political and the economic life of a number of countries. It has links with most of the basic problems of the times, being able both to capitalize on and to promote social distress of all kinds.

A record total of 2,773 terrorist incidents occurred worldwide in 1980, according to Risks International, a firm that surveys political violence in depth. Nearly one-third of these cases involved a business target. But certain kinds of attack were even more heavily concentrated on the commercial community: 46 percent of the 124 kidnappings involved businessmen victims, for example, and nearly 49 percent of the bombings targeted business properties. Only 100 of the 859 business-related incidents involved foreign firms, but nearly half of these (42) were American.

This, then, is the general nature of the threat that confronts international business. There is little comfort in a recent slack in the targeting of foreigners while, overall, terrorism continues unabated. The threat remains, and the

techniques and tactics of terrorist groups are being refined.
Given this state of the art, how can corporations evaluate
their vulnerability to attack?

Assessing vulnerability is anything but an exact science.
It does not lend itself to quantification, and one must be wary
of mathematical models and comparisons; the variables are too
numerous. But there are certain considerations which, when
examined each in its own context and then in combination, can
give a valid overall picture of a company's exposure to attack.
At the same time, such an evaluation suggests where specific
improvements in defense can be made.

Following are five general factors in corporate vulnerability which can be systematically analyzed for any facility that
might be targeted. The components under each major heading
are necessarily limited by space considerations here, but they
indicate areas that should be examined in detail. When the
whole exercise is completed, the potential exposure of the
facility to targeting will be evident.

COMPANY VISIBILITY

The first factor to consider in assessing a company's vulnerability to terrorist attack is its general visibility. Since
political terrorists rank propaganda and other psychological
effects high among their objectives, any conspicuous symbol of
capitalistic enterprise offers an attractive target. Among the
questions one should ask are the following:

1. Is the facility obviously American? If so, it may well
have a better-than-average chance of being hit. This is not
because organized terrorists need a sign to point out American
interests; they have rather sophisticated intelligence methods
to help in their targeting. The low-profile American company
abroad, with a local name and perhaps local management, is
not invisible to political terrorists, but it is not likely to be a
prime target because of its obscurity.

When an American subsidiary "flies the flag," however, it
risks providing a propaganda incentive for attack because
terrorists can make the point of striking at "U.S. imperialism."
Depending upon popular attitudes in the host country, this
type of target may be selected to reinforce a growing xeno-
phobia or otherwise to stimulate anticapitalistic sentiments.
The target thus can provide a rallying point for radical
agitation. The fact that two out of every five international
terrorist incidents in the past decade have involved U.S.
property or citizens as targets testifies to the symbolic appeal
of anything conspicuously American.

Certain company names are synonymous with an obviously
American product (Coca-Cola), or suggest superior American

technical achievement (IBM), or otherwise project a distinctly American image. Firms of this kind tend to be choice targets of terrorist groups seeking to demonstrate opposition to U.S. political power, or even just to any foreign influence. Despite spectacular inroads into world markets by Germany (which also has been targeted by terrorists abroad) and Japan – and the traditional commercial role of such countries as Great Britain, France and the Netherlands – the United States remains the preeminent symbol of "capitalism" and "imperialism" to Marxist-oriented extremists.

2. Is the company regarded as a "multinational"? Although all companies with operations in several countries are by definition "multinational," some are clearly more so than others for political propaganda purposes. Firms engaged in extractive operations (oil production, mining), for example, are singled out by radicals as being particularly exploitative. So are companies involved in defense-related production or in the computer electronics field.

The symbolic multinational corporation in recent years has been criticized in liberal, noncommunist circles in industrial countries because of its ability to "shop around" for favorable production or marketing conditions in less-developed countries and for being able to operate largely beyond the control of national governments. To capitalize on this negative sentiment, and to suggest common cause with moderate socialist and social-democratic groups, terrorists have found the multinational corporation an especially attractive target.

Beyond this consideration, however, the international corporation is seen universally by Marxists as a key element of capitalism and a source of economic power to the developed Western nations. The degree to which any company can be portrayed as a "typical multinational," therefore, has a bearing on its vulnerability to targeting by left-wing terrorists.

3. Is the product symbolic? Certain products, as already noted, have developed a negative social connotation among political critics, who often use and enjoy the very same products. Thus, one hears of the "Coca-Cola (or Pepsi) civilization," denoting an all-pervasive, materialistic, Philistine culture of America being exported around the world. Radical propagandists are quick to exploit any such symbolic linkage, trying to reduce complex attitudes toward the United States to simple slogans.

Other product associations that are singled out for attention by radicals – and hence by terrorists as well – center on military production of any kind. Thus, a chemical company that produced napalm during the Vietnam War is constantly identified with that product, although its product line includes hundreds of items with a vast range of utility.

4. Does the company have local management? If so, this is no guarantee that the plant will not be hit or the manager

targeted. But the locally run subsidiary is generally a less
inviting target than a branch run by expatriates, when the
aim is to emphasize the "foreign" enemy. Much depends on
how the local population perceives the enterprise and identifies
with it. (Of course, any native company can be hit by terrorists in its own right.)

IMAGE FACTORS

Another set of criteria for measuring corporate vulnerability is
what might simply be called image factors, or how the company
is regarded by the surrounding community. These might be
broken down into four categories for analysis.

Labor Relations

Are there any current union difficulties, or have there been
any significant strikes in the past that have left emotional
scars? What about lay-offs? Have these been accomplished
with minimum worker bitterness? What sort of cushion exists
to tide over those who are temporarily out of work? Answers
to these questions may reveal possible seeds of trouble.
  Political agitators are quick to exploit any festering
dissatisfaction among workers, and the company should ask
itself how well prepared it is to detect early signs of such
agitation and what it can do to blunt the effect. In this
regard, the level of plant vandalism and sabotage should be
watched carefully. Even if the damage is relatively small, a
growing incidence of such activity can indicate the beginning
of an orchestrated campaign by political terrorists that can
spell serious trouble ahead.

Health, Safety, and Environmental Impact

This is an area of particular importance because it involves the
entire social panorama around the company plant or facility.
What about past accidents in which there may have been loss
of life or community property damage? Have the social and
emotional effects been outlived? Is the company still blamed
for some past incident, such as a mine cave-in? Are there
embittered individuals who feel they have a score to settle with
the company, no matter how unreasonable this attitude may be?
Here may lie fertile grounds for agitprop exploitation and a
chance for a terrorist group to penetrate the plant with spies
or saboteurs.

On another plane is the question of continuing occupational hazards.   Has the company taken steps to minimize the
sometimes inevitable consequences of dealing with toxic or otherwise harmful substances?   What is the general employee view
of the company's measures to protect workers and take care of
them if they develop occupational disorders?

Environmental concerns affect not only the "company
family" but the surrounding community as well.   Does the
plant generate water, soil, or air pollution?   Is this pollution
within tolerable limits, or is the condition likely to get worse?
To what degree is there local political or academic-professional
opposition, and how much publicity is being given to the
problem?   Within the past three years there has been a discernible growth of political violence in Europe around environmental issues, centering on antinuclear sentiment but
extending to other charges of pollution and contamination.
Terrorist organizations have also shown tendencies to exploit
these broader-based protest movements.

Community Relations

The role relationship of the company to the community around
it is of utmost importance in determing the potential terrorist
threat.   Again, there are no simple answers.   A company with
fine community relations may be targeted in order to intimidate
the population as a whole or to cause the townspeople, out of
fear, to avoid contact with the company.   The political counterpart to this tactic is to attack municipal officials,
suggesting in the process that any ordinary citizen who has
contact with them may also become a target.

In general, however, strong community relations will help
any company and cannot possibly hurt it.   In societies that
have not reached a point at which terrorist activity is so
massive and pervasive that it can exercise a countergovern-
ment authority, communal social pressure can minimize the
terrorist threat to respected institutions and industrial
facilities in the neighborhood.

Terrorist groups usually seek to exploit existing grievances and identify with a popular cause, thus earning the
grudging support of persons who are otherwise repelled by
their violent methods, and perhaps also winning recruits from
among disgruntled youth.   If one plant does not offer much
opportunity for such exploitation, there is always another that
will.

Some touchstones for evaluating community relations with
the plant include: company tax contributions - does the populace consider these to be reasonable and fair?   Social services
- is the company seen as contributing to them or drawing
excessively from them?   Role as an institution - is the firm

socially integrated with the community or does it stand physically and institutionally apart?

To raise all these questions is not necessarily to imply a remedy. The optimum role of a company in any society depends upon cultural, sociological, psychological, and even historical circumstances. Overparticipation in community activities in some cases can arouse popular concern about company domination or dictation. Excessive support for certain projects - such as building a community center - can lead paradoxically to resentment and rejection of the company's self-assigned role. This is the lesson learned on a larger scale, incidentally, by foreign-aid programs of large countries in the developing world. Institutional largesse must be handled with great care to avoid creating an intolerable psychological obligation on the part of the recipient, which can be a whole community.

As a rule, however, reciprocal benefits between company and community can operate effectively within the economic sphere. When the population at large regards the company's contribution to the community as commensurate with the benefit the company receives (in labor availability, public services, etc.), a firm basis for good relations is established. If there are further offsetting factors, such as plant-generated pollution or the inhibition of other commercial development because of the nature of the company's operations, still other compensation from the company side may be in order. And beyond this point, there are perhaps other modest company contributions that can enrich community life without appearing overly paternalistic or intrusive. As long as the relationship is a partnership between the community as a whole and the company, with each making its proper contribution to a mutually profitable endeavor, the danger of psychological rejection can be avoided.

While a company's popularity within its community is no assurance that it will be spared by either terrorists or radical agitators, the likelihood of trouble is certainly significantly reduced.

Political Symbolism to the Left

Akin to the direct product symbolism already mentioned is the political propaganda image of certain companies which is nurtured by international left-wing movements. Thus the International Telephone and Telegraph Corporation has been targeted by both radical groups and terrorists in various countries because of its reported financial support of opponents of Salvador Allende in Chile, in cooperation with the CIA. The attempt here has been to exploit whatever moderate socialist dissatisfaction exists against ITT while perpetuating and reinforcing the company's negative political image. This tactic

extends as well to firms which provided munitions and other
materiel during the Viet-Nam war, or which operate plants
today in South Africa. Such targeting is also appealing to left
extremists who stress what they call the worldwide "fraternity
of liberation movements."

NATURE OF THE THREAT

External threats to a company come in many forms and vary in
nature from place to place. It is therefore vital that the
general security climate be correctly evaluated for each
separate facility. Only on the basis of sound assessment of the
local threat can cost-effective and workable defense measures
be developed.

Political violence tends to follow predictable patterns,
although there can always be surprises. In general, radical
activists start with relatively mild, nonviolent actions
(demonstrations, leaflet distributions) and then move on to
more intimidating measures (blockades, sit-ins), feeling their
way and measuring the reaction at each step. When the political terrorism stage is reached, the activists tend to start with
less sophisticated operations, then gradually escalate as experience and opportunity warrant.

In terms of organizational skill and technical competence
involved, terrorist actions rank roughly in this order: Petty
vandalism; small-group "picketing" and distribution of radical
literature; mass demonstrations (which usually enlist the
participation of basically nonviolent, liberal, nonrevolutionary
students); firebombing; sabotage in easy access areas; explosive bombing; felonious assault of targeted individuals; professional sabotage of key functions; assassination; and kidnapping.

Seldom does the violence escalate abruptly from the lower
range of operations - say, from mass demonstrations or small-
group picketing - to the upper level of sophistication, such as
kidnapping or assassination. This is due in part to the
group's lack of readiness; it must train itself to take more
complex and dramatic measures in turn. But perhaps even
more important is the need to prepare the public at large to
accept a high level of violence as a political rather than an
ordinary criminal act.

The abrupt assassination of a company official by a
political group, without having first passed through lesser
stages of violence accompanied by political propaganda, might
cause a strong shock reaction in the public that could result
in a concerted action by the authorities to crush the revolutionary movement. But a long period of slowly accelerating
political violence can condition the public to accept such
measures as a fact of life.

Several other things happen in this graduated process as well. The public loses confidence in the police who are unable to end the trouble; it gradually feels more vulnerable to the threat itself (although wise terrorists carefully avoid harming "innocent" persons at the outset and try to isolate the targeted institution); and it is "educated" by the terrorists' propaganda to recognize their actions as political rather than criminal. By the time the kidnapping-assassination phase comes, the public feels both helpless and intimidated. It is no longer prepared to respond wholeheartedly and spontaneously against even cold-blooded murder.

The corporate security analyst can be guided by the principles outlined here to determine the level of threat directed at any plant or facility around the world. First, it is important to determine the general condition of stability and control in the society at large, and what the record has been for political (and, indeed, for organized criminal) violence. A simple checklist for evaluating the level of threat might include the following items.

Groups Operating in the Area

What are their political motivation, their modes of operation, their weapons-and-tactics sophistication, and their size? Also, what is the nature of their support mechanisms? Aside from members of the groups itself who provide safe houses and specialized technical and professional services, there is frequently a sympathizer element within the general population that gives invaluable moral and material support. The extent and influence of this support element - often found in professional, artistic, and academic circles - may determine how far the terrorists are likely to go.

Nature of the Violence

Where along the spectrum of possible violent acts has the terrorist group arrived now? If it is at the mass-demonstration stage (which might be predominantly of a nonviolent, radical nature rather than incipient terrorism), the threat may be contained at that level. If there is bombing, does it seek to take casualties or is it confined to causing property damage at night? In the context of prevailing public attitudes, would the group be encouraged to escalate to a more lethal form of violence?

The kind of current terrorist activity indicates, of course, what immediate defensive measures are needed. In addition, some precautions should be taken against the next likely level of violence, and contingency plans should exist for

meeting any conceivable escalation of the threat in the future.
But it is important to avoid excessive defenses; the cost can
become prohibitive and a siege mentality can be created which
will reduce the operating efficiency of the plant. The art is
to meet the current level of threat, to have some excess
capacity to meet a sudden rise in the threat level, and to be
ready to cope with more serious dangers in the future – all
without making a gross overinvestment in security.

How Have Others Coped?

No opportunity should be lost to profit from the experience of
other companies in the area of your plant, either of foreign or
domestic ownership, that have suffered terrorist threat or
attack. Learn in detail what tactics were used by the terrorists, what countermeasures were taken by the company, and
what the response of authorities was. In some respects your
own company's basic circumstances may differ from those of
the other targeted company, requiring modifications of the
lessons learned. But the information gained will be valuable
both for ascertaining the probable nature of the threat to your
facility as well as determining what measures are effective
against it.

Available Outside Assistance

If your plant is attacked, how quickly and effectively would
the police respond? Would there be military or other reserves
to call upon? Terrorists always evaluate the effectiveness of
the authorities in making their plans, and the possible victim
should do likewise. Deficiencies in police protection or in the
ability of the police to respond to an emergency might have to
be made up by the company itself. Any evidence that the
plant has compensated for inadequate police support, which
would have become evident to the terrorists through surveillance when they planned their attack, would tend to discourage an attempt.
     The quality of firefighting services should also be
assessed. In most places, the company is wise to have a considerable capability of its own to cope with arson or firebomb
attack. Even the quickest response of the community fire
department may be too slow to deal with an incendiary assault.
     In the case of either police or fire services, it is well to
remember that well-organized terrorists frequently turn in
false alarms to divert emergency services to a distant place
just before they attack, thus assuring that help will not be as
easily available.

PHYSICAL SECURITY PROFILE

Surveys of building security are routine for every large corporation, and many of the precautions taken against criminal acts or industrial sabotage apply equally well against possible terrorist attack. But the terrorist poses a threat beyond the limits of either conventional criminals or vengeful individuals trying to cause damage to the company.

Criminals normally seek personal gain; they are trying to obtain something of value. The amount of damage they do is therefore usually circumscribed by this objective (although they might in some cases cause an explosion or start a fire as a diversion). The terrorist group, on the other hand, is not seeking what is normally thought of as "selfish gain"; the aim rather is to cause damage, attract attention, create an illusion of strength, and generate fear. This mission is easier to accomplish than that of the criminal, and the consequent destruction or loss can be many times greater.

Furthermore, terrorists generally have greater resources at their command than have criminals - and than has the individual saboteur. Often the terrorists have excellent intelligence from spies within the plant, they can draw on a variety of technical skills from their members and sympathizers, they are usually well financed, and they frequently have access to particularly effective weapons and technology.

When considering defense measures against terrorism, therefore, one must look far beyond established security precautions. A physical security profile for any facility or installation under potential terrorist threat must take into account factors such as those discussed below.

Relation of the Plant to Other Possible Targets

In politically motivated mass disturbances, a facility may come under attack as an alternate or incidental target. The primary target may be nearby and less accessible, or might draw an attack that results in the damage of other property in the neighborhood.

Distance of Plant from the Street

Space between the company building and the nearest point of public access (normally a street screened off by a fence) constitutes both warning time and a territorial buffer in an emergency. Often it is not until the fence is breached and the company's "territory" invaded that a serious threat is recognized, so generally the greater the distance from the building to the front fence the better the possibility of defense against some kind of assault.

In mob actions, it is possible to perceive a threat and use both the time and space afforded by the distance from the street to take defense measures. Obviously the danger from this kind of threat is greater if there is no buffer zone or if the public has casual access to the facility itself. Retail establishments and automobile showrooms are afforded much less natural protection, and special precautions must then be taken for them in high-risk areas.

Situation of the Facility on the Grounds

Certain features of the plant layout can be important to security. If the building is less than 35 yards from the nearest public-access area, for example, it might be hit by a hand-thrown Molotov cocktail. Within that range, then, certain other circumstances must be considered. Are there large front windows (which might be wire-screened or inexpensively reinforced with Mylar or some other invisible sheet-plastic coating)? Is it advisable to move workers from the immediate window area to prevent possible injury? Is there any especially volatile or inflammable material in front of the building that can be moved elsewhere?

In any case, it is wise to consider how the building might be evacuated during a bomb threat, or even if an explosion occurs. Is there space and are there suitable exists to the rear of the building? Since about three-quarters of all actual bomb plants have been either in the public-access areas of the target building or immediately outside it, one must always consider the danger of evacuating people directly into the explosion. Rear areas are generally less accessible to strangers than are front areas (and should where possible be kept clear of receptacles where bombs might be hidden). Escape to the rear, preferably out of view from the street in front of the building, might be necessary if a mob threatens to attack from the front. Existing fire-evacuation plans, which bring the employees out through all exits, have to be modified for bomb-threat and mob-threat evacuation to avoid exposed areas.

Other points of vulnerability for a facility involve the elevation of the building and the general character of the surrounding terrain. Blind approaches, ground undulation, location and character of the shrubbery, the positioning of fences, gates, and other possible obstacles, and the layout of parking areas and access walks or roads should all be examined in the light of any possible hostile approach or infiltration.

Structural Characteristics

Particularly if fire or explosive bombing is a danger, the facility should be analyzed for fireproofing and blast resistance. Such factors as the thickness and composition of exterior walls; size and design of windows; materials used for nonstructural partitions, and load-bearing capacity of floors determine what contingency plans might be developed for various kinds of threat. The division of work functions is particularly important for limiting possible damage.

Location of Key Elements of the Facility

Certain functions constitute the very organic substance of a plant and are particularly vulnerable to attack. Among these are:

- Fuel Storage: Many factory complexes have fuel tanks on the periphery of the industrial estate, where they can readily be resupplied and pose no danger to the rest of the compound. Since terrorists frequently target fuel depots, should such tanks be relocated deeper within the fences? From a production standpoint, is there a stand-by reserve which can be drawn upon if the main tanks should be attacked?

- Power source: Is it also located near the fence, relatively accessible to the outside? Is there a reserve transformer if the main one goes out? And if the facility uses community power, is there an emergency backup system that would permit at least partial operations if the transmission lines are cut?

- Communications: Is there a radio or other backup system that could maintain external contact if the telephones went out? (Even a CB radio in a vehicle parked on the grounds would be a help in an emergency.) Is there at least one direct line that does not run through the switchboard? Is the switchboard room kept locked to all but authorized persons? (And, incidentally, are the phone operators properly instructed on handling bomb warnings and other threats?)

- Sensitive records: Is the computer in a safe area and kept under proper security control? Are duplicates of important ADP tapes available off the premises? Are key papers kept secure with access limited to designated persons? Penetration of sensitive files, both in industry and government, has been accomplished by terrorist groups in virtually every country.

- Volatile materials: Are these kept in specially shielded areas, with quantities in the plant limited to the amount

necessary for current production?   Are reserve supplies
also kept in a reasonably well-protected place?   Are
critical spare parts likewise secure?   It must be assumed
that any terrorist group contemplating sabotage will know
the potential squeeze points and bottlenecks of the plant
and its process.

Basic Security Precautions

Most of the measures to safeguard against theft and sabotage
generally apply to the terrorist threat.   The danger of political violence, however, calls for a new dimension to conventional security doctrine, enlisting the help of the personnel
and public affairs departments. Terrorism is largely a psychological weapon directed at people. Effective countermeasures
must therefore involve everyone who can be reached by terrorist propaganda.   Among the special requirements are these:

• Personnel security: The staffing of key functions has to
  be reevaluated. Is all sensitive information handled on a
  need-to-know basis?   Is there limited access to executive
  files?   Are secretaries and other clerical personnel
  properly vetted for security? (At the height of terrorist
  violence in Argentina, one American company hired only
  married women over 30 for key secretarial positions, since
  nearly all terrorists and their sympathizers were young
  and single.) In some countries the investigation of staff
  members is resented, and in Italy it is forbidden by law.
  But most companies could scrutinize their key staff more
  carefully than they have in the past.
• Rationalization of functions: Restructuring of administrative procedures and the division of labor in the executive
  suite might be advisable if leaks of information are
  suspected, or to avoid the concentration of sensitive data
  in the hands of certain clerical personnel.
• Briefing of employees: Probably a variety of orientation
  classes on the terrorist threat is required for such
  persons as secretaries of executives, phone operators,
  security personnel, safety officers, and the like.   One
  must avoid engendering undue fear, but in high-risk
  areas key staff members must be informed of their role if
  emergency contingency plans are to work.   It is helpful
  as well for everyone in what might be called a pivotal
  role, down to the receptionist at the front desk, to be
  sensitized to danger signs.   This provides an early-
  warning system to detect impending terrorist actions.
  Not the least of those needing training are executives –
  potential kidnap victims – who should be advised on how
  to detect terrorist surveillance, to evade seizure and, if
  need be, to survive as a hostage.

- <u>Intraplant access and security</u>: Since sabotage is often most easily accomplished by someone from outside a critical area who has casual access to it (the principle of "neighborly sabotage"), it might be well to declare such areas closed to routine visits. Color-coding ID cards and the screening of movement from one part of the plant to another - at least for the most vulnerable areas - could facilitate this control.
- <u>Executive movement</u>: Nearly every company can improve its measures for protecting top executives, although some of the executives themselves resist changes in their routine or work habits for the purpose of improving their security. Again in light of the oft-demonstrated ability of terrorists to penetrate corporate headquarters, it is wise not to make general distribution around the office of the executive appointments schedule. Use of the "core day" - which assures that a top executive will be on hand for the same few hours every day (permitting scheduled in-house meetings) while he varies his arrivals and departures at either end of the day in irregular fashion - is another measure that greatly reduces exposure to possible ambush while not totally disrupting daily routine. Random choice of routes to work or to other predictable stopping places also adds materially to his safety. Such "soft-security" measures are indispensable to any company's protection system.

CRISIS MANAGEMENT CAPABILITY

The ability to determine - and correct - weaknesses in the company's defense against terrorist attack is the greatest possible insurance that there will be no attack at all. This is not, however, a foolproof precaution. While studies of political terrorism show that attackers usually pick the least protected among desirable targets, well-organized groups can bring to bear the resources necessary to hit a truly prime target almost regardless of defense. When a particular target is sufficiently important for psychological or symbolic reasons, it must be assumed that terrorists can and very well may overwhelm the defenses to accomplish their mission.

What remains, then, is the ability to deal with an incident when it occurs, despite all reasonable precautions to prevent it. This requires additional contingency planning, backed by a top-level company command unit to handle such emergencies. It should be stressed that the requirement here goes beyond the need for a crisis-management system to deal with natural disasters or major accidents - nonpremeditated, impersonal events. A terrorist incident is a planned hostile act that has anticipated the probable reaction of both the company and law-enforcement agencies; there are plans for further psychological exploitation of the incident, and any countermeasure will encounter a further (and usually well-planned) terrorist response. The situation frequently constitutes a series of engagements - a dynamic, evolving campaign - built around the original attack.

How does a corporation prepare for such a problem? First, it must recognize that its normal management machinery is not able to cope. The typical business enterprise is not equipped to conduct hour-by-hour operations against a cunning and violent adversary, or to "negotiate" for the return of a kidnapped executive. But with proper foresight and realistic planning it can develop the necessary capacity.

Steps to establish this kind of capability might be outlined as follows:

1. <u>Determine the extent of the problem</u>. Based on the history of terrorism worldwide, what would realistically be the worst possible case in each category of terrorist attack to contend with? How might these threats be applied against the company's assets either at home or abroad? Any one of several consulting firms could staff out this background.

2. <u>Develop basic policies for each contingency</u>. What should be the general response to threat/extortion? Will the company pay ransom for kidnapped executives and, if so, what should be its limit? What is the policy for handling the family of a kidnap victim? Should a kidnapped executive automatically be replaced, or should the job be kept open until he or she is returned? Should the company "negotiate" with terrorists without involving the police? (Separate judgments have to be made here, depending on conditions in each place of operation.) These are among the matters that should be settled before a crisis develops, in an atmosphere free from tension and anxiety, and methodically thought out. It is exceedingly difficult to make sound decisions during an emergency, particularly if someone's life is at stake, and it is even harder to get the necessary consensus of board members or other top management officials when no basic principles have been agreed upon in advance.

3. <u>Inform managers in the field of the policy</u>. This includes advising key executives of company plans for handling a kidnapping, in general terms - whether ransom will be paid; whether the family will be removed from the scene (usually a good idea); whether the victim will be automatically replaced. By knowing the general tactics of the company, the victim is less susceptible to psychological pressure by the kidnappers, who usually try to destroy

his confidence in the company and convince him he has been abandoned.

4. Delegate necessary authority to the field. Branch managers should be instructed on how to respond to a sudden terrorist action and be given authority to act immediately when necessary (particularly in a kidnapping). Such crises cannot be managed from the outset by corporate headquarters. The very first steps taken by management at the scene in response to a kidnapping might well affect the outcome.

5. Establish a corporate crisis-response unit. This can be built upon whatever apparatus already exists for dealing with emergencies, but everyone must be aware that terrorist acts are not "normal" crises. At a minimum, the group should include the senior representatives of security, personnel, finance, legal, and public affairs. It should be headed by an executive VP or comparable official with a clear mandate from the chief executive officer.

   Proper organization and training of a crisis-response unit (CRU) is a complex matter. Effectiveness depends upon the soundness of the corporation's basic policy for dealing with terrorism, the degree of mutual confidence and respect between the CRU and the corporate leadership, the extent to which the unit melds with the organizational structure and management style of the company, and the experience it has gained (through crisis-simulation exercise, among other things) in working together under stress. Ideally the CRU should have two basic functions: to staff out the problem and provide options for decision by top management, and to supervise the execution of the decisions then reached.

Political terrorism is a fact of life in the world today, and after a decade of development and demonstration it shows no sign of going away. Companies with international operations must contend with this phenomenon as one more problem to be solved or mastered – and at additional inconvenience and expense that must be chalked up to the cost of doing business. Nothing has happened so far, despite spectacular terrorist events in the Middle East, to indicate that this mode of violent disruption will materially affect the flow of international trade. But the individual corporation that wishes to continue to operate abroad (and to some extent, at home as well), must adjust to the terroristic component of the world's lifestyle, which is certain to continue in the 1980s and perhaps beyond.

   This chapter is a revised version of a paper originally presented at a conference on "Terrorism and U.S. Business," held on December 14, 1977 at Georgetown's Center for Strategic and International Studies.

Selected Bibliography

Abdallah, King. My Memoirs Completed, trans. H.W. Glidden. Washington, D.C.: American Council of Learned Studies, 1954.

Abdel-Fadil, Mahmoud. The Political Economy of Nasserism: A Study in Employment and Income Distribution Policies in Urban Egypt, 1952-72. New York: Cambridge University Press, 1980.

A Conversation with Ernesto Mulato: The Political and Military Strength in Angola. Washington, D.C.: American Enterprise Institute for Public Policy Research, 1979.

Abdul-Hamid, Muhamed Kamal. The Middle East in Strategic Balance. Cairo: The Modern Publishing House, n.d.

Abdul-Rauf, Muhammad. The Islamic Doctrine of Economics and Contemporary Economic Thought. Washington, D.C.: American Enterprise Institute for Public Policy Research, 1979.

Abir, Mordechai. Oil, Power and Politics: Conflict in Arabia, the Red Sea and The Gulf. London: F. Cass, 1974.

Abu-Zayd, Sulayman. Africa in the Claws of Israel. Beirut: Sharikat al-Tabi walnashr al-hibnan-izya, 1964.

Afifi, Mohamed El-Hadi. The Arabs and the United Nations. London: Longmans, Green and Co., 1964.

Ajami, Fouad. The Arab Predicament: Arab Political Thought and Practice Since 1967. New York: Cambridge University Press, 1981.

Akhavi, Shahrough. Religion and Politics in Contemporary Iran: Clergy-State Relations in the Pahlavi Period. Albany: State University of New York Press, 1980.

Al-'abid, Ibrahim. The Foreign Policy of Israel. Beirut: M.B.F., 1968.

Al-Kuwari, Ali Khalifa. Oil Revenues in the Gulf Emerates. Boulder, Colorado: Westview Press, 1978.

Alexander, Yonah and Nicholas N. Kittrie, eds. Crescent and Star: Arab-Israeli Perspectives on the Middle East Conflict. New York: AMS Press, 1972.

Anthony, John Duke. The Middle East: Oil, Politics, and Development. Washington, D.C.: American Enterprise Institute, 1975.

Antonius, George. The Arab Awakening. New York: Capricorn Books, 1955.

Arberry, Arthur J., trans. The Koran Interpreted. London: Allen and Unwin, 1955.

Aronson, Shlomo. Conflict and Bargaining in the Middle East: An Israeli Perspective. Baltimore: Johns Hopkins Press, 1979.

Atiyeh, George N. Arab and American Cultures. Washington, D.C.: American Enterprise Institute, 1977.

Atkin, Muriel. Russia and Iran: 1780-1828. Minneapolis: University of Minnesota Press, 1980.

The Atlantic Council's Working Group on Security Affairs. After Afghanistan: The Long Haul. Boulder, Colorado: Praeger, 1979.

Avineri, Shlomo, ed. Israel and the Palestinians: Reflections on the Clash of Two National Movements. New York: St. Martin's Press, 1971.

Azzam, Abd-al-Rahman. The Eternal Message of Muhammad. Trans. by C.E. Farah. New York: Devin Adair, 1964.

Bain, Kenneth Ray. The March to Zion: United States Policy and the Founding of Israel. Texas: Texas A & M University Press, 1980.

Baljon, J.M.S. Modern Muslim Koran Interpretation. Leiden: E.J. Brill, 1961.

Banisadr, Abolhassan. Islamic Government. Lexington, Kentucky: Mazda Publishers, n.d.

Bar-Simon-Tov, Yaacov. The Israeli-Egyptian War of Attrition, 1969-1970: A Case Study of Limited Local War. New York: Columbia University Press, 1980.

Bauer, Yehuda. The Jewish Emergence from Powerlessness. Toronto: University of Toronto Press, 1979.

Be'eri, E. Army Officers in Arab Politics and Society. New
    York: Praeger, 1970.

Bell, J. Bowyer. The Long War: Israel and the Arabs Since
    1946. Englewood Cliffs, N.J.: Prentice-Hall, 1969.

Berger, Earl. The Covenant and the Sword: Arab-Israeli
    Relations, 1948-1956. London: Routledge and Kegan Paul,
    1956.

Berque, Jacques. The Arabs: Their History and Future.
    New York: Praeger, 1964.

Betts, Robert Brenton. Christians in the Arab East: A Polit-
    ical Study. New York: The Combined Book Exhibit,
    1979.

Binder, Leonard. The Ideological Revolution in the Middle
    East. New York: John Wiley and Sons, 1964.

Bouheiry, Marwan. Intellectual Life in the Arab East: 1890-
    1939. Syracuse, N.Y.: Syracuse University Press, 1981.

Bowman, Larry W. and Clark, Ian. The Indian Ocean in Glo-
    bal Politics. Boulder, Colorado: Westview Press, 1981.

Bradley, C. Paul. The Camp David Process: A Study of Car-
    ter Administration Policies (1977-1980). Hamden, Conn.:
    Tompson and Rutter, 1981.

_____ . Electoral Politics in Israel: the Knesset Election of
    1981. Hamden, Conn.: Tompson and Rutter, 1981.

Brecher, Michael. Decisions in Israel's Foreign Policy. Lon-
    don: Oxford University Press, 1974.

_____ . The Foreign Policy System of Israel: Setting
    Images and Process. London: Oxford University Press,
    1972.

Bullard Sir. Readu, ed. The Middle East: A Political and
    Economic Survey. 3rd edition. London and New York:
    Oxford University Press (RIIA), 1958.

Chaffetz, David. A Journey through Afghanistan: A Memorial.
    Chicago, Ill.: Regnery Gateway, Inc., 1981.

Chaliand, Gerard. People Without a Country: The Kurds and
    Kurdistan. London: Zed Press, n.d.

Churba, Joseph. U.A.R.-Israeli Rivalry Over Aid and Trade
    in Sub-Saharan Africa, 1957-1973. Doctoral dissertation,
    Columbia University, 1965.

Comay, Michael. Israel's Role in the Developing World. Ex-
    cerpts from a lecture before the Royal Commonwealth
    Society, London, on 24 February 1972. Jerusalem, Isra-
    el, Ministry for Foreign Affairs, International Cooperation
    Division, 1972.

Cook, Michael. Early Muslim Dogma: A Source-Critical History. New York: Cambridge University Press, n.d.

Copeland, Miles. The Game of Nations: The Amorality of Power Politics. London: Weidenfeld and Nicholson, 1969.

Cottam, Richard W. Nationalism in Iran. Pittsburgh: University of Pittsburgh Press, 1979.

Cottrell, Alvin J., ed. The Persian Gulf States: A General Survey. Baltimore: Johns Hopkins Press, 1980.

Crone, Patricia and Cook, Michael. Hagarism: The Making of the Islamic World. New York: Cambridge University Press, 1980.

Crone, Patricia. Slaves on Horses: The Evolution of the Islamic Polity. New York: Cambridge University Press, 1980.

Curtis, Michael. People and Politics in the Middle East. New Brunswick: Transaction Books, 1971.

Curtis, Michael and Getelson, Susan A., eds. Israel in the Third World. New Brunswick: Transaction Books, 1976.

Davison, W. Phillips. International Political Communication. New York: Praeger, 1965.

Davis, John H. The Evasive Peace. London: John Murray, 1968.

Dawn, C. Ernest. From Ottomanism to Arabism. Urbana: University of Illinois Press, 1973.

De Planhol, Xavier. The World of Islam. Ithaca, N.Y.: Cornell University Press, 1959.

Dodd, Clement Henry. Democracy and Development in Turkey. New Humberside, England: The Eothen Press, 1979.

Dodge, Bayard. Al-Azhar: A Millenium of Muslim Learning. Washington, D.C.: Middle East Institute, 1961.

Donaldson, Robert H. The Soviet Union in the Third World. Boulder, Colo.: Praeger, 1980.

Drabek, Ann Gordon and Wilfred Knapp. The Politics of African and Middle Eastern States, An Annotated Bibliography. New York: Pergamon Press, 1976.

Eger, Akiva. Israel and the Emerging Nations. New York: American Histradrut Cultural Exchange Institute, 1971.

Egypt, Ministry of National Guidance. The Egyptian Cultural Revolution in Five Years. Cairo: Political Books Committee, 1957.

El-Haki, Ali A. The Middle Eastern States and the Law of the Sea. Syracuse: Syracuse University Press, 1979.

El Mallakh, Ragaei. Kuwait: Trade and Investment. Boulder, Colo.: Westview Press, 1979.

Elazar, Daniel J. The Camp David Framework for Peace: Toward Shared Rule. Washington, D.C.: American Enterprise Institute for Public Policy Research, 1979.

Eliav, Arie. Between Hammer and Sickle. New York: Signet Books, 1969.

Entelis, John Pierre. Comparative Politics of North Africa: Algeria, Morocco, and Tunisia. Syracuse: Syracuse University Press, 1980.

Esposito, John L. Islam and Development: Religion and Socio-Political Change. Syracuse: Syracuse University Press, 1980.

Faris, Nabhi A. and Mohammed T. Husayn. The Crescent in Crisis. Lawrence: University of Kansas Press, 1955.

Fishcher, Michael, M.J. Iran: From Religious Dispute to Revolution. Cambridge, Mass.: Harvard University Press, 1980.

Flapon, Simah. When Enemies Dare to Talk: On Israeli-Palestinian Debate. New York: The Combined Book Exhibit, 1979.

Gaube, Heinz. Iranian Cities. New York: New York University Press, 1979.

Gellhorn, Martha. The Arabs of Palestine. New York: New York American Jewish Committee, 1962.

Gerson, Allan. Israel: The West Bank and International Law. Totowa, N.J.: Biblio Distribution Centre, 1978.

Ghanim, Muhammad Hafiz. Arab International Relations. Cairo: Nahdhat Misr, 1965.

Gibb, Hamilton, A.R. Mohammedanism: An Historical Survey. New York: Oxford University Press, 1962.

Ginat, Joseph. Women in Muslim Rural Society. New Brunswick, N.J.: Rutgers University, Transaction Books, 1980.

Giniewski, Paul. Israel devant l'Afrique at l'Asie. Paris: Librarie Durlacher, 1958.

Ginsburg, Norton Sidney. Atlas of Economic Development. Chicago: University of Chicago Press, 1961.

Glubb, Sir John Bagot. A Soldier With the Arabs. London: Hodder and Stoughton, 1957.

Goldschmidt, Arthur, Jr. A Concise History of the Middle East. Boulder, Colo.: Praeger, 1979.

Grabill, Joseph L. Protestant Diplomacy and the Near East Missionary Influence on American Policy, 1810-1927. Minneapolis: University of Minnesota Press, 1971.

Grayson, Benson. United States-Iranian Relations. Washington, D.C.: University Press of America, Inc., 1981.

Griffiths, John. Afghanistan: Key to a Continent. Boulder, Colo.: Westview Press, 1981.

Grunebaum, Von Gustave. Modern Islam: The Search for Cultural Identity. Berkeley: University of California Press, 1962.

Hadawi, Sami. Bitter Harvest. New York: New World Press, 1967.

Haim, Sylvia G., ed. Arab Nationalism and a Wider World. New York: American Association for Peace in the Middle East, 1971.

Haley, Edward P. and Lewis W. Snider. Lebanon in Crisis: Participants and Issues. Syracuse, N.Y.: Syracuse University Press, 1979.

Halpern, Ben. The Idea of the Jewish State. Cambridge, Mass.: Harvard University Press, 1961.

Harkabi, Yehoshafat. The Arabs' Position in Their Conflict with Israel. Jerusalem: Israel Universities Press, 1972.

Higgins, Rosalyn. United Nations Peacekeeping, 1946-1967. Documents and Commentary. Oxford, London, New York, 1969. Issued under Auspices of Royal Institute of International Affairs.

Hitti, Philip K. The Arabs: A Short History. New York: Gateway, 1962.

_____. Islam: A Way of Life. Chicago: Regnery Gateway, Inc., 1970.

Holt, Peter M. and Daly, M. W. The History of the Sudan from the Coming of Islam to the Present Day. Boulder, Colo.: Westview Press, 1979.

Horn, Carl von. Soldiering for Peace. New York: Makay, 1967.

Hourani, Albert H. Arabic Thought in the Liberal Age, 1798-1939. New York and London: Oxford University Press, 1962.

_____. Europe and the Middle East. Berkeley: University of California Press, 1980.

_____. The Emergence of the Modern Middle East. Berkeley: University of California Press, 1980.

Howard, Harry N. Middle East and North Africa: A Bibliography for Undergraduate Libraries. Williamsport, Penna.: Bro-Dart Publishing Co., 1971.

Hudson, Michael C. Arab Politics: The Search for Legitimacy. New Haven: Yale University Press, 1977.

Ismael, Tareq Y. The Middle East in World Politics: A Study of Contemporary International Relations. Syracuse: Syracuse University Press, 1974.

_____. The UAR in Africa: Egypt's Policy under Nasser. Evanston, Ill.: Northwestern University Press, 1971.

_____. The Arab Left. Syracuse: Syracuse University Press, n.d.

Israel Ministry of Commerce and Industry, Department of External Trade. Israel's Trade with Africa, Asia, Oceania and South America. Jerusalem: 1972.

Issawi, Charles, ed. The Economic History of the Middle East, 1800-1914. Chicago: University of Chicago Press, 1966.

_____. The Economic History of Turkey, 1800-1914. Chicago: University of Chicago Press, 1980.

Itzkowitz, Norman. Ottoman Empire and Islamic Tradition. Chicago: University of Chicago Press, 1980.

Jabbari, Ahmad and Olson, Robert. Iran: Essays on a Revolution in the Making. Lexington, Kentucky: Mazda Publishers, 1981.

Jequier, Nicholas. Israel's Foreign Aid. Cambridge, Mass.: Harvard University Press, 1969.

Joseph, Suad and Pillsbury, Barbara. Muslm-Christian Conflicts: Economic, Political and Social Origins. Boulder, Colo.: Westview Press, 1979.

Jureidini, Paul and R.D. McLaurin. Beyond Camp David: Emerging Alignments and Leaders in the Middle East. Syracuse: Syracuse University Press, 1981.

Jurji, Eduard. The Middle East: Its Religion and Culture. Philadelphia: Westminster, 1956.

Kaminker, Benjamin. The Histadrut and Developing Countries. Tel-Aviv: Histradrut, Political Department, n.d.

Keddie, Nikki. Iran: Religion, Politics and Society. Totowa, N.J.: Biblio Distribution Centre, 1981.

_____. Roots of Revolution: An Interpretive History of Modern Iran. New Haven, Conn.: Yale University Press, 1981.

Kelley, John B. Arabia, the Gulf and the West: A Critical View of Arabs and Their Oil Policy. New York: The Combined Book Exhibit, 1980.

Kennedy, Hugh. The Early Abbasid Caliphate. Totowa, N.J.: Barnes and Noble Books, 1981.

Khalaf, Samir. Persistance and Change in 19th Century Lebanon: A Sociological Essay. Syracuse: Syracuse University Press, 1979.

Khalidi, Walid and Abish Yusuf. Arab Political Documents 1963. Political Studies and Public Administration Department AUB Beirut: The American University of Beirut, 1964.

Khalifa, Ali Mohammed. The United Arab Emirates: Unity in Fragmentation. Boulder, Colo.: Westview Press, 1979.

Kimche, David and Dan Bawly. The Six-Day War -- Problems and Aftermath. New York: Stein and Day, 1971.

Kleiman, Aaron S. Soviet Russia and the Middle East. Baltimore: Johns Hopkins Press, 1970.

Kour, Z.H. The History of Aden: 1839-1872. Totowa, N.J.: Biblio Distribution Centre, 1981.

Koury, Enver M. The Crisis in the Lebanese System: Confessionalism and Chaos. Washington, D.C.: American Enterprise Institute, 1976.

Krausz, Ernest. Studies of Israeli Society. Volume 1, Migration, Ethnicity and Community. New Brunswick, N.J.: Rutgers University, Transaction Books, 1980.

Lall, Arthur. The U.N. and the Middle East Crisis, 1967. Rev. ed. New York: Columbia University Press, 1970.

Laqueur, Walter. The Struggle for the Mideast. London: Rutledge and Kegan Paul, 1969.

Lenczowski, George. Soviet Advances in the Middle East. Washington, D.C.: American Enterprise Institute, 1972.

_____ . Political Elites in the Middle East. Washington, D.C.: American Enterprise Institute, 1975.

_____ . The Middle East in World Affairs. Ithaca, N.Y.: Cornell University Press, 1980.

Lesch, Ann Mosley. Arab Politics in Palestine, 1917-1939. Ithaca. N.Y.: Cornell University Press, 1979.

Lewis, Bernard. The Arabs in History. New York: Harper, 1960.

Lewis, Jesse W. The Strategic Balance in the Mediterranean. Washington, D.C.: American Enterprise Institute, 1976.

Long, David E., ed. The Government: Politics of the Middle East and North Africa. Boulder, Colo.: Praeger, 1980.

Long, David E., ed. The Middle East in Transition. New York: Praeger, 1958.

Mabro, Robert. The Egyptian Economy, 1952-1972. New York: Oxford University Press, 1979.

MacDonald, Robert. The League of Arab States. Princeton: Princeton University Press, 1965.

MacDonald, Charles G. Iran, Saudi Arabia and the Law of the Sea. Westport, Conn.: The Greenwood Press, 1980.

Malkin, Ahuva and Zev Goldberg, eds. Israel's Relations with the Developing Countries. Tel-Aviv: Beit Berl Center for Education, Studies and Research, 1963.

Mansfield, Peter. Nasser's Egypt. Baltimore: Penguin Books, 1965.

_____. The Middle East: A Political and Economic Survey. New York: Oxford University Press, 1980. (1973)

Marlowe, John. Arab Nationalism and British Imperialism. New York: Praeger, 1961.

Mazrui, Ali A. Africa's International Relations. Boulder, Colo.: Praeger, 1979.

Mehdi, M.T. Peace in the Middle East. New York: New World, 1967.

Middle East Negotiations: A Conversation with Joseph Sisco. Washington, D.C.: American Enterprise Institute, 1980.

Miller, Aaron David. Search for Security: Saudi Arabian Oil and American Foreign Policy, 1939-1949. Chapel Hill, N.C.: University of North Carolina Press, 1980.

Monroe, Elizabeth. Britain's Moment in the Middle East, 1914-1956. Baltimore: Johns Hopkins Press, 1963.

Muinis, Husain. Egypt and its Mission. Cairo: Al-Namudtha-jiyza Press, 1954.

Nakhleh, Emile A. Arab-American Relations in the Persian Gulf. Washington, D.C.: American Enterprise Institute, 1975.

_____, ed. A Palestinian Agenda for the West Bank and Gaza. Washington, D.C.: American Enterprise Institute, 1980.

_____. The United States and Saudi Arabia. Washington, D.C.: American Enterprise Institute, 1975.

Nasser, Munir K. Press, Politics and Power: Egypt's Heikal and Al-Ahram. Ames: Iowa State University Press, 1979.

Nast, Seyyed Hossein. Ideals and Realities of Islam. New York: Praeger, 1967.

Nevakivi, Jukka. Britain, France, and the Arab Middle East, 1914-1920. London: Oxford University Press, 1969.

Nore, Peter and Turner, Terisa. Oil and Class Struggle. London: Zed Press, n.d.

Novik, Minrod and Joyce Starr. Challenges in the Middle East. Washington, D.C.: Praeger Special Studies, 1981.

Nuseibeh, Hazem Zaki. The Ideas of Arab Nationalism. Ithaca, N.Y.: Cornell University Press, 1956.

Patai, Raphael. Golden River to Golden Road: Society, Culture and Change in the Mideast. Philadelphia: University of Pennsylvannia Press, 1962.

Penniman, Howard. Israel at the Polls: the Knesset Elections of 1977. Washington, D.C.: American Enterprise Institute, 1978.

Penrose, Edith. Iraq: International Relations and National Development. Boulder, Colo.: Westview Press, 1978.

Peretz, Don. The Government and Politics of Israel. Boulder, Colo.: Praeger, 1979.

Pfeff, Richard H. Jerusalem: Keystone of an Arab-Israeli Settlement. Washington, D.C.: American Enterprise Institute, 1969.

Pipes, Daniel. Slave Soldiers and Islam: The Genesis of a Military System. New Haven: Yale University Press, 1981.

Plascov, Avi. The Palestinian Refugees in Jordan 1948-1957. Totowa, N.J.: Biblio Distribution Centre, 1981.

Polk, William R. The Arab World. Cambridge, Mass.: Harvard University Press, 1980.

Proctor, Harris, ed. Islam and International Relations. New York: Praeger, 1964.

Pryce-Jones, David. The Face of Defeat. New York: Holt, Rinehart and Winston, 1973.

Records of the Joint Chiefs of Staff: 1946-1953: The Middle East. Washington, D.C.: University Publications of America, Inc., 1980.

Record, Jeffrey. The Rapid Deployment Force and U.S. Military Intervention in the Persian Gulf. Cambridge, Mass.: Institute for Foreign Policy Analysis, Inc.: 1981.

Roi, Yaacov. Soviet Decision-Making in Practice: The USSR and Israel, 1947-1954. New Brunswick, N.J.: Rutgers University, Transaction Books, 1980.

Reich, Bernard. Israel's Foreign Policy: A Case Study in Small State Diplomacy. Doctoral dissertation, University of Virginia, 1964.

Reisman, Michael. The Art of the Possible: Diplomatic Alternatives in the Mideast. Princeton: Princeton University Press, 1970.

Rivlin, Benjamin, ed., and Joseph S. Szyliowicz. The Contemporary Middle East: Tradition and Innovation. New York: Random House, 1965.

Rodinson, Maxime. The Arabs. Chicago: University of Chicago Press, 1981.

_____. Marxism and the Muslim World. London: Zed Press, n.d.

Rokach, Livia. Israel's Sacred Terrorism. Belmont, Mass.: Association of Arab American University Graduates, 1980.

Rozner, Shlomo. Israel and the Developing Nations, Explanatory Pages for Lecturers. Jerusalem: Prime Minister's Office, Information Center, 1967.

Rubin, Barry. The Arab States in the Palestinian Conflict. Syracuse: Syracuse University Press, 1981.

_____. Paved with Good Intentions: the American Experience and Iran. New York: Oxford University Press, 1980.

Rugh, William A. The Arab Press: News Media and Political Process in the Arab World. Syracuse: Syracuse University Press, 1979.

Ryan, John and Saad, Adib T. Agricultural Education for Development in the Middle East. Syracuse: Syracuse University Press, 1980.

Safran, Nadav. From War to War: The Arab-Israeli Confrontation, 1948-67. New York: Pegasus, 1969.

Savory, Roger M. Introduction to Islamic Civilization. New York: Cambridge University Press, 1976.

_____. Iran Under the Safavids. New York: Cambridge University Press, 1980.

Sayeh, Fayez A. The Dynamics of Neutralism in the Arab World: A Symposium. San Francisco: Chandler Publishing Co., 1964.

Schacht, Joseph. Legacy of Islam. New York: Oxford University Press, n.d.

Segre, Dan. A Crisis of Identity. New York: Oxford University Press, 1980.

Shaked, Houmi. The Middle East and the United States: Perceptions and Policies. New Brunswick, N.J.: Rutgers University, Transaction Books, 1980.

Sharabi, Hisham B. Nationalism and Revolution in the Arab World. Princeton: D. Van Nostrand, 1966.

Shichor, Yitzhak. The Middle East in China's Foreign Policy, 1949-1977. New York: Cambridge University Press, 1979.

Spencer, William. Political Evolution in the Middle East. Philadelphia: J.B. Lippincott, George Washington University, 1962.

Smith, Wilfred C. Islam in Modern History. New York: New American Library, 1957.

Stein, Janice Gross and Raymond Tanter. Rational Decision-Making: Israel's Security Choices. Columbus: Ohio State University, 1980.

_____. The United States and Israel. Cambridge, Mass.: Harvard University Press, 1963.

Stoddard, Philip H. and Cuthell, David C. and Sullivan, Margaret W. Change and the Muslim World. Syracuse: Syracuse University Press, n.d.

Stookley, Robert W. Yemen: the Politics of the Yemen Arab Republic. Boulder, Colo.: Westview Press, 1978.

Swanson, Jon C. Emigration and Economic Development: The Case of the Yemen Arab Republic. Boulder, Colo.: Westview Press, 1979.

Tahtinen, Dale R. National Security Challenges to Saudi Arabia. Washington, D.C.: American Enterprise Institute, 1978.

Thompson, Josh H. and Robert D. Reischauer, eds. Modernization of the Arab World. Princeton, N.J.: Journal of International Affairs, 1966.

Thompson, Virginia and Adloff, Richard. The Western Saharans: Background to Conflict. Totowa, N.J.: Barnes and Noble Books, 1980.

Trade and Credit in the Middle East and North Africa: Problems and Resolutions. New York: Chase Trade Information Corp., 1981.

Tritton, A.S. Islam. London: Hutchinson University Press, 1968.

Vatikiotis, P.J. The Modern History of Egypt. Baltimore: Johns Hopkins Press, 1980.

Udovitch, Abraham L. The Islamic Middle East, 700-1900:
    Studies in Economic and Social History. Princeton, N.J.:
    The Darwin Press, Inc., 1981.

Walstedt, Bertil. State Manufacturing Enterprise in a Mixed
    Economy: The Turkish Case. Baltimore: Johns Hopkins
    Press, 1980.

Waterbury, John. Egypt: Burdens of the Past; Options for
    the Future. Hanover, N.H.: The American Universities
    Field Staff, 1977.

_____. Hydropolitics of the Nile Valley. Syracuse: Syra-
    cuse University Press, 1979.

Wells, Donald A. Saudi Arabian Development Strategy. Wash-
    ington, D.C.: American Enterprise Institute, 1976.

Wilson, Evan. Decision on Palestine: How the U.S. Came to
    Recognize Israel. Stanford, Calif.: Hoover Institution
    Press, 1979.

Wise and Charles Issawi. Middle East Perspectives: The Next
    Twenty Years. Princeton, N.J.: The Darwin Press, Inc.
    1981.

Wolfe, Ronald G., ed. The United States, Arabia, and the
    Gulf. Georgetown University, Washington, D.C.: Center
    for Contemporary Arab Studies.

Yogev, Gedalia. Political and Diplomatic Documents of the
    State of Israel December 1947-May 1948. New Brunswick,
    N.J.: Rutgers University, Transaction Books, 1980.

Index

About the Authors

RIAD A. AJAMI is an assistant professor of International Business and Management, College of Administrative Science, Ohio State University. He is a member of the Academy of International Business, and the Academy of Management.

Professor Ajami received his Ph.D. from Pennsylvania State University. Ajami's most recent book is Arab Response to the Multinationals. He has had articles published in the Journal of International Business Studies, Management International Review, Strategic Management Journal, Journal of Contemporary Business, Middle East Management Review, and Business and Society Review.

YONAH ALEXANDER is professor of International Studies and Director of the Institute for Studies in International Terrorism at the State University of New York at Oneonta. He is also a senior staff associate of the Center for Strategic and International Studies, Georgetown University, and fellow, Institute of Social and Behavioral Pathology (University of Chicago). An author, editor, and co-editor of fifteen books, Dr. Alexander is editor-in-chief of Terrorism and Political Communication and Persuasion, both international journals.

HOSSEIN ASKARI is currently President of Askari, Jalal & Sheshunoff International. From 1978-1981 he was advisor on International Economics and Financial Matters to the Minister of Finance and National Economy of Saudi Arabia and advisor to the Executive Director of the International Monetary Fund; prior to this he was professor of Business at the University of Texas at Austin. He is the author of numerous books and articles. His most recent book is entitled Taxation and Tax Policies in the Middle East (Butterworth), to be published in 1982. He received all of his university education at the

Massachusetts Institute of Technology, where he obtained a
B.S. in Civil Engineering, attended the Sloan School of Management and received his Ph.D. in Economics.

WALDO H. DUBBERSTEIN is a Defense Intelligence officer in
the Defense Intelligence Agency, Department of Defense. He
has had nearly 40 years of intelligence experience in the Department of Defense and in the Central Intelligence Agency.
Dr. Dubberstein has also served two years as Professor of
International Relations on the faculty of the National War College, Department of Defense and at the University of Chicago
and The George Washington University. Having received his
B.A. at St. John's College with an emphasis on languages and
classical studies, Dr. Dubberstein went on to receive his M.A.
in History and his Ph.D. in Oriental Studies and Archaeology
both from the University of Chicago.

PETER B. HALE is the Director of the Office of Country Marketing. He joined the Commerce Department as a Management
Intern in 1964. In January 1966, he became the Turkey Desk
Officer in the Bureau of International Commerce, a position he
held for five years. Mr. Hale subsequently served as Desk
Officer for Iran, as Deputy Regional Marketing Director for
Western Europe, and as Regional Marketing Director for Southern Europe. In 1974, Mr. Hale became Director of the Commerce Action Group for the Near East. In 1976, Mr. Hale
received the Department's Silver Medal Award "for innovative
leadership in organizing and administering" the Department's
major new program of Near East export expansion. Mr. Hale
received his B.A. degree in economics in 1962 from Oberlin
College, Oberlin, Ohio. In 1964, he was awarded an M.B.A.
from the University of Michigan at Ann Arbor.

ROBERT A. KILMARX is Senior Vice President International of
Frazier Associates, a Washington D.C. consulting firm. Prior
to this he was Director of Business and Defense Studies at the
Center for Strategic and International Studies of Georgetown
University and Director of BKW Associates, Inc., a management consulting firm. He served many years as an intelligence
specialist with the Department of Defense, and is a professional lecturer on economic and business topics.

CHERIE A. LOUSTAUNAU joined the Department of Commerce's
Near East/South Asia Division in 1967 after serving as a re-
search assistant in the Economics Department of the World
Bank. She joined the Commerce Action Group for the Near
East in 1974, serving on the Business Facilitation Staff and
bringing information on major projects in the region to the
attention of U.S. companies. She recently became the Regional
Marketing Manager for Iran/Israel/Egypt/North Africa in

CAGNE and is responsible for developing and implementing U.S. commercial policy in the region and for advising U.S. firms on trade and investment opportunities and methods of doing business in these countries. Ms. Loustaunau received a bachelors degree in international affairs from Georgetown University's School of Foreign Service and a Masters degree in economics from Georgetown.

CHARLES G. MACDONALD is an Assistant Professor of International Relations at Florida International University in North Miami, Florida. During the 1979-80 academic year he held a visiting appointment in the Woodrow Wilson Department of Government and Foreign Affairs at the University of Virginia. He is author of Iran, Saudi Arabia, and the Law of the Sea (Greenwood Press, 1980). Revolution in Iran: A Reappraisal, edited with Enver M. Koury, is forthcoming in 1982. In addition, his articles have appeared in the Middle East Journal, Naval War College Review, Journal of South Asian and Middle Eastern Studies, and Levant (Pakistan).

BROOKS McCLURE is Director of Operations for the International Management and Resources Corporation, Washington, D.C. A veteran of the U.S. Foreign Service, he served with the Commerce Department's Working Group on Terrorism. A graduate of the University of Maryland and the Naval War College, Mr. McClure is the author of The Dynamics of Terrorism and a contributor to International Terrorism in the Contemporary World and Contemporary Terrorism.

IBRAHIM M. OWEISS has been Professor of Economics at Georgetown University since 1967. He is a founding member of the Center for Contemporary Arab Studies at Georgetown University as well as a member of its Executive Committee. Prior to his present position at Georgetown University, Professor Oweiss taught at various other institutions in Egypt and in the United States. He specialized in the economics of energy and oil, and in the economics of the Middle East. He served as First Undersecretary of State for Economic Affairs in Egypt and as Chief of the Egyptian Economic Mission to the United States. The term "petrodollars" was coined by him when he first introduced the study on the subject in 1973.

MALCOLM C. PECK is Director of Programs at the Middle East Institute in Washington, D.C. He holds an A.B. degree (with honors) and an A.M. in Middle East Studies from Harvard University. He earned his Ph.D. from the Fletcher School of Law and Diplomacy. Before joining the staff of MEI in 1970, Dr. Peck taught at the University of Tennessee at Chattanooga and was a post-doctoral research fellow at the Harvard University Center for Middle Eastern Studies. Author of a number of

articles on Middle East subjects, he is currently preparing a
book on the United Arab Emirates for Westview Press and
serving as consulting editor to Garland Publishing for a series
called "Outstanding Monographs in Middle Eastern Studies."
He serves on several boards including the National Committee
to Honor the Fourteenth Centennial of Islam.

ROGER M. SAVORY is Professor of Islamic history in the University of Toronto's Department of Middle East and Islamic
Studies, of which he is a former chairman (1968-73).   He
earned degrees from Oxford and the University of London,
having earlier served in Iran with the British Army and Foreign Service.   His principal field of interest is Iranian history
and culture, on which he has published widely.   His recent
publications include Iran under the Safavids, Cambridge University Press 1980; Turmoil in Iran, in Middle East Focus,
March 1979; and The Problem of Sovereignty in an Ithna Ashari ("Twelver") Shi'i State, in Middle East Review, Summer 1979
(reprinted in Michael Curtis (ed.), Religion and Politics in the
Middle East, Westview Special Studies on the Middle East,
1980).   An earlier work edited by Professor Savory, Introduction to Islamic Civilization, Cambridge University Press 1976,
has been widely adopted in the United States in a range of
courses dealing with the civilization and history of the Middle East.